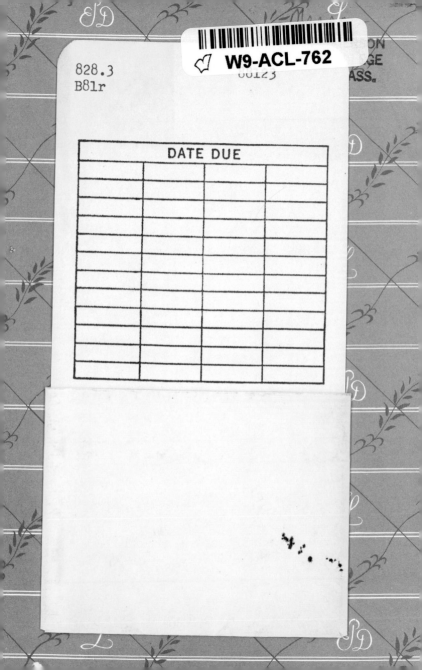

RELIGIO MEDICI
AND OTHER WRITINGS

THE WORLD'S MOST COMPREHENSIVE
LIBRARY OF GREAT BOOKS

There are nearly 1000 titles in Everyman's Library. This world's
largest series of great books was founded 1906 by J. M. Dent
and Sons, Ltd., London and E. P. Dutton & Co., Inc., New York.
The number of the series followed by A, thus 953A, designates
the American editions of Everyman's Library in a large format
and uniform typography. A catalogue of all the volumes in print
in Everyman's Library is available from the publishers, E. P.
Dutton & Co., Inc., 300 Fourth Avenue, New York 10, N. Y.

PHILOSOPHY AND THEOLOGY
92A

RELIGIO MEDICI
AND OTHER WRITINGS

BY

SIR THOMAS BROWNE

WITH A NEW INTRODUCTION
BY FRANK L. HUNTLEY

NEW YORK: E. P. DUTTON AND COMPANY, INC.
LONDON: J. M. DENT AND SONS, LIMITED

This new American Edition published 1951
by E. P. Dutton & Co., Inc.

All rights reserved.

Printed in U.S.A.
from new plates made from type completely reset.

———

With a new Introduction by Frank L. Huntley
Copyright 1951 by E. P. Dutton & Co., Inc.

———

American Editions Uniform with this Format:

AQUINAS—Selected Writings
  (953A)
ARISTOTLE—Nichomachean
  Ethics (547A)
Aucassin and Nicolette (497A)
AUSTEN—Pride and Prejudice
  (22A)
BROOKS—New England: Indian
  Summer (641A)
BROOKS—The World of Wash-
  ington Irving (642A)
BROWNE—Religio Medici
  (92A)
COOPER—The Last of the
  Mohicans (79A)
DESCARTES—A Discourse on
  Method (570A)
DICKENS—Great Expectations
  (234A)
GOLDSMITH—The Vicar of
  Wakefield (295A)
HARDY—Far from the Madding
  Crowd (644A)

HOBBES—Leviathan (691A)
HOWELLS—Indian Summer
  (643A)
LUCRETIUS—Of the Nature of
  Things (750A)
MARLOWE—Plays and Poems
  (383A)
MELVILLE—Moby-Dick (179A)
MILL—Utilitarianism (482A)
PAINE—The Rights of Man
  (718A)
PLATO—The Republic (64A)
ROUSSEAU—The Social Con-
  tract (660A)
ST. AUGUSTINE—Confessions
  (200A)
ST. FRANCIS, The Little
  Flowers of (485A)
THUCYDIDES—Peloponnesian
  War (455A)
ZOLA—Germinal (897A)

The new American Editions of Everyman's Library are for sale only
in the United States of America, the Philippine Islands, Cuba and
Mexico.

Printed and bound by The Colonial Press Inc., Clinton, Mass.

SIR THOMAS BROWNE, born in 1605 and edu-
cated at Winchester and Oxford. Studied at con-
tinental universities and practised medicine at
Norwich. Knighted on account of his Royalist
sympathies in the Civil War. Died in 1682.

CONTENTS

INTRODUCTION

THE writings of Sir Thomas Browne are honored and loved not only by men of letters and academic specialists, but by doctors, lawyers, merchants, and priests, who find in this man's learning, imagination, humor, and reverence a satisfactory answer to the problems which perplex thoughtful men in all generations. One who speaks with authority in science and with humility in faith and reconciles these two worlds, speaks to us all.

Thomas Browne was born in Cheapside, London, in 1605, three years before Milton was born in the same parish. From his father, a pious and prosperous mercer, the child absorbed a natural godliness. And from the mercer's craft of weaving cloth, an imagery with overtones of religion pervaded his imagination—warp and woof, the thread of life, the body's tender filaments, fabric, and the glome or bottom of our days—an imagery which in later years he wove into his patterned prose.

Although he was raised under the shadow of St. Paul's School, young Thomas attended Winchester. We have very little record of him, however, until he entered Pembroke College at Oxford, then known as Broadgates Hall.

At Oxford two great teachers seem to have cast for him the direction of his future life: Dr. Thomas Clayton, M.D., energetic and ambitious; and the Rev. Thomas Lushington, radical in theology and notoriously convivial. Regius Professor of Physic, Dr. Clayton was "the ornament of Oxford medical men" and Master of Pembroke. Through his influence young Browne read Galen, heard lectures on the human body, curative herbs, and the wonders of terrestrial science. At Oxford's first museum the future doctor must have gazed at the skin of a woman "flayed in America by Indians," "a mermaid's hand," and "the pizzle of a dragon," exhibits that would fascinate even today. From his tutor Dr. Lushington, on the other hand, he learned mathematics, the mystery of numbers, and neo-Platonic theology. Philosophy as it emanated from the Platonic Academy of Ficino in Florence was as beautiful in its abstractions as anatomy was elegantly concrete. These two worlds Browne fortunately discovered at Oxford: one visible, the other invisible; one finite, the other infinite; one ending in decay, the other gloriously incorruptible. Not unnaturally, for the rest of his life he marveled at man's being "that great and true amphibium."

His father died while Browne was very young, and his mother remarried. With an ample patrimony he was able to pursue his studies on the continent, fortunately for an ambitious student, since Oxford was far behind in medical education. Browne went first to Montpellier in France, and then to Padua, the finest medical school in Europe. Here in Italy, under Europe's great masters in the Vesalian tradition, he received the kind of medical training which had enabled Harvey fifteen years before to discover the circulation of the blood. Here also he added Italian to his French, fostered a love of painting and architecture, and lived amicably with people of a Christian faith different from his own. Finally, he went to Leyden, to get his medical degree at a Protestant university.

At the age of thirty, engaged in beginning the practice of medicine in England, he set down for his own profit and delight his ideas on religion, compelled, as it were, to resolve the paradox first perceived at Oxford and inherent, finally, in the very title of his book, *Religio Medici*. Are the soaring claims of Christian neo-Platonism valid for a man who diagnoses disease through the color of urine and watches the decay of human tissue? His Anglican yet humanly sceptical answer in the affirmative so delighted the friends who read it in manuscript that seven years later, in 1642, one of its copies fell into the hands of a printer and was published without the author's permission. The corrected version of the following year made Browne famous, and the Latin translation in 1644 gave him a European reputation. In a period of religious strife, Browne's first published book was an irenic masterpiece.

The two parts of *Religio Medici* are clearly enough connected, yet one cannot always see by logic just where, in each part, Browne takes us. Part One is man's relation to God, expressed in the first and great commandment— "Love thy God with all thy heart"; and Part Two concerns his relation to his fellow men on earth, or the second commandment, "Love thy neighbor as thyself." He proceeds from the *One* to the *Many*. With delightful digression and yet with a unity of feeling and metaphor, Browne takes us from sense, through reason, into the infinite realms of faith; then speaks to us of human affection. Sense, reason, and faith are rebels against each other, but they are also inseparable allies. Though the doctor's sense perceptions are unusually well trained, he must yet eke them out with his reason. Similarly, his reason, even after the best and most expensive education Europe could give a man, is still imperfect: faith must come to its aid. In the neo-Platonic hierarchy we ascend from the microcosm to the macrocosm, from the visible to the invisible, from the manifest to the secret—and back again. Hence Browne's favorite image is the circle, that ancient emblem of perfection in which all things meet and in which there is no beginning and no end. Each point thereon—and God is imaged as a mighty geometrician—is both alpha and omega. Man's smaller circle must move in harmony with it. According to the Platonic theory of the participation of things in ideal forms, our imperfect lives can reflect God.

Browne had meantime moved to Norwich, attracted there, no doubt, by the residence nearby of his old Oxford tutor, Dr. Lushington, and several of his Pembroke contemporaries. The busy city offered a medical practice which easily sustained him for the rest of his long life. In 1641, he married Dorothy Mileham, of a good Norfolk family. She was, Browne's earliest biographer tells us, of "such symmetrical proportion to her worthy husband, both in the graces of her body and mind, that they seemed to come together by a kind of natural magnetism." They had ten children, but the infant mortality rate was such that, even in a physician's family, only four survived their childhood. Edward Browne, the oldest, acquired a medical education even superior to his father's, and rose in fame to deliver the Harveian oration before the College of Physicians and to become personal medical advisor to His Majesty, Charles the Second.

In Norwich Browne wrote his second book, *Pseudodoxia Epidemica. An Enquiry into Vulgar Errors,* as it was called, answered Bacon's plea in *The Advancement of Learning* and the *Novum Organum* for a "calendar of old errors," necessary as purgation before there could be a sound method of experimental reasoning. In no sense is the work a dogmatic assertion of truth. The emphasis lies, in the spirit of Renaissance Pyrrhonism, upon the "enquiry." After the opening chapters, which echo Bacon's sources of human error in the idols of the mind, Browne examines the "vulgar error" in each chapter of the "books" devoted to minerals, animals, man, paintings, geography and history, and Scriptural interpretation in this general order: (1) authorities who persist in the error and those who, more enlightened, deny it; (2) an appeal to our common sense and reason; (3) a report of an actual experiment Despite its many old-fashioned ideas, the work not only shows Browne to have been in the forefront of such sciences as optics, magnetism, and biological as well as botanical generation, but also contains some advanced higher Biblical criticism. It was Browne's scientific *magnum opus,* and was corrected in edition after edition from 1646 to 1672.

A Letter to a Friend upon Occasion of the Death of his Intimate Friend, the next selection in the present volume, though bringing Browne no fame during his life, has had perhaps more readers than the imposing *Vulgar Errors.* Published posthumously, it was long thought to have been composed in Browne's later years, since the advice which ends it was incorporated at the beginning of his *Christian Morals.* Walter Pater and Paul Elmer More, however, felt that its sympathetic collocation would be with *Urn Burial* rather than with *Christian Morals.* Of the death of the young man which Browne describes in such clinical detail and with such Christian grace, Pater wrote:

> There has been, in this case, a tardiness and reluctancy in the circumstances of dissolution, which had permitted [Browne], in the character of a physician, as it were, to assist at the spiritualizing of the bodily frame by natural process; a wonderful new type of a kind of mortified grace being evolved by the way.

A chain of circumstantial evidence points to the year 1656 for its first drafting.

In *Hydriotaphia or Urn Burial* (1658), Browne's mind, heart, and soul take full flight. The book begins on a low note:

> In a Field of old Walsingham, not many months past, were digged up between forty and fifty urns, deposited in a dry and sandy soil, not a yard deep, nor far from one another: . . . some containing two pounds of bones, distinguished in skulls, ribs, jaws, thigh-bones, and teeth. . . .

And it ends in one of the most glorious passages of English prose:

> Now since these dead bones have already outlasted the living ones of Methuselah, and in a yard under ground, and thin walls of clay, out-worn all the strong and specious buildings above it; and quietly rested under the drums and tramplings of three conquests; what Prince can promise such diuturnity unto his Reliques, or might not gladly say, 'Sic ego componi versus in ossa velim.'[1] Time which antiquates Antiquities, and hath an art to make dust of all things, hath yet spared these *minor* Monuments.

The paradoxical argument of *Urn Burial* springs from that sentence of Tertullian, so important in *Religio Medici*, "Credo quia impossibile est." This does not mean that one believes a thing by virtue of its sheer incredibility; rather, it serves to define the boundaries of faith. In faith, those things are true which appear contrary to one's senses and not demonstrable by one's reason. Reason would have these bones obliterated despite man's pathetically rational effort to perpetuate himself after death. Hence the first four chapters of *Urn Burial* pile up in detail all the modes of sepulture known to Browne the antiquarian, and assail immortality with all the evidence which Browne as scientist and philosopher can bring against it. Then in the fifth chapter, he overthrows this array of learning, and does so by a simple paradox: every proud effort of man to build his immortality in tombs is futile; Christian faith is the only "patent from oblivion." Here again his intellect, which can prove that we perish, he raises to faith in an *O altitudo*.

With *Urn Burial* Browne published *The Garden of Cyrus* or *The Quincuncial Lozenge*. Whereas the former piece shows us the futility of things here on earth, the

---

[1] Tibullus: I might wish to be thus laid to rest, when I am turned to bones.

latter serves to lift us from earth to heaven. Each has five chapters. In *The Garden of Cyrus* Browne admires the planting of trees in five's, one in the center and four at the corners of a rectangle so that the trees in rows form a lattice-work. But the essay on the *quincunx,* the odd word he found for this kind of planting, is only superficially a disquisition on gardening and botany. Proclus, Dr. Lushington's favorite neo-Platonist, had raised the science of geometry to the heights of theology, as had also Dr. John Dee in the introduction to the first English translation of Euclid's *Elements* (1570). In his *Religio* Browne confessed that he had "often admired the mystical way of Pythagoras and the secret Magick of numbers." Thus the real meaning of the essay, anticipated on the title page, is the Garden of Cyrus, "artificially, naturally, and mystically considered." These divisions are so important to the whole that in early editions of it they mark the chapters in running titles: chapter 1, the Garden of Cyrus; chapter 2, the figure "in sundry *artificial* contrivances"; chapter 3, *"natural* examples"; and chapters 4 and 5, the quincunx *mystically* enlarged upon. The beginnings of each chapter point up this three-fold hierarchy. Like Plato's famous painting of a bed, the emblematic quincunx is first described for itself as an "imitation" in gardening; then it is taken back to the nature which the gardener "imitates"; and finally it is equated with the archetypal design that lies beyond even nature. At the close Browne writes: "All things begin in order, so shall they end, and so shall they begin again; according to the ordainer of order and mystical Mathematicks of the City of Heaven." The "out-lasting" of the poor bones in *Urn Burial* was not "design" but historical accident.

Thus Browne's enormous learning in the most esoteric parts of history, art, philosophy, mathematics, geography, anatomy, botany, physics, and astronomy only served to make more steadfast his Christian faith. His way of thinking and his mode of expression are more devotional than theological, more poetic than syllogistic. A symbol or picture always held for him a more lively meaning than an abstract or logical definition. Like parables, metaphors make epistemic relations between the two worlds for this man of imagination. Hence the quincunxial figure in the Garden of Cyrus forms a circle, once more, like the "definition" of God which he got from Hermes Trismegistus, that God is a circle whose center is nowhere and whose circumference is everywhere. The circle is the emblem of perfection and immortality; the right line drawn through its center becomes the mortal diameter. The whole figure is the Greek letter *theta*, θ, standing for *thanatos*, death. Yet in death, by death, through death, over death stands always that ever-living perfection of God in whose image we are made:

> Nature tells me I am the Image of God, as well as Scripture: he that understands not thus much, hath not his introduction or first lesson, and is yet to begin the Alphabet of man.

His last book, *Christian Morals,* is a series of meditations on religion and ethics collected from the private notebooks of a lifetime. It is to be read not at one sitting, like the shorter pieces, nor with an index like *Vulgar Errors,* but like Pascal's *Pensées,* Marcus Aurelius' *Meditations,* or Thomas à Kempis' *The Imitation of Christ.* With no thought of sustained exposition or argument, Browne places before us in this work his first and last thoughts on the meaning of being a Christian. Whatever else Dr. Browne was, he was this; and *Christian Morals* is charged with passages of his most seasoned thought expressed in some of his greatest prose:

> Let not the sun in Capricorn go down upon thy wrath, but write thy wrongs in ashes. Draw the curtain of night upon injuries, shut them up in the tower of oblivion, and let them be as though they had not been. To forgive our enemies, yet hope that God will punish them, is not to forgive enough; to forgive

them ourselves, and not to pray God to forgive them, is a partial piece of Charity. . . .

The gentle stoicism of the book is perhaps summarized in
this sentence: "Be a moralist of the Mount, an Epictetus
in the Faith, and christianize thy notions."

In 1671 Charles the Second, visiting Norwich, honored
the city's most famous Royalist citizen. The erudite and
amiable physician—neither fat nor lean, dressed to keep
himself always warm, brown hair flowing around his
sensitive face with its habitual blush—rose from his knee
Sir Thomas Browne. He spent his last years visiting the
sick, corresponding with experts on innumerable matters, managing a rich household, tending one of the best
herbal gardens in England, collecting for his own museum, and drafting inaugural speeches for his famous
but less gifted son Dr. Edward Browne. He died on his
seventy-seventh birthday, October 19, 1682, thus, strangely
and appropriately, completing his own circle.

Although we have come a long way in science since Sir
Thomas corresponded with the founders of the Royal
Society, our age, because of this one-sided progress, has
become increasingly aware of the religious temper of the
seventeenth century. Among men like Milton, Donne,
Taylor, Herbert, and Crashaw, Browne is loved for the
quality of his faith. He never preaches at us or argues
with us, but persuades with a gentle and ironic humor.
On the metaphysical problem of causation, for example,
he observes that to deny the action of the soul upon the
body is

> To devolve the honour of the principal agent upon the instru-
> ment, which, if with reason we may do, then let our hammers
> rise up and boast that they have built our houses, and our pens
> receive the honour of our writings.

Nor was he tortured by religion into giving up his family,
his home, or his chosen profession. In science he is no

Harvey; in philosophy, no Descartes; in religion, no Pascal. Yet in being part of all of these, and still a doctor, scholar, husband, father, he is a devout layman, and withal a consummate artist.

The concept of style as the antiseptic of decay is peculiarly appropriate to this physician's literary work. His prose startles while it informs. No statistical analysis or historical category can describe it. Whoever desires to become more sensitive to style will have to read it for himself, alert to perceive how its rhetorical elements exactly define, not ornamentally falsify, the character of the man and the essence of his thought. Some of his style is "high," and some "low," and very often the two are purposefully juxtaposed as the anatomist becomes lost in wonder of the Creator. A principle of much of his writing is plenitude: not one word or phrase but two are used, each sounding a separate, a polar note. This is more than "richness," and the critical cliché "organ tones" is a commentary on only half of it.

In single sentences, in paragraphs, in whole works, Browne takes us from earth to heaven and from heaven to earth, as though his whole mind were concentrating on the paradox of man's body of flesh that can house an immortal soul.

Frank L. Huntley

University of Michigan
    1951

BIBLIOGRAPHY

The definitive edition of Browne's complete works is that by Geoffrey Keynes, 6 volumes, London, 1928-31.

The biographies of Browne are (1) the early "Minutes" written by his friend, the Rev. John Whitefoot; (2) a sensitive life by Samuel Johnson prefixed to his edition of *Christian Morals* (London, 1756); (3) the first life using modern methods of investigation, by Simon Wilkin (London, 1836); (4) the "English Men of Letters" biography by Sir Edmund Gosse (London and New York, 1905); and (5) the latest life, by Jeremiah S. Finch (New York, 1950), with a bibliography. Whitefoot's "Minutes" appear in Johnson and Wilkin.

In 1924 Geoffrey Keynes published his *Bibliography of Sir Thomas Browne* (Cambridge, 1924). A short annotated bibliography for students is that by Douglas Bush at the end of his *English Literature in the Earlier Seventeenth Century* (Oxford, 1945).

Intelligent criticism of Browne permeates the pages of Douglas Bush's history. Other perceptive essays are by Coleridge in *Literary Remains* (London, 1836); Walter Pater, *Appreciations* (London and New York, 1889); Sir William Osler, *An Alabama Student* (Oxford, 1909); and Paul Elmer More, *Shelburne Essays,* 6th series (New York and London, 1909).

For Browne's scientific achievements the student should begin with G. K. Chalmer's "Sir Thomas Browne, True Scientist," in *Osiris,* volume II (1936), and Finch's excellent biography; for Browne's philosophy of religion, the revised edition of William P. Dunn's classic essay, *Sir*

Thomas Browne (Minneapolis 1950). On Browne's recon-ciliation or division of the two worlds, the student should read Basil Willey, *The Seventeenth Century Background* (London, 1934) and D. K. Ziegler, *In Divided and Dis-tinguished Worlds* (Cambridge, Mass., 1943)—both with some caution; and finally Joseph Needham, *The Great Amphibium* (New York, 1932).

More specialized studies are: J. M. Cline's analysis of *Hydriotaphia* in *University of California Publications in English* (Berkeley, 1940); Margaret L. Wiley, "Sir Thomas Browne and the Genesis of Paradox," *Journal of the His-tory of Ideas* (June, 1948); and Frank L. Huntley's argu-ment for identifying the persons in *A Letter to a Friend,* in *Modern Philology* (February, 1951).

The best essay on Browne's style is that by Austin Warren in *The Kenyon Review* (Autumn 1951).

RELIGIO MEDICI
1643

TO THE READER

CERTAINLY that man were greedy of Life, who should
desire to live when all the world were at an end; and he
must needs be very impatient, who would repine at death
in the society of all things that suffer under it. Had not
almost every man suffered by the Press, or were not
the tyranny thereof become universal, I had not wanted
reason for complaint: but in times wherein I have lived
to behold the highest perversion of that excellent invention, the name of his Majesty defamed, the Honour of
Parliament depraved, the Writings of both depravedly,
anticipatively, counterfeitly imprinted; complaints may
seem ridiculous in private persons; and men of my condition may be as incapable of affronts, as hopeless of their
reparations. And truely, had not the duty I owe unto the
importunity of friends, and the allegiance I must ever
acknowledge unto truth, prevailed with me, the inactiv-
ity of my disposition might have made these sufferings
continual, and time, that brings other things to light,
should have satisfied me in the remedy of its oblivion.
But because things evidently false are not onely printed,
but many things of truth most falsely set forth, in this
latter I could not but think my self engaged: for, though
we have no power to redress the former, yet in the other
the reparation being within our selves, I have at present
represented unto the world a full and intended Copy
of that Piece, which was most imperfectly and surrepti-
tiously published before.

This, I confess, about seven years past, with some
others, of affinity thereto, for my private exercise and
satisfaction, I had at leisurable hours composed; which

being communicated unto one, it became common unto many, and was by Transcription successively corrupted, untill it arrived in a most depraved Copy at the Press. He that shall peruse that work, and shall take notice of sundry particularities and personal expressions therein, will easily discern the intention was not publick; and, being a private Exercise directed to my self, what is delivered therein, was rather a memorial unto *me*, than an Example or Rule unto any other; and therefore, if there be any singularity therein correspondent unto the private conceptions of any man, it doth not advantage them; or if dissentaneous thereunto, it no way overthrows them. It was penned in such a place, and with such disadvantage, that, (I protest,) from the first setting of pen unto paper, I had not the assistance of any good Book whereby to promote my invention or relieve my memory; and therefore there might be many real lapses therein, which others might take notice of, and more than I suspected my self. It was set down many years past, and was the sense of my conceptions at that time, not an immutable Law unto my advancing judgement at all times; and therefore there might be many things therein plausible unto my passed apprehension, which are not agreeable unto my present self. There are many things delivered Rhetorically, many expressions therein meerly Tropical, and as they best illustrate my intention; and therefore also there are many things to be taken in a soft and flexible sense, and not to be called unto the rigid test of Reason. Lastly, all that is contained therein is in submission unto maturer discernments; and, as I have declared, shall no further father them than the best and learned judgments shall authorize them: under favour of which considerations I have made its secrecy publick, and committed the truth thereof to every Ingenuous Reader.

THO. BROWNE.

RELIGIO MEDICI

THE FIRST PART

FOR my Religion, though there be several Circumstances that might perswade the World I have none at all, (as the general scandal of my Profession, the natural course of my Studies, the indifferency of my Behaviour and Discourse in matters of Religion, neither violently Defending one, nor with that common ardour and contention Opposing another;) yet, in despight hereof, I dare without usurpation assume the honourable Stile of a Christian. Not that I meerly owe this Title to the Font, my Education, or the clime wherein I was born, (as being bred up either to confirm those Principles my Parents instilled into my unwary Understanding, or by a general consent proceed in the Religion of my Country;) but having in my riper years and confirmed Judgment seen and examined all, I find my self obliged by the Principles of Grace, and the Law of mine own Reason, to embrace no other Name but this. Neither doth herein my zeal so far make me forget the general Charity I owe unto Humanity, as rather to hate than pity Turks, Infidels, and (what is worse,) Jews; rather contenting my self to enjoy that happy Stile, than maligning those who refuse so glorious a Title.

But, because the Name of a Christian is become too

general to express our Faith, (there being a Geography
of Religions as well as Lands, and every Clime distinguished not only by their Laws and Limits, but circumscribed by their Doctrines and Rules of Faith;) to be
particular, I am of that Reformed new-cast Religion,
wherein I dislike nothing but the Name; of the same
belief our Saviour taught, the Apostles disseminated, the
Fathers authorized, and the Martyrs confirmed; but by
the sinister ends of Princes, the ambition and avarice
of Prelates, and the fatal corruption of times, so decayed,
impaired, and fallen from its native Beauty, that it required the careful and charitable hands of these times
to restore it to its primitive Integrity. Now the accidental
occasion whereupon, the slender means whereby, the low
and abject condition of the Person by whom so good a
work was set on foot, which in our Adversaries beget contempt and scorn, fills me with wonder, and is the very
same Objection the insolent Pagans first cast at CHRIST
and His Disciples.

Yet have I not so shaken hands with those desperate
Resolutions, (who had rather venture at large their decayed bottom, than bring her in to be new trimm'd in
the Dock; who had rather promiscuously retain all, than
abridge any, and obstinately be what they are, than what
they have been,) as to stand in Diameter and Swords
point with them. We have reformed from them, not
against them; for (omitting those Improperations and
Terms of Scurrility betwixt us, which only difference our
Affections, and not our Cause,) there is between us one
common Name and Appellation, one Faith and necessary
body of Principles common to us both; and therefore I am
not scrupulous to converse and live with them, to enter
their Churches in defect of ours, and either pray with
them, or for them. I could never perceive any rational
Consequence from those many Texts which prohibit the
Children of Israel to pollute themselves with the Temples

of the Heathens; we being all Christians, and not divided by such detested impieties as might prophane our Prayers, or the 'place wherein we make them; or that a resolved Conscience may not adore her Creator any where, especially in places devoted to His Service; where, if *their* Devotions offend Him, mine may please Him; if theirs prophane it, mine may hallow it. Holy-water and Crucifix (dangerous to the common people,) deceive not my judgment, nor abuse my devotion at all. I am, I confess, naturally inclined to that which misguided Zeal terms *Superstition*. My common conversation I do acknowledge austere, my behaviour full of rigour, sometimes not without morosity; yet at my Devotion I love to use the civility of my knee, my hat, and hand, with all those outward and sensible motions which may express or promote my invisible Devotion. I should violate my own arm rather than a Church; nor willingly deface the name of Saint or Martyr. At the sight of a Cross or Crucifix I can dispense with my hat, but scarce with the thought or memory of my Saviour. I cannot laugh at, but rather pity, the fruitless journeys of Pilgrims, or contemn the miserable condition of Fryars; for, though misplaced in Circumstances, there is something in it of Devotion. I could never hear the Ave-Mary Bell without an elevation; or think it a sufficient warrant, because *they* erred in one circumstance, for me to err in all, that is, in silence and dumb contempt. Whilst, therefore, they directed their Devotions to *Her,* I offered mine to GOD, and rectified the Errors of their Prayers by rightly ordering mine own. At a solemn Procession I have wept abundantly, while my consorts, blind with opposition and prejudice, have fallen into an excess of scorn and laughter. There are, questionless, both in Greek, Roman, and African Churches, Solemnities and Ceremonies, whereof the wiser Zeals do make a Christian use, and stand condemned by us, not as evil in themselves, but as allurements and baits of superstition to those vulgar heads that look asquint on the face of Truth, and those unstable Judgments that cannot consist in the narrow point and centre of Virtue without a reel or stagger to the Circumference.

As there were many Reformers, so likewise many Reformations; every Country proceeding in a particular way and method, according as their national Interest, together with their Constitution and Clime, inclined them; some angrily, and with extremity; others calmly, and with mediocrity; not rending, but easily dividing the community, and leaving an honest possibility of a reconciliation; which though peaceable Spirits do desire, and may conceive that revolution of time and the mercies of GOD may effect, yet that judgment that shall consider the present antipathies between the two extreams, their contrarieties in condition, affection, and opinion, may with the same hopes expect an union in the Poles of Heaven.

But (to difference my self nearer, and draw into a lesser Circle,) there is no Church whose every part so squares unto my Conscience; whose Articles, Constitutions, and Customs seem so consonant unto reason, and as it were framed to my particular Devotion, as this whereof I hold my Belief, the Church of England; to whose Faith I am a sworn Subject, and therefore in a double Obligation subscribe unto her Articles, and endeavour to observe her Constitutions. Whatsoever is beyond, as points indifferent, I observe according to the rules of my private reason, or the humour and fashion of my Devotion; neither believing this, because Luther affirmed it, or disproving that, because Calvin hath disavouched it. I condemn not all things in the Council of Trent, nor approve all in the Synod of Dort. In brief, where the Scripture is silent, the Church is my Text; where that speaks, 'tis but my Comment: where there is a joynt silence of both, I borrow not the rules of my Religion from Rome or Geneva, but the dictates of my own reason. It is an unjust scandal of our adversaries, and a gross errour in our selves, to compute the Nativity of our Religion from Henry the Eighth, who, though he rejected the Pope, refus'd not the faith of Rome, and effected no more than what his own Predecessors desired and assayed in Ages past, and was conceived the State of Venice would have attempted in our days. It is as uncharitable a point in *us* to fall upon those popular scurrilities and opprobrious scoffs of the Bishop of Rome, to whom, as a temporal Prince, we owe the duty of good language. I confess there is cause of passion between us: by his sentence I stand excommunicated; *Heretick* is the best language he affords me; yet can no ear witness I ever returned him the name of *Antichrist, Man of Sin,* or *Whore of Babylon.* It is the method of Charity to suffer without reaction: those usual Satyrs and invectives of the Pulpit may perchance produce a good effect on the vulgar, whose ears are opener to Rhetorick than Logick; yet do they in no wise confirm the faith of wiser Believers, who know that a good cause needs not to be patron'd by passion, but can sustain it self upon a temperate dispute.

I could never divide my self from any man upon the difference of an opinion, or be angry with his judgment for not agreeing with me in that from which perhaps within a few days I should dissent my self. I have no Genius to disputes in Religion, and have often thought it wisdom to decline them, especially upon a disadvantage, or when the cause of Truth might suffer in the weekness of my patronage. Where we desire to be informed, 'tis good to contest with men above our selves; but to confirm and establish our opinions, 'tis best to argue with judgments below our own, that the frequent spoils and Victories over their reasons may settle in ourselves an esteem and confirmed Opinion of our own. Every man is not a proper Champion for Truth, nor fit to take up the Gauntlet in the cause of Verity: many, from the ignorance of these Maximes, and an inconsiderate Zeal unto Truth, have too rashly charged the troops of Error, and remain as Trophies unto the enemies of Truth. A man may be in as just possession of Truth as of a City, and yet be forced to surrender; 'tis therefore far better to enjoy her with peace, than to hazzard her on a battle. If, therefore, there rise any doubts in my way, I do forget them, or at least defer them till my better setled judgement and more manly reason be able to resolve them; for I perceive every man's own reason is his best (Œdipus, and will, upon a reasonable truce, find a way to loose those bonds wherewith the subtleties of error have enchained our more flexible and tender judgements. In Philosophy, where Truth seems double-fac'd, there is no man more Paradoxical than my self: but in Divinity I love to keep the Road; and, though not in an implicite, yet an humble faith, follow the great wheel of the Church, by which I move, not reserving any proper Poles or motion from the Epicycle of my own brain. By this means I leave no gap for Heresies, Schismes, or Errors, of which at present I hope I shall not injure Truth to say I have no taint or tincture. I must confess my greener studies have been polluted with two or three; not any begotten in the latter Centuries, but old and obsolete, such as could never have been revived, but by such extravagant and irregular heads as mine: for indeed Heresies perish not with their Authors, but, like the river Arethusa, though they lose their currents in one place, they rise up again in another. One General Council is not able to extirpate one single Heresie: it may be cancell'd for the present; but revolution of time, and the like aspects from Heaven, will restore it, when it will flourish till it be condemned again. For as though there were a Metempsuchosis, and the soul of one man passed into another, Opinions do find, after certain Revolutions, men and minds like those that first begat them. To see our selves again, we need not look for Plato's year: every man is not only himself; there hath been many Diogenes, and as many Timons, though but few of that name: men are liv'd over again, the world is now as it was in Ages past; there was none then, but there hath been some one since that parallels him, and is, as it were, his revived self.

Now the first of mine was that of the Arabians, That the Souls of men perished with their Bodies, but should yet be raised again at the last day. Not that I did absolutely conceive a mortality of the Soul; but if that were, (which Faith, not Philosophy, hath yet throughly disproved,) and that both entred the grave together, yet I held the same conceit thereof that we all do of the body, that it should rise again. Surely it is but the merits of our unworthy Natures, if we sleep in darkness until the last Alarum. A series reflex upon my own unworthiness did make me backward from challenging this prerogative of my Soul: so that I might enjoy my Saviour at the last, I could with patience be nothing almost unto Eternity.

The second was that of Origen, That GOD would not persist in His vengeance for ever, but after a definite time of His wrath, He would release the damned Souls from torture. Which error I fell into upon a serious contemplation of the great Attribute of GOD, His Mercy; and did a little cherish it in my self, because I found therein no malice, and a ready weight to sway me from the other extream of despair, whereunto Melancholy and Contemplative Natures are too easily disposed.

A third there is, which I did never positively maintain or practise, but have often wished it had been consonant to Truth, and not offensive to my Religion, and that is, the Prayer for the Dead; whereunto I was inclin'd from some charitable inducements, whereby I could scarce contain my Prayers for a friend at the ringing of a Bell, or behold his Corps without an Orison for his Soul. 'Twas a good way, methought, to be remembered by posterity, and far more noble than an History.

These opinions I never maintained with pertinacy, or endeavoured to enveagle any mans belief unto mine, nor so much as ever revealed or disputed them with my dearest friends; by which means I neither propagated them in others, nor confirmed them in my self; but suffering them to flame upon their own substance, without addition of new fuel, they went out insensibly of themselves. Therefore these Opinions, though condemned by lawful Councels, were not Heresies in me, but bare Errors, and single Lapses of my understanding, without a joynt depravity of my will. Those have not onely depraved understandings, but diseased affections, which cannot enjoy a singularity without an Heresie, or be the Author of an Opinion without they be of a Sect also. This was the villany of the first Schism of Lucifer, who was not content to err alone, but drew into his Faction many Legions of Spirits; and upon this experience he tempted only Eve, as well understanding the Communicable nature of Sin, and that to deceive but one, was tacitely and upon consequence to delude them both.

That Heresies should arise, we have the Prophesie of CHRIST; but that old ones should be abolished, we hold no prediction. That there must be Heresies, is true, not only in our Church, but also in any other: even in doctrines heretical, there will be super-heresies; and Arians not only divided from their Church, but also among themselves. For heads that are disposed unto Schism and complexionally propense to innovation, are naturally indisposed for a community, nor will be ever confined unto the order or œconomy of one body; and, therefore, when they separate from others, they knit but loosely among themselves; nor contented with a general breach or dichotomy with their Church do subdivide and mince themselves almost into Atoms. 'Tis true, that men of singular parts and humours have not been free from singular opinions and conceits in all Ages; retaining something, not only beside the opinion of his own Church or any other, but also any particular Author; which, notwithstanding, a sober Judgment may do without offence or heresie; for there is yet, after all the Decrees of Councils and the niceties of the Schools, many things untouch'd, unimagin'd, wherein the liberty of an honest reason may play and expatiate with security, and far without the circle of an Heresie.

As for those wingy Mysteries in Divinity, and airy subtleties in Religion, which have unhing'd the brains of better heads, they never stretched the *Pia Mater* of mine. Methinks there be not impossibilities enough in Religion for an active faith; the deepest Mysteries ours contains have not only been illustrated, but maintained, by Syllogism and the rule of Reason. I love to lose my self in a mystery, to pursue my Reason to an *O altitudo!* 'Tis my solitary recreation to pose my apprehension with those involved Ænigmas and riddles of the Trinity, with Incarnation, and Resurrection. I can answer all the Objections of Satan and my rebellious reason with that odd resolution I learned of Tertullian, *Certum est, quia impossibile est*. I desire to exercise my faith in the difficultest point; for to credit ordinary and visible objects is not faith, but perswasion. Some believe the better for seeing CHRIST's Sepulchre; and, when they have seen the Red Sea, doubt not of the Miracle. Now, contrarily, I bless my self and am thankful that I lived not in the days of Miracles, that I never saw CHRIST nor His Disciples. I would not have been one of those Israelites that pass'd the Red Sea, nor one of CHRIST's patients on whom

He wrought His wonders; then had my faith been thrust upon me, nor should I enjoy that greater blessing pronounced to all that believe and saw not. 'Tis an easie and necessary belief, to credit what our eye and sense hath examined. I believe He was dead, and buried, and rose again; and desire to see Him in His glory, rather than to contemplate Him in His Cenotaphe or Sepulchre. Nor is this much to believe; as we have reason, we owe this faith unto History: *they* only had the advantage of a bold and noble Faith, who lived before His coming, who upon obscure prophesies and mystical Types could raise a belief, and expect apparent impossibilities.

'Tis true, there is an edge in all firm belief, and with an easie Metaphor we may say, the *Sword* of Faith; but in these obscurities I rather use it in the adjunct the Apostle gives it, a *Buckler;* under which I conceived a wary combatant may lye invulnerable. Since I was of understanding to know we knew nothing, my reason hath been more pliable to the will of Faith; I am now content to understand a mystery without a rigid definition, in an easie and Platonick description. That allegorical description of Hermes pleaseth me beyond all the Metaphysical definitions of Divines. Where I cannot satisfy my reason, I love to humour my fancy: I had as live you tell me that *anima est angelus hominis, est Corpus* DEI, as *Entelechia;—Lux est umbra* DEI, as *actus perspicui.* Where there is an obscurity too deep for our Reason, 'tis good to sit down with a description, periphrasis, or adumbration; for by acquainting our Reason how unable it is to display the visible and obvious effects of Nature, it becomes more humble and submissive unto the subtleties of Faith; and thus I teach my haggard and unreclaimed Reason to stoop unto the lure of Faith. I believe there was already a tree whose fruit our unhappy Parents tasted, though, in the same Chapter when GOD forbids it, 'tis positively said, the plants of the field were not yet

grown, *for* GOD *had not caus'd it to rain upon the earth.*
I believe that the Serpent, (if we shall literally understand it,) from his proper form and figure, made his motion on his belly before the curse. I find the tryal of the
Pucellage and virginity of Women, which GOD ordained
the Jews, is very fallible. Experience and History informs me, that not onely many particular Women, but
likewise whole Nations, have escaped the curse of Child-
birth, which GOD seems to pronounce upon the whole
Sex. Yet do I believe that all this is true, which indeed my Reason would perswade me to be false; and
this I think is no vulgar part of Faith, to believe a thing
not only above but contrary to Reason, and against the
Arguments of our proper Senses.

In my solitary and retired imagination

(neque enim cum porticus aut me
Lectulus accepit, desum mihi,)

I remember I am not alone, and therefore forget not to
contemplate Him and His Attributes Who is ever with
me, especially those two mighty ones, His Wisdom and
Eternity. With the one I recreate, with the other I confound, my understanding; for who can speak of Eternity
without a solœcism, or think thereof without an Extasie?
Time we may comprehend; 'tis but five days elder then
our selves, and hath the same Horoscope with the World;
but to retire so far back as to apprehend a beginning,
to give such an infinite start forwards as to conceive an
end, in an essence that we affirm hath neither the one nor
the other, it puts my Reason to St. Paul's Sanctuary. My
Philosophy dares not say the Angels can do it. GOD hath
not made a Creature that can comprehend Him; 'tis a
privilege of His own nature. I AM THAT I AM, was His
own definition unto Moses; and 'twas a short one, to confound mortality, that durst question GOD, or ask Him
what He was. Indeed, He onely is; all others have and

shall be. But in Eternity there is no distinction of Tenses; and therefore that terrible term *Predestination,* which hath troubled so many weak heads to conceive, and the wisest to explain, is in respect to GOD no prescious determination of our Estates to come, but a definitive blast of His Will already fulfilled, and at the instant that He first decreed it; for to His Eternity, which is indivisible and all together, the last Trump is already sounded, the reprobates in the flame, and the blessed in Abraham's bosome. St. Peter speaks modestly, when he saith, *a thousand years to* GOD *are but as one day;* for, to speak like a Philosopher, those continued instances of time which flow into a thousand years, make not to Him one moment: what to us is to come, to His Eternity is present, His whole duration being but one permanent point, without Succession, Parts, Flux, or Division.

There is no Attribute that adds more difficulty to the mystery of the Trinity, where, though in a relative way of Father and Son, we must deny a priority. I wonder how Aristotle could conceive the World eternal, or how he could make good two Eternities. His similitude of a Triangle comprehended in a square doth somewhat illustrate the Trinity of our Souls, and that the Triple Unity of GOD; for there is in us not three, but a Trinity of Souls; because there is in us, if not three distinct Souls, yet differing faculties, that can and do subsist apart in different Subjects, and yet in us are so united as to make but one Soul and substance. If one Soul were so perfect as to inform three distinct Bodies, that were a petty Trinity: conceive the distinct number of three, not divided nor separated by the intellect, but actually comprehended in its Unity, and that is a perfect Trinity. I have often admired the mystical way of Pythagoras, and the secret Magick of numbers. *Beware of Philosophy,* is a precept not to be received in too large a sense; for in this Mass of Nature there is a set of things that carry in their

Front (though not in Capital Letters, yet in Stenography and short Characters,) something of Divinity, which to wiser Reasons serve as Luminaries in the Abyss of Knowledge, and to judicious beliefs as Scales and Roundles to mount the Pinacles and highest pieces of Divinity. The severe Schools shall never laugh me out of the Philosophy of Hermes, that this visible World is but a Picture of the invisible, wherein, as in a Pourtraict, things are not truely, but in equivocal shapes, and as they counterfeit some more real substance in that invisible fabrick.

That other Attribute wherewith I recreate my devotion, is His Wisdom, in which I am happy; and for the contemplation of this only, do not repent me that I was bred in the way of Study: the advantage I have of the vulgar, with the content and happiness I conceive therein, is an ample recompence for all my endeavours, in what part of knowledge soever. Wisdom is His most beauteous Attribute; no man can attain unto it, yet Solomon pleased GOD when he desired it. He is wise, because He knows all things; and He knoweth all things, because He made them all: but His greatest knowledge is in comprehending *that* He made not, that is, Himself. And this is also the greatest knowledge in man. For this do I honour my own profession, and embrace the Counsel even of the Devil himself: had he read such a Lecture in Paradise as he did at Delphos, we had better known our selves, nor had we stood in fear to know *him*. I know He is wise in all, wonderful in what we conceive, but far more in what we comprehend not; for we behold Him but asquint, upon reflex or shadow; our understanding is dimmer than Moses Eye; we are ignorant of the backparts or lower side of His Divinity; therefore to prie into the maze of His Counsels is not only folly in man, but presumption even in Angels. Like us, they are His Servants, not His Senators; He holds no Counsel, but that mystical one of the Trinity, wherein, though there be three Persons, there is but one mind that decrees without contradiction. Nor needs He any: his actions are not begot with deliberation, His Wisdom naturally knows what's best; His intellect stands ready fraught with the superlative and purest Ideas of goodness; consultation and election, which are two motions in us, make but one in Him, His actions springing from His power at the first touch of His will. These are Contemplations metaphysical: my humble speculations have another Method, and are content to trace and discover those expressions He hath left in His Creatures, and the obvious effects of Nature. There is no danger to profound these mysteries, no *sanctum sanctorum* in Philosophy. The World was made to be inhabited by Beasts, but studied and contemplated by Man: 'tis the Debt of our Reason we owe unto GOD, and the homage we pay for not being Beasts. Without this, the World is still as though it had not been, or as it was before the sixth day, when as yet there was not a Creature that could conceive or say there was a World. The Wisdom of GOD receives small honour from those vulgar Heads that rudely stare about, and with a gross rusticity admire His works: those highly magnifie Him, whose judicious inquiry into His Acts, and deliberate research into His Creatures, return the duty of a devout and learned admiration. Therefore,

> Search while thou wilt, and let thy Reason go,
> To ransome Truth, even to th' Abyss below;
> Rally the scattered Causes; and that line,
> Which Nature twists, be able to untwine.
> It is thy Makers will, for unto none
> But unto Reason can He e'er be known.
> The Devils do know Thee, but those damnèd Meteors
> Build not Thy Glory, but confound Thy Creatures.
> Teach my indeavours so Thy works to read,
> That learning them in Thee, I may proceed.
> Give Thou my reason that instructive flight,
> Whose weary wings may on Thy hands still light.

Teach me to soar aloft, yet ever so
When neer the Sun, to stoop again below.
Thus shall my humble Feathers safely hover,
And, though near Earth, more than the Heavens discover.
And then at last, when homeward I shall drive,
Rich with the Spoils of Nature, to my Hive,
There will I sit like that industrious Flie,
Buzzing Thy praises, which shall never die,
Till Death abrupts them, and succeeding Glory
Bid me go on in a more lasting story.

And this is almost all wherein an humble Creature may endeavour to requite and some way to retribute unto his Creator: for if *not he that saith, "Lord, Lord," but he that doth the will of his Father, shall be saved;* certainly our wills must be our performances, and our intents make out our Actions; otherwise our pious labours shall find anxiety in our Graves, and our best endeavours not hope, but fear, a resurrection.

There is but one first cause, and four second causes of all things. Some are without efficient, as GOD; others without matter, as Angels; some without form, as the first matter: but every Essence, created or uncreated, hath its final cause, and some positive end both of its Essence and Operation. This is the cause I grope after in the works of Nature; on this hangs the Providence of GOD. To raise so beauteous a structure as the World and the Creatures thereof, was but His Art; but their sundry and divided operations, with their predestinated ends, are from the Treasure of His Wisdom. In the causes, nature, and affections of the Eclipses of the Sun and Moon, there is most excellent speculation; but to profound farther, and to contemplate a reason why His Providence hath so disposed and ordered their motions in that vast circle as to conjoyn and obscure each other, is a sweeter piece of Reason, and a diviner point of Philosophy. Therefore sometimes, and in some things, there appears to me as much Divinity in Galen his books *De Usu Partium,* as

in Suarez Metaphysicks. Had Aristotle been as curious in
the enquiry of this cause as he was of the other, he had
not left behind him an imperfect piece of Philosophy
but an absolute tract of Divinity.

Natura nihil agit frustra, is the only indisputed Axi
ome in Philosophy. There are no Grotesques in Nature
not anything framed to fill up empty Cantons, and un
necessary spaces. In the most imperfect Creatures, and
such as were not preserved in the Ark, but, having their
Seeds and Principles in the womb of Nature, are every
where, where the power of the Sun is, in these is the Wis
dom of His hand discovered. Out of this rank Solomon
chose the object of his admiration. Indeed, what Reason
may not go to School to the wisdom of Bees, Ants, and
Spiders? what wise hand teacheth *them* to do what Rea
son cannot teach *us?* Ruder heads stand amazed at those
prodigious pieces of Nature, Whales, Elephants, Dromi
daries and Camels; these, I confess, are the Colossus and
majestick pieces of her hand: but in these narrow Engine
there is more curious Mathematicks; and the civility o
these little Citizens more neatly sets forth the Wisdom
of their Maker. Who admires not Regio-Montanus his
Fly beyond his Eagle, or wonders not more at the opera
tion of two Souls in those little Bodies, than but one in
the Trunk of a Cedar? I could never content my con
templation with those general pieces of wonder, th
Flux and Reflux of the Sea, the increase of Nile, the con
version of the Needle to the North; and have studied
to match and parallel those in the more obvious and
neglected pieces of Nature, which without further trave
I can do in the Cosmography of myself. We carry with u
the wonders we seek without us: there is all Africa and
her prodigies in us; we are that bold and adventurou
piece of Nature, which he that studies wisely learns in
compendium what others labour at in a divided piec
and endless volume.

Thus there are two Books from whence I collect my Divinity; besides that written one of GOD, another of His servant Nature, that universal and publick Manuscript, that lies expans'd unto the Eyes of all: those that never saw him in the one, have discover'd Him in the other. This was the Scripture and Theology of the Heathens: the natural motion of the Sun made *them* more admire Him than its supernatural station did the Children of Israel; the ordinary effects of Nature wrought more admiration in *them* than in the other all His Miracles. Surely the Heathens knew better how to joyn and read these mystical Letters than we Christians, who cast a more careless Eye on these common Hieroglyphicks, and disdain to suck Divinity from the flowers of Nature. Nor do I so forget GOD as to adore the name of Nature; which I define not, with the Schools, to be the principle of motion and rest, but that streight and regular line, that settled and constant course the Wisdom of GOD hath ordained the actions of His creatures, according to their several kinds. To make a revolution every day is the Nature of the Sun, because of that necessary course which GOD hath ordained it, from which it cannot swerve but by a faculty from that voice which first did give it motion. Now this course of Nature GOD seldome alters or perverts, but, like an excellent Artist, hath so contrived His work, that with the self same instrument, without a new creation, He may effect His obscurest designs. Thus He sweetneth the Water with a Wood, preserveth the Creatures in the Ark, which the blast of His mouth might have as easily created; for GOD is like a skilful Geometrician, who, when more easily and with one stroak of his Compass he might describe or divide a right line, had yet rather do this in a circle or longer way, according to the constituted and fore-laid principles of his Art. Yet this rule of His He doth sometimes pervert, to acquaint the World with His Prerogative, lest the arrogancy of our reason should question His power, and conclude He could not. And thus I call the effects of Nature the works of GOD, Whose hand and instrument she only is; and therefore to ascribe His actions unto her, is to devolve the honour of the principal agent upon the instrument; which if with reason we may do, then let our hammers rise up and boast they have built our houses, and our pens receive the honour of our writings. I hold there is a general beauty in the works of GOD, and therefore no deformity in any kind or species of creature whatsoever. I cannot tell by what Logick we call a Toad, a Bear, or an Elephant ugly; they being created in those outward shapes and figures which best express the actions of their inward forms, and having past that general Visitation of GOD, Who saw that all that He had made was good, that is, conformable to His Will, which abhors deformity, and is the rule of order and beauty. There is no deformity but in Monstrosity; wherein, notwithstanding, there is a kind of Beauty; Nature so ingeniously contriving the irregular parts, as they become sometimes more remarkable than the principal Fabrick. To speak yet more narrowly, there was never any thing ugly or mis-shapen, but the Chaos; wherein, notwithstanding, (to speak strictly,) there was no deformity, because no form; nor was it yet impregnant by the voice of GOD. Now Nature is not at variance with Art, nor Art with Nature, they being both servants of His Providence. Art is the perfection of Nature. Were the World now as it was the sixth day, there were yet a Chaos. Nature hath made one World, and Art another. In brief, all things are artificial; for Nature is the Art of GOD.

This is the ordinary and open way of His Providence, which Art and Industry have in a good part discovered; whose effects we may foretel without an Oracle: to foreshew these, is not Prophesie, but Prognostication. There is another way, full of Meanders and Labyrinths, whereof the Devil and Spirits have no exact Ephemerides; and that is a more particular and obscure method of His Providence, directing the operations of individuals and single Essences: this we call *Fortune*, that serpentine and crooked line, whereby He draws those actions His Wisdom intends, in a more unknown and secret way. This cryptick and involved method of His Providence have I ever admired; nor can I relate the History of my life, the occurrences of my days, the escapes of dangers, and hits of chance, with a *Bezo las Manos* to Fortune, or a bare *Gramercy* to my good Stars. Abraham might have thought the Ram in the thicket came thither by accident; humane reason would have said that meer chance conveyed Moses in the Ark to the sight of Pharaoh's Daughter: what a Labyrinth is there in the story of Joseph, able to convert a Stoick! Surely there are in every man's Life certain rubs, doublings, and wrenches, which pass a while under the effects of chance, but at the last, well examined, prove the meer hand of GOD. 'Twas not dumb chance, that, to discover the Fougade or Powder-plot, contrived a miscarriage in the Letter. I like the Victory of '88 the better for that one occurrence, which our enemies imputed to our dishonour and the partiality of Fortune, to wit, the tempests and contrariety of Winds. King Philip did not detract from the Nation, when he said, *he sent his Armado to fight with men, and not to combate with the Winds*. Where there is a manifest disproportion between the powers and forces of two several agents, upon a Maxime of reason we may promise the victory to the Superiour; but when unexpected accidents slip in, and unthought of occurrences intervene, these must proceed from a power that owes no obedience to those Axioms; where, as in the writing upon the wall, we may behold the hand, but see not the spring that moves it. The success of that petty Province of Holland (of which the Grand Seignour proudly said, *if they*

should trouble him as they did the Spaniard, he would
send his men with shovels and pick-axes, and throw it
into the Sea,) I cannot altogether ascribe to the ingenuity and industry of the people, but the mercy of GOD,
that hath disposed them to such a thriving Genius; and
to the will of His Providence, that disposeth her favour
to each Country in their pre-ordinate season. All cannot
be happy at once; for, because the glory of one State depends upon the ruine of another, there is a revolution
and vicissitude of their greatness, and must obey the
swing of that wheel, not moved by Intelligences, but by
the hand of GOD, whereby all Estates arise to their *Zenith*
and Vertical points according to their predestinated
periods. For the lives, not only of men, but of Commonwealths, and the whole World, run not upon an *Helix*
that still enlargeth, but on a Circle, where, arriving to
their Meridian, they decline in obscurity, and fall under
the Horizon again.

These must not therefore be named the effects of
Fortune, but in a relative way, and as we term the works
of Nature. It was the ignorance of man's reason that
begat this very name, and by a careless term miscalled
the Providence of GOD; for there is no liberty for causes
to operate in a loose and stragling way; nor any effect
whatsoever, but hath its warrant from some universal or
superiour Cause. 'Tis not a ridiculous devotion to say a
prayer before a game at Tables; for even in *sortilegies*
and matters of greatest uncertainty, there is a setled and
pre-ordered course of effects. It is we that are blind, not
Fortune: because our Eye is too dim to discover the mystery of her effects, we foolishly paint her blind, and hood-
wink the Providence of the Almighty. I cannot justifie
that contemptible Proverb, *That fools only are Fortu-*
nate, or that insolent Paradox, *That a wise man is out*
of the reach of Fortune; much less those opprobrious
epithets of Poets, *Whore, Bawd,* and *Strumpet.* 'Tis, I

confess, the common fate of men of singular gifts of mind
to be destitute of those of Fortune, which doth not any
way deject the Spirit of wiser judgements, who thoroughly
understand the justice of this proceeding; and being
inriched with higher donatives, cast a more careless eye
on these vulgar parts of felicity. It is a most unjust ambition to desire to engross the mercies of the Almighty,
not to be content with the goods of mind, without a possession of those of body or Fortune; and it is an error
worse than heresie, to adore these complemental and
circumstantial pieces of felicity, and undervalue those
perfections and essential points of happiness wherein we
resemble our Maker. To wiser desires it is satisfaction
enough to deserve, though not to enjoy, the favours of
Fortune: let Providence provide for Fools. 'Tis not partiality, but equity in GOD, Who deals with us but as our
natural Parents: those that are able of Body and Mind
He leaves to their deserts; to those of weaker merits He
imparts a larger portion, and pieces out the defect of
one by the excess of the other. Thus have we no just
quarrel with Nature for leaving us naked; or to envy the
Horns, Hoofs, Skins, and Furs of other Creatures, being
provided with Reason, that can supply them all. We
need not labour with so many Arguments to confute
Judicial Astrology; for, if there be a truth therein, it doth
not injure Divinity. If to be born under *Mercury* disposeth us to be witty, under *Jupiter* to be wealthy; I do
not owe a Knee unto these, but unto that merciful
Hand that hath ordered my indifferent and uncertain
nativity unto such benevolous Aspects. Those that hold
that all things are governed by Fortune, had not erred,
had they not persisted there. The Romans, that erected
a Temple to Fortune, acknowledged therein, though in
a blinder way, somewhat of Divinity; for, in a wise supputation, all things begin and end in the Almighty. There
is a nearer way to Heaven than Homer's Chain; an easie

Logic may conjoyn Heaven and Earth in one Argument, and with less than a *Sorites* resolve all things into GOD. For though we christen effects by their most sensible and nearest Causes, yet is GOD the true and infallible Cause of all; whose concourse, though it be general, yet doth it subdivide itself into the particular Actions of every thing, and is that Spirit, by which each singular Essence not only subsists, but performs its operation.

The bad construction and perverse comment on these pair of second Causes, or visible hands of GOD, have perverted the Devotion of many unto Atheism; who, forgetting the honest Advisoes of Faith, have listened unto the conspiracy of Passion and Reason. I have therefore always endeavoured to compose those Feuds and angry Dissentions between Affection, Faith, and Reason; for there is in our Soul a kind of Triumvirate, or triple Government of three Competitors, which distract the Peace of this our Commonwealth, not less than did that other the State of Rome.

As Reason is a Rebel unto Faith, so Passion unto Reason: as the propositions of Faith seem absurd unto Reason, so the Theorems of Reason unto Passion, and both unto Reason. Yet a moderate and peaceable discretion may so state and order the matter, that they may be all Kings, and yet make but one Monarchy, every one exercising his Soveraignty and Prerogative in a due time and place, according to the restraint and limit of circumstance. There is, as in Philosophy, so in Divinity, sturdy doubts and boisterous Objections, wherewith the unhappiness of our knowledge too nearly acquainteth us. More of these no man hath known than myself, which I confess I conquered, not in a martial posture, but on my Knees. For our endeavours are not only to combat with doubts, but always to dispute with the Devil. The villany of that Spirit takes a hint of Infidelity from our Studies, and, by demonstrating a naturality in one way, makes us mistrust a miracle in another. Thus, having perused the *Archidoxis* and read the secret Sympathies of things, he would disswade my belief from the miracle of the Brazen Serpent, make me conceit that Image worked by Sympathy, and was but an Ægyptian trick to cure their Diseases without a miracle. Again, having seen some experiments of *Bitumen,* and having read far more of *Naphtha,* he whispered to my curiosity the fire of the Altar might be natural; and bid me mistrust a miracle in Elias, when he entrenched the Altar round with Water; for that inflamable substance yields not easily unto Water, but flames in the Arms of its Antagonist. And thus would he inveagle my belief to think the combustion of Sodom might be natural, and that there was an Asphaltick and Bituminous nature in that Lake before the Fire of Gomorrah. I know that *Manna* is now plentifully gathered in Calabria; and Josephus tells me, in his days it was as plentiful in Arabia; the Devil therefore made the *quære, Where was then the miracle in the days of Moses? the Israelites saw but that in his time, the Natives of those Countries behold in ours.* Thus the Devil played at Chess with me, and yielding a Pawn, thought to gain a Queen of me, taking advantage of my honest endeavours; and whilst I laboured to raise the structure of my Reason, he strived to undermine the edifice of my Faith.

Neither had these or any other ever such advantage of me, as to incline me to any point of Infidelity or desperate positions of Atheism; for I have been these many years of opinion there was never any. Those that held Religion was the difference of Man from Beasts, have spoken probably, and proceed upon a principle as inductive as the other. That doctrine of Epicurus, that denied the Providence of GOD, was no Atheism, but a magnificent and high strained conceit of His Majesty, which he deemed too sublime to mind the trivial Actions of those inferiour Creatures. That *aftal Necessity* of the Stoicks is nothing but the immutable Law of His Will. Those that heretofore denied the Divinity of the HOLY GHOST, have been condemned but as Hereticks; and those that now deny our Saviour, (though more than Hereticks,) are not so much as Atheists; for, though they deny two persons in the Trinity, they hold, as we do, there is but one GOD.

That Villain and Secretary of Hell, that composed that miscreant piece *Of the Three Impostors,* though divided from all Religions, and was neither Jew, Turk, nor Christian, was not a positive Atheist. I confess every Country hath its Machiavel, every Age its Lucian, whereof common Heads must not hear, nor more advanced Judgments too rashly venture on: it is the Rhetorick of Satan, and may pervert a loose or prejudicate belief.

I confess I have perused them all, and can discover nothing that may startle a discreet belief; yet are there heads carried off with the Wind and breath of such motives. I remember a Doctor in Physick, of Italy, who could not perfectly believe the immortality of the Soul, because Galen seemed to make a doubt thereof. With another I was familiarly acquainted in France, a Divine, and a man of singular parts, that on the same point was so plunged and gravelled with three lines of Seneca, that all our Antidotes, drawn from both Scripture and Philosophy, could not expel the poyson of his errour. There are a set of Heads, that can credit the relations of Mariners, yet question the Testimonies of St. Paul; and peremptorily maintain the traditions of Ælian or Pliny, yet in Histories of Scripture raise Queries and Objections, believing no more than they can parallel in humane Authors. I confess there are in Scripture Stories that do exceed the Fables of Poets, and to a captious Reader sound like *Garagantua* or *Bevis.* Search all the Legends of times past, and the fabulous conceits of these present and 'twill be hard to find one that deserves to carry the

Buckler unto Sampson; yet is all this of an easie possibility, if we conceive a Divine concourse, or an influence but from the little Finger of the Almighty. It is impossible that either in the discourse of man, or in the infallible Voice of GOD, to the weakness of our apprehensions, there should not appear irregularities, contradictions, and antimonies: my self could shew a Catalogue of doubts, never yet imagined nor questioned, as I know, which are not resolved at the first hearing; not fantastick Queries or Objections of Air; for I cannot hear of Atoms in Divinity. I can read the History of the Pigeon that was sent out of the Ark, and returned no more, yet not question how she found out her Mate that was left behind: that Lazarus was raised from the dead, yet not demand where in the interim his Soul awaited; or raise a Law-case, whether his Heir might lawfully detain his inheritance bequeathed unto him by his death, and he, though restored to life, have no Plea or Title unto his former possessions. Whether Eve was framed out of the left side of Adam, I dispute not; because I stand not yet assured which is the right side of a man, or whether there be any such distinction in Nature: that she was edified out of the Rib of Adam I believe, yet raise no question who shall arise with that Rib at the Resurrection. Whether Adam was an Hermaphrodite, as the Rabbins contend upon the Letter of the Text, because it is contrary to reason, there should be an Hermaphrodite before there was a Woman, or a composition of two Natures before there was a second composed. Likewise, whether the World was created in Autumn, Summer, or the Spring, because it was created in them all; for whatsoever Sign the Sun possesseth, those four Seasons are actually existent. It is the nature of this Luminary to distinguish the several Seasons of the year, all which it makes at one time in the whole Earth, and successive in any part thereof. There are a bundle of curiosities, not only in Philosophy, but in

Divinity, proposed and discussed by men of most supposed abilities, which indeed are not worthy our vacant
hours, much less our serious Studies: Pieces only fit to be
placed in *Pantagruel's* Library, or bound up with Tartaretus *De modo Cacandi.*

These are niceties that become not those that peruse
so serious a Mystery. There are others more generally
questioned and called to the Bar, yet methinks of an easie
and possible truth.

'Tis ridiculous to put off or drown the general Flood
of Noah in that particular inundation of Deucalion. That
there was a Deluge once, seems not to me so great a Miracle, as that there is not one always. How all the kinds of
Creatures, not only in their own bulks, but with a com-
petency of food and sustenance, might be preserved in
one Ark, and within the extent of three hundred Cubits,
to a reason that rightly examines it, will appear very
feasible. There is another secret, not contained in the
Scripture, which is more hard to comprehend, and put
the honest Father to the refuge of a Miracle; and that
is, not only how the distinct pieces of the World, and
divided Islands, should be first planted by men, but inhabited by Tigers, Panthers, and Bears. How America
abounded with Beasts of prey and noxious Animals, yet
contained not in it that necessary Creature, a Horse, is
very strange. By what passage those, not only Birds, but
dangerous and unwelcome Beasts, came over; how there
be Creatures there, which are not found in this Triple
Continent; (all which must needs be strange unto us, that
hold but one Ark, and that the Creatures began their
progress from the Mountains of Ararat:) they who, to
salve this, would make the Deluge particular, proceed
upon a principle that I can no way grant; not only upon
the negative of Holy Scriptures, but of mine own Reason, whereby I can make it probable, that the world was
as well peopled in the time of Noah as in ours; and fif-

teen hundred years to people the World, as full a time for them, as four thousand years since have been to us.

There are other assertions and common Tenents drawn from Scripture, and generally believed as Scripture, whereunto, notwithstanding, I would never betray the liberty of my Reason. 'Tis a Postulate to me, that Methusalem was the longest liv'd of all the Children of Adam; and no man will be able to prove it, when, from the process of the Text, I can manifest it may be otherwise. That Judas perished by hanging himself, there is no certainty in Scripture: though in one place it seems to affirm it, and by a doubtful word hath given occasion to translate it; yet in another place, in a more punctual description, it makes it improbable, and seems to overthrow it. That our Fathers, after the Flood, erected the Tower of Babel to preserve themselves against a second Deluge, is generally opinioned and believed; yet is there another intention of theirs expressed in Scripture: besides, it is improbable from the circumstance of the place, that is, a plain in the Land of Shinar. These are no points of Faith, and therefore may admit a free dispute.

There are yet others, and those familiarly concluded from the text, wherein (under favour,) I see no consequence. The Church of Rome confidently proves the opinion of Tutelary Angels from that Answer, when Peter knockt at the Door, *'Tis not he, but his Angel;* that is, (might some say,) his *Messenger,* or some body from him; for so the Original signifies, and is as likely to be the doubtful Families meaning. This exposition I once suggested to a young Divine, that answered upon this point; to which I remember the Franciscan Opponent replyed no more, but *That it was a new, and no authentick interpretation.*

These are but the conclusions and fallible discourses of man upon the Word of God, for such I do believe the Holy Scriptures: yet, were it of man, I could not chuse but say, it was the singularest and superlative piece that hath been extant since the Creation. Were I a Pagan, I should not refrain the Lecture of it; and cannot but commend the judgment of Ptolomy, that thought not his Library compleat without it. The Alcoran of the Turks (I speak without prejudice,) is an ill composed Piece, containing in it vain and ridiculous Errors in Philosophy, impossibilities, fictions, and vanities beyond laughter, maintained by evident and open Sophisms, the Policy of Ignorance, deposition of Universities, and banishment of Learning, that hath gotten Foot by Arms and violence: this without a blow hath disseminated it self through the whole Earth. It is not unremarkable what Philo first observed, that the Law of Moses continued two thousand years without the least alteration; whereas, we see the Laws of other Common-weals do alter with occasions; and even those that pretended their original from some Divinity, to have vanished without trace or memory. I believe, besides Zoroaster, there were divers that writ before Moses, who, notwithstanding, have suffered the common fate of time. Mens Works have an age like themselves; and though they out-live their Authors, yet have they a stint and period to their duration: this only is a work too hard for the teeth of time, and cannot perish but in the general Flames, when all things shall confess their Ashes.

I have heard some with deep sighs lament the lost lines of Cicero; others with as many groans deplore the combustion of the Library of Alexandria: for my own part, I think there be too many in the World, and could with patience behold the urn and ashes of the Vatican, could I, with a few others, recover the perished leaves of Solomon. I would not omit a Copy of Enoch's Pillars, had they many nearer Authors than Josephus, or did not relish somewhat of the Fable. Some men have written more than others have spoken; Pineda quotes more

Authors in one work, than are necessary in a whole World. Of those three great inventions in Germany, there are two which are not without their incommodities, and 'tis disputable whether they exceed not their use and commodities. 'Tis not a melancholy *Utinam* of my own, but the desires of better heads, that there were a general Synod; not to unite the incompatible difference of Religion, but for the benefit of learning, to reduce it as it lay at first, in a few and solid Authors; and to condemn to the fire those swarms and millions of Rhapsodies, begotten only to distract and abuse the weaker judgements of Scholars, and to maintain the trade and mystery of Typographers.

I cannot but wonder with what exception the Samaritans could confine their belief to the Pentateuch, or five Books of Moses. I am ashamed at the Rabbinical Interpretation of the Jews upon the Old Testament, as much as their defection from the New: and truly it is beyond wonder, how that contemptible and degenerate issue of Jacob, once so devoted to Ethnick Superstition, and so easily seduced to the Idolatry of their Neighbours, should now in such an obstinate and peremptory belief adhere unto their own Doctrine, expect impossibilities, and, in the face and eye of the Church, persist without the least hope of Conversion. This is a vice in *them,* that were a vertue in *us;* for obstinacy in a bad Cause is but constancy in a good. And herein I must accuse those of my own Religion, for there is not any of such a fugitive Faith, such an unstable belief, as a Christian; none that do so oft transform themselves, not unto several shapes of Christianity and of the same Species, but unto more unnatural and contrary Forms of Jew and Mahometan; that, from the name of *Saviour,* can condescend to the bare term of *Prophet;* and, from an old belief that He is come, fall to a new expectation of His coming. It is the promise of CHRIST to make us all one Flock; but

how and when this Union shall be, is as obscure to me
as the last day. Of those four Members of Religion we
hold a slender proportion. There are, I confess, some new
additions, yet small to those which accrew to our Adversaries, and those only drawn from the revolt of Pagans,
men but of negative Impieties, and such as deny CHRIST,
but because they never heard of Him. But the Religion
of the Jew is expressly against the Christian, and the
Mahometan against both. For the Turk, in the bulk
he now stands, he is beyond all hope of conversion; if
he fall asunder, there may be conceived hopes, but not
without strong improbabilities. The Jew is obstinate in
all fortune; the persecution of fifteen hundred years hath
but confirmed them in their Errour: they have already
endured whatsoever may be inflicted, and have suffered
in a bad cause, even to the condemnation of their enemies. Persecution is a bad and indirect way to plant Religion: it hath been the unhappy method of angry Devotions, not only to confirm honest Religion, but wicked
Heresies, and extravagant Opinions. It was the first stone
and Basis of our Faith; none can more justly boast of Per-
secutions, and glory in the number and valour of Martyrs. For, to speak properly, those are true and almost
only examples of fortitude: those that are fetch'd from
the field, or drawn from the actions of the Camp, are not
oft-times so truely precedents of valour as audacity, and
at the best attain but to some bastard piece of fortitude.
If we shall strictly examine the circumstances and req-
uisites which Aristotle requires to true and perfect
valour, we shall find the name only in his Master, Alexander, and as little in that Roman Worthy, Julius Cæsar;
and if any in that easie and active way have done so
nobly as to deserve that name, yet in the passive and
more terrible piece these have surpassed, and in a more
heroical way may claim the honour of that Title. 'Tis not
in the power of every honest Faith to proceed thus far, or

pass to Heaven through the flames. Every one hath it not
in that full measure, nor in so audacious and resolute a
temper, as to endure those terrible tests and trials; who,
notwithstanding, in a peaceable way, do truely adore
their Saviour, and have (no doubt,) a Faith acceptable in
the eyes of GOD.

Now, as all that dye in the War are not termed *Souldiers;* so neither can I properly term all those that suffer
in matters of Religion, *Martyrs*. The Council of Con-
stance condemns John Huss for an Heretick; the Stories
of his own Party stile him a Martyr: he must needs offend the Divinity of both, that says he was neither the one
nor the other. There are many (questionless,) canon-
ized on earth, that shall never be Saints in Heaven; and
have their names in Histories and Martyrologies, who
in the eyes of GOD are not so perfect Martyrs as was that
wise Heathen, Socrates, that suffered on a fundamental
point of Religion, the Unity of GOD. I have often pitied
the miserable Bishop that suffered in the cause of Antipodes; yet cannot chuse but accuse *him* of as much madness, for exposing his living on such a trifle, as those of
ignorance and folly, that condemned him. I think my
conscience will not give me the lye, if I say there are not
many extant that in a noble way fear the face of death
less than myself; yet, from the moral duty I owe to the
Commandment of GOD, and the natural respects that I
tender unto the conservation of my essence and being,
I would not perish upon a Ceremony, Politick points,
or indifference: nor is my belief of that untractible temper, as not to bow at their obstacles, or connive at matters wherein there are not manifest impieties. The
leaven, therefore, and ferment of all, not only civil but
Religious actions, is Wisdom; without which, to commit
ourselves to the flames is Homicide, and (I fear,) but to
pass through one fire into another.

That Miracles are ceased, I can neither prove, nor

absolutely deny, much less define the time and period of their cessation. That they survived CHRIST, is manifest upon the Record of Scripture; that they outlived the Apostles also, and were revived at the Conversion of Nations many years after, we cannot deny, if we shall not question those Writers whose testimonies we do not controvert in points that make for our own opinions. Therefore that may have some truth in it that is reported by the Jesuites of their Miracles in the Indies; I could wish it were true, or had any other testimony than their own Pens. *They* may easily believe those Miracles abroad, who daily conceive a greater at home, the transmutation of those visible elements into the Body and Blood of our Saviour. For the conversion of Water into Wine, which He wrought in Cana, or, what the Devil would have had Him done in the Wilderness, of Stones into Bread, compared to this, will scarce deserve the name of a Miracle: though indeed, to speak properly, there is not one Miracle greater than another, they being the extraordinary effects of the Hand of GOD, to which all things are of an equal facility; and to create the World, as easie as one single Creature. For this is also a Miracle, not onely to produce effects against or above Nature, but before Nature; and to create Nature, as great a Miracle as to contradict or transcend her. We do too narrowly define the Power of GOD, restraining it to our capacities. I hold that GOD can do all things; how He should work contradictions, I do not understand, yet dare not therefore deny. I cannot see why the Angel of GOD should question Esdras to recal the time past, if it were beyond His own power; or that GOD should pose mortality in that which He was not able to perform Himself. I will not say GOD cannot, but He will not, perform many things, which we plainly affirm He cannot. This, I am sure, is the mannerliest proposition, wherein, notwithstanding, I hold no Paradox; for, strictly, His power is the same with His will, and they both, with all the rest, do make but one GOD.

Therefore that Miracles have been, I do believe; that they may yet be wrought by the living, I do not deny; but have no confidence in those which are fathered on the dead. And this hath ever made me suspect the efficacy of reliques, to examine the bones, question the habits and appurtenances of Saints, and even of CHRIST Himself. I cannot conceive why the Cross that Helena found, and whereon CHRIST Himself dyed, should have power to restore others unto life. I excuse not Constantine from a fall off his Horse, or a mischief from his enemies, upon the wearing those nails on his bridle, which our Saviour bore upon the Cross in His Hands. I compute among your *Piæ fraudes,* nor many degrees before consecrated Swords and Roses, that which Baldwyn, King of Jerusalem, returned the Genovese for their cost and pains in his War, to wit, the ashes of John the Baptist. Those that hold the sanctity of their Souls doth leave behind a tincture and sacred faculty on their bodies, speak naturally of Miracles, and do not salve the doubt. Now one reason I tender so little Devotion unto Reliques, is, I think, the slender and doubtful respect I have always held unto Antiquities. For that indeed which I admire, is far before Antiquity, that is, Eternity; and that is, GOD Himself; Who, though He be styled *the Ancient of Days,* cannot receive the adjunct of Antiquity; Who was before the World, and shall be after it, yet is not older than it; for in His years there is no Climacter; His duration is Eternity, and far more venerable than Antiquity.

But above all things I wonder how the curiosity of wiser heads could pass that great and indisputable Miracle, the cessation of Oracles; and in what swoun their Reasons lay, to content themselves and sit down with such a far-fetch'd and ridiculous reason as Plutarch

alleadgeth for it. The Jews, that can believe the supernatural Solstice of the Sun in the days of Joshua, have yet
the impudence to deny the Eclipse, which every Pagan
confessed, at His death: but for this, it is evident beyond
all contradiction, the Devil himself confessed it. Certainly it is not a warrantable curiosity, to examine the
verity of Scripture by the concordance of humane history, or seek to confirm the Chronicle of Hester or Daniel, by the authority of Megasthenes or Herodotus. I confess, I have had an unhappy curiosity this way, till I
laughed my self out of it with a piece of Justine, where
he delivers that the Children of Israel for being scabbed
were banished out of Egypt. And truely since I have
understood the occurrences of the World, and know in
what counterfeit shapes and deceitful vizards times present represent on the stage things past, I do believe them
little more then things to come. Some have been of my
opinion, and endeavoured to write the History of their
own lives; wherein Moses hath outgone them all, and left
not onely the story of his life, but (as some will have it,)
of his death also.

It is a riddle to me, how this story of Oracles hath not
worm'd out of the World that doubtful conceit of Spirits
and Witches; how so many learned heads should so far
forget their Metaphysicks, and destroy the ladder and
scale of creatures, as to question the existence of Spirits.
For my part, I have ever believed and do now know, that
there are Witches: they that doubt of these, do not onely
deny *them,* but Spirits; and are obliquely and upon consequence a sort not of Infidels, but Atheists. Those that
to confute their incredulity desire to see apparitions, shall
questionless never behold any, nor have the power to be
so much as Witches; the Devil hath them already in a
heresie as Capital as Witchcraft; and to appear to them,
were but to convert them. Of all the delusions wherewith
he deceives mortality, there is not any that puzzleth me

more than the Legerdemain of Changelings. I do not credit those transformations of reasonable creatures into beasts, or that the Devil hath a power to transpeciate a man into a Horse, who tempted CHRIST (as a trial of His Divinity,) to convert but stones into bread. I could believe that Spirits use with man the act of carnality, and that in both sexes; I conceive they may assume, steal, or contrive a body, wherein there may be action enough to content decrepit lust, or passion to satisfie more active veneries; yet, in both, without a possibility of generation: and therefore that opinion that Antichrist should be born of the Tribe of Dan by conjunction with the Divil, is ridiculous, and a conceit fitter for a Rabbin than a Christian. I hold that the Devil doth really possess some men, the spirit of Melancholly others, the spirit of Delusion others; that, as the Devil is concealed and denyed by some, so GOD and good Angels are pretended by others, whereof the late defection of the Maid of Germany hath left a pregnant example.

Again, I believe that all that use sorceries, incantations, and spells, are not Witches, or, as we term them, *Magicians.* I conceive there is a traditional Magick, not learned immediately from the Devil, but at second hand from his Scholars, who, having once the secret betrayed, are able, and do emperically practise without his advice, they both proceeding upon the principles of Nature; where actives, aptly conjoyned to disposed passives, will under any Master produce their effects. Thus I think at first a great part of Philosophy was Witchcraft; which, being afterward derived to one another, proved but Philosophy, and was indeed no more but the honest effects of Nature: what, invented by us, is Philosophy, learned from him, is Magick. We do surely owe the discovery of many secrets to the discovery of good and bad Angels. I could never pass that sentence of Paracelsus without an asterisk or annotation; *Ascendens constel-*

latum multa revelat quærentibus magnalia naturæ, (i.e. *opera* DEI.) I do think that many mysteries ascribed to our own inventions have been the courteous revelations of Spirits; (for those noble essences in Heaven bear a friendly regard unto their fellow Natures on Earth;) and therefore believe that those many prodigies and ominous prognosticks, which fore-run the ruines of States, Princes, and private persons, are the charitable premonitions of good Angels, which more careless enquiries term but the effects of chance and nature.

Now, besides these particular and divided Spirits, there may be (for ought I know,) an universal and common Spirit to the whole World. It was the opinion of Plato, and it is yet of the Hermetical Philosophers. If there be a common nature that unites and tyes the scattered and divided individuals into one species, why may there not be one that unites them all? However, I am sure there is a common Spirit that plays within us, yet makes no part of us; and that is, the Spirit of GOD, the fire and scintillation of that noble and mighty Essence, which is the life and radical heat of Spirits, and those essences that know not the vertue of the Sun; a fire quite contrary to the fire of Hell. This is that gentle heat that brooded on the waters, and in six days hatched the World; this is that irradiation that dispels the mists of Hell, the clouds of horrour, fear, sorrow, despair; and preserves the region of the mind in serenity. Whosoever feels not the warm gale and gentle ventilation of this Spirit, though I feel his pulse, I dare not say he lives: for truely, without this, to me there is no heat under the Tropick; nor any light, though I dwelt in the body of the Sun.

> As, when the labouring Sun hath wrought his track
> Up to the top of lofty Cancers back,
> The ycie Ocean cracks, the frozen pole
> Thaws with the heat of the Celestial coale;

So, when Thy absent beams begin t' impart
Again a Solstice on my frozen heart,
My winter's ov'r, my drooping spirits sing,
And every part revives into a Spring.
But if Thy quickning beams a while decline,
And with their light bless not this Orb of mine,
A chilly frost surpriseth every member,
And in the midst of June I feel December.
O how this earthly temper both debase
The noble Soul, in this her humble place;
Whose wingy nature ever doth aspire
To reach that place whence first it took its fire.
These flames I feel, which in my heart do dwell,
Are not Thy beams, but take their fire from Hell:
O quench them all, and let Thy Light divine
Be as the Sun to this poor Orb of mine;
And to Thy sacred Spirit convert those fires,
Whose earthly fumes choak my devout aspires.

Therefore for Spirits, I am so far from denying their existence, that I could easily believe, that not onely whole Countries, but particular persons, have their Tutelary and Guardian Angels. It is not a new opinion of the Church of Rome, but an old one of Pythagoras and Plato; there is no heresie in it; and if not manifestly defin'd in Scripture, yet is it an opinion of a good and wholesome use in the course and actions of a mans life, and would serve as an Hypothesis to salve many doubts, whereof common Philosophy affordeth no solution. Now, if you demand my opinion and Metaphysicks of their natures, I confess them very shallow; most of them in a negative way, like that of GOD; or in a comparative, between ourselves and fellow-creatures; for there is in this Universe a Stair, or manifest Scale of creatures, rising not disorderly, or in confusion, but with a comely method and proportion. Between creatures of meer existence, and things of life, there is a large disproportion of nature; between plants, and animals or creatures of sense, a wider difference; between them and Man, a far greater: and if the proportion hold one, between Man and Angels there should be yet a greater. We do not comprehend their natures, who retain the first definition of Porphyry, and distinguish them from our selves by immortality; for before his Fall, 'tis thought, Man also was Immortal; yet must we needs affirm that he had a different essence from the Angels. Having therefore no certain knowledge of their Natures, 'tis no bad method of the Schools, whatsoever perfection we find obscurely in our selves, in a more compleat and absolute way to ascribe unto them. I believe they have an extemporary knowledge, and upon the first motion of their reason do what we cannot without study or deliberation; that they know things by their forms, and define by specifical difference what we describe by accidents and properties; and therefore probabilities to us may be demonstrations unto them: that they have knowledge not onely of the specifical, but numerical forms of individuals, and understand by what reserved difference each single Hypostasis (besides the relation to its species,) becomes its numerical self: that, as the Soul hath a power to move the body it informs, so there's a faculty to move any, though inform none: ours upon restraint of time, place, and distance; but that invisible hand that conveyed Habakkuk to the Lyons Den, or Philip to Azotus, infringeth this rule, and hath a secret conveyance, wherewith mortality is not acquainted. If they have that intuitive knowledge, whereby as in reflexion they behold the thoughts of one another, I cannot peremptorily deny but they know a great part of ours. They that, to refute the Invocation of Saints, have denied that they have any knowledge of our affairs below, have proceeded too far, and must pardon my opinion, till I can thoroughly answer that piece of Scripture, *At the conversion of a sinner the Angels in Heaven rejoyce.* I cannot, with those in that great Father, securely interpret the work of the first day, *Fiat lux,* to the creation of Angels; though I confess, there is not any creature that hath so neer a glympse of their nature as light in the Sun and Elements. We stile it a bare accident; but, where it subsists alone, 'tis a spiritual Substance, and may be an Angel: in brief, conceive light invisible, and that is a Spirit.

These are certainly the Magisterial and masterpieces of the Creator, the Flower, or (as we may say,) the best part of nothing; actually existing, what we are but in hopes and probability. We are onely that amphibious piece between a corporal and spiritual Essence, that middle form that links those two together, and makes good the Method of GOD and Nature, that jumps not from extreams, but unites the incompatible distances by some middle and participating natures. That we are the breath and similitude of GOD, it is indisputable, and upon record of Holy Scripture; but to call ourselves a Microcosm, or little World, I thought it only a pleasant trope of Rhetorick, till my neer judgement and second thoughts told me there was a real truth therein. For first we are a rude mass, and in the rank of creatures which onely are, and have a dull kind of being, not yet priviledged with life, or preferred to sense or reason; next we live the life of Plants, the life of Animals, the life of Men, and at last the life of Spirits, running on in one mysterious nature those five kinds of existences, which comprehend the creatures, not onely of the World, but of the Universe. Thus is Man that great and true *Amphibium,* whose nature is disposed to live, not onely like other creatures in divers elements, but in divided and distinguished worlds: for though there be but one to sense, there are two to reason, the one visible, the other invisible; whereof Moses seems to have left description, and of the other so obscurely, that some parts thereof are yet in controversie. And truely, for the first chapters of Genesis, I must confess a great deal of obscurity; though Divines have to the power of humane reason endeavoured to make all

go in a literal meaning, yet those allegorical interpretations are also probable, and perhaps the mystical method
of Moses bred up in the Hieroglyphical Schools of the
Egyptians.

Now for that immaterial world, methinks we need not
wander so far as beyond the first moveable; for even in
this material Fabrick the Spirits walk as freely exempt
from the affection of time, place, and motion, as beyond
the extreamest circumference. Do but extract from the
corpulency of bodies, or resolve things beyond their first
matter, and you discover the habitation of Angels, which
if I call the ubiquitary and omnipresent Essence of GOD,
I hope I shall not offend Divinity: for before the
Creation of the World GOD was really all things. For the
Angels He created no new World, or determinate mansion, and therefore they are everywhere where is His
Essence, and do live at a distance even in Himself. That
GOD made all things for Man, is in some sense true, yet
not so far as to subordinate the Creation of those purer
Creatures unto ours, though as *ministring Spirits* they
do, and are willing to fulfil the will of GOD in these lower
and sublunary affairs of Man. GOD made all things for
Himself, and it is impossible He should make them for
any other end than His own Glory; it is all He can receive, and all that is without Himself. For, honour being
an external adjunct, and in the honourer rather than
in the person honoured, it was necessary to make a Creature, from whom He might receive this homage; and that
is, in the other world, Angels, in this, Man; which when
we neglect, we forget the very end of our Creation, and
may justly provoke GOD, not onely to repent that He
hath made the World, but that He hath sworn He would
not destroy it. That there is but one World, is a conclusion of Faith: Aristotle with all his Philosophy hath not
been able to prove it, and as weakly that the World was
eternal. That dispute much troubled the Pen of the an-

cient Philosophers, but Moses decided that question, and all is salved with the new term of a *Creation*, that is, a production of something out of nothing. And what is that? whatsoever is opposite to something; or more exactly, that which is truely contrary unto GOD: for He onely is, all others have an existence with dependency, and are something but by a distinction. And herein is Divinity conformant unto Philosophy, and generation not onely founded on contrarieties, but also creation; GOD, being all things, is contrary unto nothing, out of which were made all things, and so nothing became something, and Omneity informed Nullity into an Essence.

The whole Creation is a Mystery, and particularly that of Man. At the blast of His mouth were the rest of the Creatures made, and at His bare word they started out of nothing: but in the frame of Man (as the Text describes it,) He played the sensible operator, and seemed not so much to create, as make him. When He had separated the materials of other creatures, there consequently resulted a form and soul; but, having raised the walls of Man, He was driven to a second and harder creation of a substance like Himself, an incorruptible and immortal Soul. For these two affections we have the Philosophy and opinion of the Heathens, the flat affirmative of Plato, and not a negative from Aristotle. There is another scruple cast in by Divinity concerning its production, much disputed in the Germane auditories, and with that indifferency and equality of arguments, as leave the controversie undetermined. I am not of Paracelsus mind, that boldly delivers a receipt to make a man without conjunction; yet cannot but wonder at the multitude of heads that do deny traduction, having no other argument to confirm their belief then that Rhetorical sentence and *Antimetathesis* of Augustine, *Creando infunditur, infundendo creatur.* Either opinion will consist well enough with Religion: yet I should rather incline to this, did not one

objection haunt me, (not wrung from speculations and
subtilties, but from common sense and observation; not
pickt from the leaves of any Author, but bred amongst
the weeds and tares of mine own brain;) and this is a conclusion from the equivocal and monstrous productions
in the conjunction of Man with Beast: for if the Soul
of man be not transmitted and transfused in the seed
of the Parents, why are not those productions meerly
beasts, but have also an impression and tincture of reason in as high a measure as it can evidence it self in those
improper Organs? Nor, truely, can I peremptorily deny
that the Soul, in this her sublunary estate, is wholly and
in all acceptions inorganical; but that for the perform-
ance of her ordinary actions there is required not onely a
symmetry and proper disposition of Organs, but a Crasis
and temper correspondent to its operations: yet is not
this mass of flesh and visible structure the instrument
and proper corps of the Soul, but rather of Sense, and
that the hand of Reason. In our study of Anatomy there
is a mass of mysterious Philosophy, and such as reduced
the very Heathens to Divinity: yet, amongst all those
rare discoveries and curious pieces I find in the Fabrick
of Man, I do not so much content myself, as in that I find
not, there is no Organ or Instrument for the rational
Soul; for in the brain, which we term the seat of Reason,
there is not any thing of moment more than I can discover in the crany of a beast: and this is a sensible and
no inconsiderable argument of the inorganity of the Soul,
at least in that sense we usually so receive it. Thus we are
men, and we know not how: there is something in us
that can be without us, and will be after us; though it is
strange that it hath no history what it was before us, nor
cannot tell how it entred in us.

Now, for these walls of flesh, wherein the Soul doth
seem to be immured before the Resurrection, it is nothing but an elemental composition, and a Fabrick that

must fall to ashes. *All flesh is grass,* is not onely metaphorically, but litterally, true; for all those creatures we behold are but the herbs of the field, digested into flesh in them, or more remotely carnified in our selves. Nay further, we are what we all abhor, *Anthropophagi* and Cannibals, devourers not onely of men, but of our selves; and that not in an allegory, but a positive truth; for all this mass of flesh which we behold, came in at our mouths; this frame we look upon, hath been upon our trenchers; in brief, we have devour'd our selves. I cannot believe the wisdom of Pythagoras did ever positively, and in a literal sense, affirm his Metempsychosis, or impossible transmigration of the Souls of men into beasts. Of all Metamorphoses or transmigrations, I believe only one, that is of Lots wife; for that of Nebuchodonosor proceeded not so far: in all others I conceive there is no further verity than is contained in their implicite sense and morality. I believe that the whole frame of a beast doth perish, and is left in the same state after death as before it was materialled unto life: that the Souls of men know neither contrary nor corruption; that they subsist beyond the body, and outlive death by the priviledge of their proper natures, and without a Miracle; that the Souls of the faithful, as they leave Earth, take possession of Heaven: that those apparitions and ghosts of departed persons are not the wandring souls of men, but the unquiet walks of Devils, prompting and suggesting us unto mischief, blood, and villainy; instilling and stealing into our hearts that the blessed Spirits are not at rest in their graves, but wander sollicitous of the affairs of the World. But that those phantasms appear often, and do frequent Cœmeteries, Charnel-houses, and Churches, it is because those are the dormitories of the dead, where the Devil, like an insolent Champion, beholds with pride the spoils and Trophies of his Victory over Adam.

This is that dismal conquest we all deplore, that makes

us so often cry, *O Adam, quid fecisti?* I thank GOD I have
not those strait ligaments, or narrow obligations to the
World, as to dote on life, or be convulst and tremble at
the name of death. Not that I am insensible of the dread
and horrour thereof; or by raking into the bowels of
the deceased, continual sight of Anatomies, Skeletons,
or Cadaverous reliques, like Vespilloes, or Grave-makers,
I am become stupid or have forgot the apprehension
of Mortality; but that, marshalling all the horrours, and
contemplating the extremities thereof, I find not anything therein able to daunt the courage of a man, much
less a well-resolved Christian; and therefore am not angry
at the errour of our first Parents, or unwilling to bear
a part of this common fate, and like the best of them to
dye, that is, to cease to breathe, to take a farewel of the
elements, to be a kind of nothing for a moment, to be
within one instant of a Spirit. When I take a full view
and circle of my self without this reasonable moderator,
and equal piece of Justice, Death, I do conceive my self
the miserablest person extant. Were there not another
life that I hope for, all the vanities of this World should
not intreat a moments breath from me: could the Devil
work my belief to imagine I could never dye, I would not
outlive that very thought. I have so abject a conceit of
this common way of existence, this retaining to the Sun
and Elements, I cannot think this is to be a Man, or to
live according to the dignity of humanity. In exspectation
of a better, I can with patience embrace this life, yet in
my best meditations do often defie death; I honour any
man that contemns it, nor can I highly love any that is
afraid of it: this makes me naturally love a Souldier, and
honour those tattered and contemptible Regiments that
will die at the command of a Sergeant. For a Pagan there
may be some motives to be in love with life; but for a
Christian to be amazed at death, I see not how he can

escape this Dilemma, that he is too sensible of this life, or hopeless of the life to come.

Some Divines count Adam thirty years old at his Creation, because they suppose him created in the perfect age and stature of man. And surely we are all out of the computation of our age, and every man is some months elder than he bethinks him; for we live, move, have a being, and are subject to the actions of the elements, and the malice of diseases, in that other World, the truest Microcosm, the Womb of our Mother. For besides that general and common existence we are conceived to hold in our Chaos, and whilst we sleep within the bosome of our causes, we enjoy a being and life in three distinct worlds, wherein we receive most manifest graduations. In that obscure World and Womb of our Mother, our time is short, computed by the Moon, yet longer than the days of many creatures that behold the Sun; our selves being not yet without life, sense, and reason; though for the manifestation of its actions, it awaits the opportunity of objects, and seems to live there but in its root and soul of vegetation. Entring afterwards upon the scene of the World, we arise up and become another creature, performing the reasonable actions of man, and obscurely manifesting that part of Divinity in us; but not in complement and perfection, till we have once more cast our secondine, that is, this slough of flesh, and are delivered into the last World, that is, that ineffable place of Paul, that proper *ubi* of Spirits. The smattering I have of the Philosophers Stone (which is something more then the perfect exaltation of gold,) hath taught me a great deal of Divinity, and instructed my belief, how that immortal spirit and incorruptible substance of my Soul may lye obscure, and sleep a while within this house of flesh. Those strange and mystical transmigrations that I have observed in Silkworms, turned my Philosophy into Divinity. There is in these works of nature, which seem to puzzle reason, something Divine, and hath more in it than the eye of a common spectator doth discover.

I am naturally bashful; nor hath conversation, age, or travel, been able to effront or enharden me; yet I have one part of modesty which I have seldom discovered in another, that is, (to speak truely,) I am not so much afraid of death, as ashamed thereof. 'Tis the very disgrace and ignominy of our natures, that in a moment can so disfigure us, that our nearest friends, Wife, and Children, stand afraid and start at us: the Birds and Beasts of the field, that before in a natural fear obeyed us, forgetting all allegiance, begin to prey upon us. This very conceit hath in a tempest disposed and left me willing to be swallowed up in the abyss of waters, wherein I had perished unseen, unpityed, without wondering eyes, tears of pity, Lectures of mortality, and none had said,

Quantum mutatus ab illo!

Not that I am ashamed of the Anatomy of my parts, or can accuse Nature for playing the bungler in any part of me, or my own vitious life for contracting any shameful disease upon me, whereby I might not call my self as wholesome a morsel for the worms as any.

Some, upon the courage of a fruitful issue, wherein, as in the truest Chronicle, they seem to outlive themselves, can with greater patience away with death. This conceit counterfeit subsisting in our progenies seems to me a meer fallacy, unworthy the desires of a man that can but conceive a thought of the next World; who, in a nobler ambition, should desire to live in his substance in Heaven, rather than his name and shadow in the earth. And therefore at my death I mean to take a total adieu of the World, not caring for a Monument, History, or Epitaph, not so much as the bare memory of my name to be found any where but in the universal Register of

GOD. I am not yet so Cynical as to approve the Testament of Diogenes; nor do I altogether allow that *Rodomon-ado* of Lucan,

—— *Cælo tegitur, qui non habet urnam.*

He that unburied lies wants not his Herse,
For unto him a Tomb's the Universe.

but commend in my calmer judgement those ingenu-ous intentions that desire to sleep by the urns of their Fathers, and strive to go the neatest way unto corruption. I do not envy the temper of Crows and Daws, nor the numerous and weary days of our Fathers before the Flood. If there be any truth in Astrology, I may outlive a Jubilee: as yet I have not seen one revolution of Saturn, nor hath my pulse beat thirty years; and yet, excepting one, have seen the Ashes and left under ground all the Kings of Europe; have been contemporary to three Emperours, four Grand Signiours, and as many Popes. Methinks I have outlived my self, and begin to be weary of the Sun; I have shaken hands with delight, in my warm blood and Canicular days, I perceive I do antici-pate the vices of age; the World to me is but a dream or mock-show, and we all therein but Pantalones and Anticks, to my severer contemplations.

It is not, I confess, an unlawful Prayer to desire to surpass the days of our Saviour, or wish to outlive that age wherein He thought fittest to dye; yet if (as Divinity affirms,) there shall be no gray hairs in Heaven, but all shall rise in the perfect state of men, we do but outlive those perfections in this World, to be recalled unto them by a greater Miracle in the next, and run on here but to be retrograde hereafter. Were there any hopes to outlive vice, or a point to be superannuated from sin, it were worthy our knees to implore the days of Methuselah. But age doth not rectify, but incurvate our natures, turn-ing bad dispositions into worser habits, and (like dis-

eases,) brings on incurable vices; for every day as we grow
weaker in age, we grow stronger in sin, and the number
of our days doth but make our sins innumerable. The
same vice committed at sixteen, is not the same, though
it agree in all other circumstances, at forty, but swells
and doubles from the circumstance of our ages; wherein,
besides the constant and inexcusable habit of transgress-
ing, the maturity of our judgment cuts off pretence unto
excuse or pardon. Every sin, the oftner it is committed,
the more it acquireth in the quality of evil; as it succeeds
in time, so it proceeds in degrees of badness; for as they
proceed they ever multiply, and, like figures in Arithmetick, the last stands for more than all that went before
it. And though I think no man can live well once, but
he that could live twice, yet for my own part I would not
live over my hours past, or begin again the thread of
my days: not upon Cicero's ground, because I have lived
them well, but for fear I should live them worse. I find
my growing Judgment daily instruct me how to be better,
but my untamed affections and confirmed vitiosity make
me daily do worse. I find in my confirmed age the same
sins I discovered in my youth; I committed many then
because I was a Child; and because I commit them still
I am yet an infant. Therefore I perceive a man may be
twice a Child, before the days of dotage; and stand in
need of Æsons Bath before threescore.

    And truly there goes a great deal of providence to pro-
duce a mans life unto threescore: there is more required
than an able temper for those years; though the radical
humour contain in it sufficient oyl for seventy, yet I perceive in some it gives no light past thirty: men assign not
all the causes of long life, that write whole Books thereof.
They that found themselves on the radical balsome, or
vital sulphur of the parts, determine not why Abel lived
not so long as Adam. There is therefore a secret glome
or bottome of our days: 'twas His wisdom to determin

hem, but His perpetual and waking providence that
ulfils and accomplisheth them; wherein the spirits, our-
elves, and all the creatures of GOD in a secret and dis-
)uted way do execute His will. Let *them* not therefore
omplain of immaturity that die about thirty; they fall
)ut like the whole World, whose solid and well-composed
ubstance must not expect the duration and period of its
onstitution: when all things are completed in it, its age
s accomplished; and the last and general fever may as
laturally destroy it before six thousand, as me before
orty. There is therefore some other hand that twines
he thread of life than that of Nature: we are not onely
gnorant in Antipathies and occult qualities; our ends
re as obscure as our beginnings; the line of our days is
lrawn by night, and the various effects therein by a pensil
hat is invisible; wherein though we confess our igno-
ance, I am sure we do not err if we say it is the hand of
iOD.

I am much taken with two verses of Lucan, since I have
)een able not onely, as we do at School, to construe, but
inderstand:

> *Victurosque Dei celant, ut vivere durent,*
> *Felix esse mori.*

> We're all deluded, vainly searching ways
> To make us happy by the length of days;
> For cunningly to make's protract this breath,
> The Gods conceal the happiness of Death.

here be many excellent strains in that Poet, wherewith
is Stoical Genius hath liberally supplied him; and truely
here are singular pieces in the Philosophy of Zeno, and
octrine of the Stoicks, which I perceive, delivered in a
'ulpit, pass for current Divinity: yet herein are they in
xtreams, than can allow a man to be his own Assassine,
nd so highly extol the end and suicide of Cato. This is
ndeed not to fear death, but yet to be afraid of life.
t is a brave act of valour to contemn death; but where

life is more terrible than death, it is then the trues
valour to dare to live. And herein Religion hath taugh
us a noble example; for all the valiant acts of Curtius
Scevola, or Codrus, do not parallel or match that on
of Job; and sure there is no torture to the rack of a dis
ease, nor any Ponyards in death it self like those in th
way or prologue to it.

Emori nolo, sed me esse mortuum nihil curo.
I would not die, but care not to be dead.

Were I of Cæsar's Religion, I should be of his desires, an
wish rather to go off at one blow, then to be sawed i
pieces by the grating torture of a disease. Men that loo
no farther than their outsides, think health an appurte
nance unto life, and quarrel with their constitutions fo
being sick; but I, that have examined the parts of mar
and know upon what tender filaments that Fabrick hang
do wonder that we are not always so; and, considerin
the thousand doors that lead to death, do thank my Go
that we can die but once. 'Tis not onely the mischie
of diseases, and the villany of poysons, that make an en
of us; we vainly accuse the fury of Guns, and the ne
inventions of death; it is in the power of every hand t
destroy us, and we are beholding unto every one we mee
he doth not kill us. There is therefore but one comfo
left, that, though it be in the power of the weakest art
to take away life, it is not in the strongest to deprive
of death: GOD would not exempt Himself from that, th
misery of immortality in the flesh, He undertook not tha
was immortal. Certainly there is no happiness within th
circle of flesh, nor is it in the Opticks of these eyes to be
hold felicity. The first day of our Jubilee is Death; th
Devil hath therefore failed of his desires: we are happie
with death than we should have been without it: the
is no misery but in himself, where there is no end
misery; and so indeed, in his own sense, the Stoick is

the right. He forgets that he can dye who complains of misery; we are in the power of no calamity while death is in our own.

Now, besides this literal and positive kind of death, there are others whereof Divines make mention, and those, I think, not meerly Metaphorical, as mortification, dying unto sin and the World. Therefore, I say, every man hath a double Horoscope, one of his humanity, his birth; another of his Christianity, his baptism; and from this do I compute or calculate my Nativity, not reckoning those *Horæ combustæ* and odd days, or esteeming my self any thing, before I was my Saviours, and inrolled in the Register of CHRIST. Whosoever enjoys not this life, I count him but an apparition, though he wear about him the sensible affections of flesh. In these moral accep- tions, the way to be immortal is to dye daily: nor can I think I have the true Theory of death, when I contem- plate a skull, or behold a Skeleton, with those vulgar imaginations it casts upon us; I have therefore enlarged that common *Memento mori,* into a more Christian memorandum, *Memento quatuor Novissima,* those four inevitable points of us all, Death, Judgement, Heaven, and Hell. Neither did the contemplations of the Hea- thens rest in their graves, without a further thought of Rhadamanth, or some judicial proceeding after death, though in another way, and upon suggestion of their natural reasons. I cannot but marvail from what Sibyl or Oracle they stole the Prophesie of the Worlds destruction by fire, or whence Lucan learned to say,

> *Communis mundo superest rogus, ossibus astra*
> *Misturus.*

> There yet remains to th' World one common Fire,
> Wherein our bones with stars shall make one Pyre.

I believe the World grows near its end, yet is neither old nor decayed, nor shall ever perish upon the ruines of its own Principles. As the work of Creation was above Nature, so is its adversary, annihilation; without which the World hath not its end, but its mutation. Now what force should be able to consume it thus far, without the breath of GOD, which is the truest consuming flame, my Philosophy cannot inform me. Some believe there went not a minute to the Worlds creation, nor shall there go to its destruction; those six days, so punctually described, make not to them one moment, but rather seem to manifest the method and Idea of the great work of the intellect of GOD, than the manner how He proceeded in its operation. I cannot dream that there should be at the last day any such Judicial proceeding, or calling to the Bar, as indeed the Scripture seems to imply, and the literal Commentators do conceive: for unspeakable mysteries in the Scriptures are often delivered in a vulgar and illustrative way; and. being written unto man, are delivered, not as they truely are, but as they may be understood; wherein, notwithstanding, the different interpretations according to different capacities may stand firm with our devotion, nor be any way prejudicial to each single edification.

Now to determine the day and year of this inevitable time, is not onely convincible and statute-madness, but also manifest impiety. How shall we interpret Elias six thousand years, or imagine the secret communicated to a Rabbi, which GOD hath denyed unto His Angels? It had been an excellent Quære to have posed the Devil of Delphos, and must needs have forced him to some strange amphibology. It hath not onely mocked the predictions of sundry Astrologers in Ages past, but the prophesies of many melancholy heads in these present; who, neither understanding reasonably things past or present, pretend a knowledge of things to come; heads ordained onely to manifest the incredible effects of melancholy, and to fulfil old prophecies rather than be the authors of new. *In*

those days there shall come Wars and rumours of Wars,
to me seems no prophecy, but a constant truth, in all
times verified since it was pronounced. *There shall be*
signs in the Moon and Stars; how comes He then *like*
a Thief in the night, when He gives an item of His
coming? That common sign drawn from the revelation
of Antichrist, is as obscure as any: in our common compute He hath been come these many years: but for my
own part, (to speak freely,) I am half of opinion that
Antichrist is the Philosopher's stone in Divinity, for the
discovery and invention whereof, though there be prescribed rules and probable inductions, yet hath hardly
any man attained the perfect discovery thereof. That
general opinion that the World grows near its end, hath
possessed all ages past as nearly as ours. I am afraid that
the Souls that now depart, cannot escape that lingring
expostulation of the Saints under the Altar, *Quousque,*
DOMINE? *How long,* O LORD? and groan in the expectation of that great Jubilee.

This is the day that must make good that great attribute of GOD, His Justice; that must reconcile those
unanswerable doubts that torment the wisest understandings; and reduce those seeming inequalities and respective distributions in this world, to an equality and recom-
pensive Justice in the next. This is that one day, that shall
include and comprehend all that went before it; wherein,
as in the last scene, all the Actors must enter, to compleat
and make up the Catastrophe of this great piece. This is
the day whose memory hath onely power to make us
honest in the dark, and to be vertuous without a witness.

Ipsa sui pretium virtus sibi,

that Vertue is her own reward, is but a cold principle,
and not able to maintain our variable resolutions in a
constant and settled way of goodness. I have practised
that honest artifice of Seneca, and in my retired and

solitary imaginations, to detain me from the foulness
of vice, have fancied to my self the presence of my dear
and worthiest friends, before whom I should lose my
head, rather than be vitious: yet herein I found that
there was nought but moral honesty, and this was not
to be vertuous for His sake Who must reward us at the
last. I have tryed if I could reach that great resolution
of his, to be honest without a thought of Heaven or Hell:
and indeed I found, upon a natural inclination and in-
bred loyalty unto virtue, that I could serve her without
a livery; yet not in that resolved and venerable way, but
that the frailty of my nature, upon an easie temptation,
might be induced to forget her. The life, therefore, and
spirit of all our actions is the resurrection, and a stable
apprehension that our ashes shall enjoy the fruit of our
pious endeavours: without this, all Religion is a Fallacy,
and those impieties of Lucian, Euripides, and Julian,
are no blasphemies, but subtle verities, and Atheists have
been the onely Philosophers.

How shall the dead arise, is no question of my Faith;
to believe only possibilities, is not Faith, but meer Philosophy. Many things are true in Divinity, which are neither
inducible by reason, nor confirmable by sense; and many
things in Philosophy confirmable by sense, yet not inducible by reason. Thus it is impossible by any solid or
demonstrative reasons to perswade a man to believe the
conversion of the Needle to the North; though this
be possible, and true, and easily credible, upon a single
experiment unto the sense. I believe that our estranged
and divided ashes shall unite again; that our separated
dust, after so many Pilgrimages and transformations into
the parts of Minerals, Plants, Animals, Elements, shall
at the Voice of God return into their primitive shapes,
and joyn again to make up their primary and predesti-
nate forms. As at the Creation there was a separation of

that confused mass into its species; so at the destruction
thereof there shall be a separation into its distinct individuals. As at the Creation of the World, all the distinct
species that we behold lay involved in one mass, till the
fruitful Voice of GOD separated this united multitude
into its several species; so at the last day, when those
corrupted reliques shall be scattered in the Wilderness
of forms, and seem to have forgot their proper habits,
GOD by a powerful Voice shall command them back into
their proper shapes, and call them out by their single
individuals. Then shall appear the fertility of Adam,
and the magick of that sperm that hath dilated into so
many millions. I have often beheld as a miracle, that
artificial resurrection and revivification of Mercury, how
being mortified into a thousand shapes, it assumes again
its own, and returns into its numerical self. Let us speak
naturally and like Philosophers, the forms of alterable
bodies in these sensible corruptions perish not; nor, as
we imagine, wholly quit their mansions, but retire and
contract themselves into their secret and unaccessible
parts, where they may best protect themselves from the
action of their Antagonist. A plant or vegetable consumed to ashes to a contemplative and school-Philoso-
pher seems utterly destroyed, and the form to have taken
his leave for ever; but to a sensible Artist the forms are
not perished, but withdrawn into their incombustible
part, where they lie secure from the action of that
devouring element. This is made good by experience,
which can from the Ashes of a Plant revive the plant,
and from its cinders recall it into its stalk and leaves again.
What the Art of man can do in these inferiour pieces,
what blasphemy is it to affirm the finger of GOD cannot
do in these more perfect and sensible structures! This is
that mystical Philosophy, from whence no true Scholar
becomes an Atheist, but from the visible effects of nature

grows up a real Divine, and beholds not in a dream, as Ezekiel, but in an ocular and visible object, the types of his resurrection.

Now, the necessary Mansions of our restored selves are those two contrary and incomparable places we call *Heaven* and *Hell*. To define them, or strictly to determine what and where these are, surpasseth my Divinity. That elegant Apostle, which seemed to have a glimpse of Heaven, hath left but a negative description thereof; *which neither eye hath seen, nor ear hath heard, nor can enter into the heart of man:* he was translated out of himself to behold it; but, being returned into himself, could not express it. St. John's description by Emerals, Chrysolites, and precious Stones, is too weak to express the material Heaven we behold. Briefly therefore, where the Soul hath the full measure and complement of happiness; where the boundless appetite of that spirit remains compleatly satisfied, that it can neither desire addition nor alteration; that, I think, is truly Heaven: and this can onely be in the injoyment of that essence, whose infinite goodness is able to terminate the desires of it self, and the unsatiable wishes of ours: wherever GOD will thus manifest Himself, there is Heaven, though within the circle of this sensible world. Thus the Soul of man may be in Heaven any where, even within the limits of his own proper body; and when it ceaseth to live in the body, it may remain in its own soul, that is, its Creator: and thus we may say that St. Paul, *whether in the body, or out of the body,* was yet in Heaven. To place it in the Empyreal, or beyond the tenth sphear, is to forget the world's destruction; for, when this sensible world shall be destroyed, all shall then be here as it is now there, an Empyreal Heaven, a *quasi* vacuity; when to ask where Heaven is, is to demand where the presence of GOD is, or where we have the glory of that happy vision. Moses, that was bred up in all the learning of the

Egyptians, committed a gross absurdity in Philosophy, when with these eyes of flesh he desired to see GOD, and petitioned his Maker, that is, Truth it self, to a contradiction. Those that imagine Heaven and Hell neighbours, and conceive a vicinity between those two extreams, upon consequence of the Parable, where Dives discoursed with Lazarus in Abraham's bosome, do too grosly conceive of those glorified creatures, whose eyes shall easily out-see the Sun, and behold without a perspective the extreamest distances: for if there shall be in our glorified eyes, the faculty of sight and reception of objects, I could think the visible species there to be in as unlimitable a way as now the intellectual. I grant that two bodies placed beyond the tenth sphear, or in a vacuity, according to Aristotle's Philosophy, could not behold each other, because there wants a body or Medium to hand and transport the visible rays of the object unto the sense; but when there shall be a general defect of either Medium to convey, or light to prepare and dispose that Medium, and yet a perfect vision, we must suspend the rules of our Philosophy, and make all good by a more absolute piece of opticks.

I cannot tell how to say that fire is the essence of Hell: I know not what to make of Purgatory, or conceive a flame that can either prey upon, or purifie the substance of a Soul. Those flames of sulphur mention'd in the Scriptures, I take not to be understood of this present Hell, but of that to come, where fire shall make up the complement of our tortures, and have a body or subject wherein to manifest its tyranny. Some, who have had the honour to be textuary in Divinity, are of opinion it shall be the same specifical fire with ours. This is hard to conceive; yet can I make good how even that may prey upon our bodies, and yet not consume us: for in this material World there are bodies that persist invincible in the powerfullest flames; and though by the action of fire they

fall into ignition and liquation, yet will they never suffer
a destruction. I would gladly know how Moses with an
actual fire calcined or burnt the Golden Calf unto powder: for that mystical metal of Gold, whose solary and
celestial nature I admire, exposed unto the violence of
fire, grows onely hot, and liquifies, but consumeth not;
so, when the consumable and volatile pieces of our bodies
shall be refined into a more impregnable and fixed temper like Gold, though they suffer from the action of
flames, they shall never perish, but lye immortal in the
arms of fire. And surely, if this frame must suffer onely
by the action of this element, there will many bodies
escape; and not onely Heaven, but Earth will not be at
an end, but rather a beginning. For at present it is not
earth, but a composition of fire, water, earth, and air;
but at that time, spoiled of these ingredients, it shall
appear in a substance more like it self, its ashes. Philosophers that opinioned the worlds destruction by fire, did
never dream of annihilation, which is beyond the power
of sublunary causes; for the last and proper action of that
element is but vitrification, or a reduction of a body into
glass; and therefore some of our Chymicks facetiously
affirm, that at the last fire all shall be christallized and
reverberated into glass, which is the utmost action of that
element. Nor need we fear this term, *annihilation,* or
wonder that GOD will destroy the works of his Creation;
for man subsisting, who is, and will then truely appear,
a Microcosm, the world cannot be said to be destroyed.
For the eyes of GOD, and perhaps also of our glorified
selves, shall as really behold and contemplate the World
in its Epitome or contracted essence, as now it doth at
large and in its dilated substance. In the seed of a Plant
to the eyes of GOD, and to the understanding of man,
there exists, though in an invisible way, the perfect
leaves, flowers, and fruit thereof; for things that are *in
posse* to the sense, are actually existent to the understand-

ing. Thus God beholds all things, Who contemplates as fully His works in their Epitome, as in their full volume; and beheld as amply the whole world in that little compendium of the sixth day, as in the scattered and dilated pieces of those five before.

Men commonly set forth the torments of Hell by fire, and the extremity of corporal afflictions, and describe Hell in the same method that Mahomet doth Heaven. This indeed makes a noise, and drums in popular ears: but if this be the terrible piece thereof, it is not worthy to stand in diameter with Heaven, whose happiness consists in that part that is best able to comprehend it, that immortal essence, that translated divinity and colony of God, the Soul. Surely, though we place Hell under Earth, the Devil's walk and purlue is about it: men speak too popularly who place it in those flaming mountains, which to grosser apprehensions represent Hell. The heart of man is the place Devils dwell in: I feel sometimes a Hell within my self; Lucifer keeps his Court in my breast, Legion is revived in me. There are as many Hells, as Anaxagoris conceited worlds. There was more than one Hell in Magdalene, when there were seven Devils, for every Devil is an Hell unto himself; he holds enough of torture in his own *ubi,* and needs not the misery of circumference to afflict him: and thus a distracted Conscience here, is a shadow or introduction unto Hell hereafter. Who can but pity the merciful intention of those hands that do destroy themselves? the Devil, were it in his power, would do the like; which being impossible, his miseries are endless, and he suffers most in that attribute wherein he is impassible, his immortality.

I thank God, and with joy I mention it, I was never afraid of Hell, nor never grew pale at the description of that place. I have so fixed my contemplations on Heaven, that I have almost forgot the idea of Hell, and am afraid rather to lose the Joys of the one, than endure the misery of the other: to be deprived of them is a perfect Hell, and needs, methinks, no addition to compleat our afflictions. That terrible term hath never detained me from sin, nor do I owe any good action to the name thereof. I fear GOD, yet am not afraid of Him: His Mercies make me ashamed of my sins, before His Judgements afraid thereof. These are the forced and secondary method of His wisdom, which He useth but as the last remedy, and upon provocation; a course rather to deter the wicked, than incite the virtuous to His worship. I can hardly think there was ever any sacred into Heaven; they go the fairest way to Heaven that would serve GOD without a Hell; other Mercenaries, that crouch into Him in fear of Hell, though they term themselves the servants, are indeed but the slaves, of the Almighty.

And to be true, and speak my soul, when I survey the occurrences of my life, and call into account the Finger of GOD, I can perceive nothing but an abyss and mass of mercies, either in general to mankind, or in particular to my self. And (whether out of the prejudice of my affection, or an inverting and partial conceit of His mercies, I know not; but) those which others term crosses, afflictions, judgements, misfortunes, to me, who inquire farther into them than their visible effects, they both appear, and in event have ever proved, the secret and dissembled favors of His affection. It is a singular piece of Wisdom to apprehend truly, and without passion, the Works of GOD, and so well to distinguish His Justice from His Mercy, as not to miscall those noble Attributes: yet it is likewise an honest piece of Logick, so to dispute and argue the proceedings of GOD, as to distinguish even His judgments into mercies. For GOD is merciful unto all, because better to the worst than the best deserve; and to say He punisheth none in this World, though it be a Paradox, is no absurdity. To one that hath committed Murther, if the Judge should only ordain a Fine, it were a madness to call this a punishment, and to repine at the sentence, rather than admire the clemency of the Judge. Thus, our offences being mortal, and deserving not only Death, but Damnation, if the goodness of God be content to traverse and pass them over with a loss, misfortune, or disease, what frensie were it to term this a punishment rather than an extremity of mercy, and to groan under the rod of His Judgements, rather than admire the Scepter of His Mercies! Therefore to adore, honour, and admire Him, is a debt of gratitude due from the obligation of our nature, states, and conditions; and with these thoughts, He that knows them best, will not deny that I adore Him. That I obtain Heaven, and the bliss thereof, is accidental, and not the intended work of my devotion; it being a felicity I can neither think to deserve, nor scarce in modesty to expect. For these two ends of us all, either as rewards or punishments, are mercifully ordained and disproportionably disposed unto our actions; the one being so far beyond our deserts, the other so infinitely below our demerits.

There is no Salvation to those that believe not in CHRIST, that is, say some, since His Nativity, and, as Divinity affirmeth, before also; which makes me much apprehend the ends of those honest Worthies and Philosophers which dyed before His Incarnation. It is hard to place those Souls in Hell, whose worthy lives do teach us Virtue on Earth; methinks, amongst those many subdivisions of Hell, there might have been one Limbo left for these. What a strange vision will it be to see their Poetical fictions converted into Verities, and their imagined and fancied Furies into real Devils! How strange to them will sound the History of Adam, when they shall suffer for him they never heard of! when they who derive their genealogy from the Gods, shall know they are the unhappy issue of sinful man! It is an insolent part of reason, to controvert the Works of God, or question the Justice of His proceedings. Could Humility teach others, as it hath instructed me, to contemplate the infinite and incomprehensible distance betwixt the Creator and the Creature; or did we seriously perpend that one simile of St. Paul, *Shall the Vessel say to the Potter, "Why hast thou made me thus?"* it would prevent these arrogant disputes of reason; nor would we argue the definitive sentence of GOD, either to Heaven or Hell. Men that live according to the right rule and law of reason, live but in their own kind, as beasts do in theirs; who justly obey the prescript of their natures, and therefore cannot reasonably demand a reward of their actions, as onely obeying the natural dictates of their reason. It will, therefore, and must at last appear, that all salvation is through CHRIST; which verity, I fear, these great examples of virtue must confirm, and make it good how the perfectest actions of earth have no title or claim unto Heaven.

Nor truely do I think the lives of these, or of any other, were ever correspondent, or in all points conformable, unto their doctrines. It is evident that Aristotle transgressed the rule of his own Ethicks. The Stoicks that condemn passion, and command a man to laugh in Phalaris his Bull, could not endure without a groan a fit of the Stone or Colick. The Scepticks that affirmed they knew nothing, even in that opinion confute themselves, and thought they knew more than all the World beside. Diogenes I hold to be the most vain-glorious man of his time, and more ambitious in refusing all Honours, than Alexander in rejecting none. Vice and the Devil put a Fallacy upon our Reasons, and, provoking us too hastily to run from it, entangle and profound us deeper in it. The Duke of Venice, that weds himself unto the Sea by a Ring of Gold, I will not argue of prodigality, because it is a solemnity of good use and consequence in the State: but the Philosopher that threw his money into the Sea to avoid Avarice, was a notorious prodigal. There is no

road or ready way to virtue: it is not an easie point of
art to disentangle our selves from this riddle, or web of
Sin. To perfect virtue, as to Religion, there is required a
Panoplia, or compleat armour; that, whilst we lye at
close ward against one Vice, we lye not open to the venny
of another. And indeed wiser discretions that have the
thred of reason to conduct them, offend without pardon; whereas under-heads may stumble without dishonour. There go so many circumstances to piece up one
good action, that it is a lesson to be good, and we are
forced to be virtuous by the book. Again, the Practice of
men holds not an equal pace, yea, and often runs counter
to their Theory: we naturally know what is good, but
naturally pursue what is evil: the Rhetorick wherewith
I perswade another, cannot perswade my self. There is a
depraved appetite in us, that will with patience hear the
learned instructions of Reason, but yet perform no farther than agrees to its own irregular humour. In brief, we
all are monsters, that is, a composition of Man and Beast,
wherein we must endeavour to be as the Poets fancy that
wise man Chiron, that is, to have the Region of Man
above that of Beast, and Sense to sit but at the feet of
Reason. Lastly, I do desire with GOD that all, but yet affirm with men that few, shall know Salvation; that the
bridge is narrow, the passage strait, unto life: yet those
who do confine the Church of GOD, either to particular
Nations, Churches, or Families, have made it far narrower than our Saviour ever meant it.

The vulgarity of those judgements that wrap the
Church of GOD in Strabo's *cloak,* and restrain it unto
Europe, seem to me as bad Geographers as Alexander,
who thought he had Conquer'd all the World, when he
had not subdued the half of any part thereof. For we
cannot deny the Church of GOD both in Asia and Africa,
if we do not forget the Peregrinations of the Apostles,
the deaths of the Martyrs, the Sessions of many and

(even in our reformed judgement) lawful Councils, held in those parts in the minority and nonage of ours. Nor must a few differences, more remarkable in the eyes of man than perhaps in the judgement of GOD, excommunicate from Heaven one another; much less those Christians who are in a manner all Martyrs, maintaining their Faith in the noble way of persecution, and serving GOD in the Fire, whereas we honour him but in the Sunshine. 'Tis true we all hold there is a number of Elect, and many to be saved; yet, take our Opinions together, and from the confusion thereof there will be no such thing as salvation, nor shall any one be saved. For first, the Church of Rome condemneth us, we likewise them; the Subreformists and Sectaries sentence the Doctrine of our Church as damnable; the Atomist, or Familist, reprobates all these; and all these, them again. Thus, whilst the Mercies of GOD do promise us Heaven, our conceits and opinions exclude us from that place. There must be, therefore, more than one St. Peter: particular Churches and Sects usurp the gates of Heaven, and turn the key against each other; and thus we go to Heaven against each others wills, conceits, and opinions, and, with as much uncharity as ignorance, do err, I fear, in points not only of our own, but one anothers salvation.

I believe many are saved, who to man seem reprobated; and many are reprobated, who, in the opinion and sentence of man, stand elected. There will appear at the Last day strange and unexpected examples both of His Justice and His Mercy; and therefore to define either, is folly in man, and insolency even in the Devils. Those acute and subtil spirits, in all their sagacity, can hardly divine who shall be saved; which if they could Prognostick, their labour were at an end, nor need they compass the earth *seeking whom they may devour*. Those who, upon a rigid application of the Law, sentence Solomon unto damnation, condemn not onely him, but themselves, and the whole World: for, by the Letter and written Word of GOD, we are without exception in the state of Death; but there is a prerogative of GOD, and an arbitrary pleasure above the Letter of His own Law, by which alone we can pretend unto Salvation, and through which Solomon might be as easily saved as those who condemn him.

The number of those who pretend unto Salvation, and those infinite swarms who think to pass through the eye of this Needle, have much amazed me. That name and compellation of *little Flock,* doth not comfort, but deject, my Devotion; especially when I reflect upon mine own unworthiness, wherein, according to my humble apprehensions, I am below them all. I believe there shall never be an Anarchy in Heaven; but, as there are Hierarchies amongst the Angels, so shall there be degrees of priority amongst the Saints. Yet is it (I protest,) beyond my ambition to aspire unto the first ranks; my desires onely are (and I shall be happy therein,) to be but the last man, and bring up the Rere in Heaven.

Again, I am confident and fully perswaded, yet dare not take my oath, of my Salvation. I am as it were sure, and do believe without all doubt, that there is such a City as Constantinople; yet for me to take my Oath thereon were a kind of Perjury, because I hold no infallible warrant from my own sense to confirm me in the certainty thereof. And truly, though many pretend an absolute certainty of their Salvation, yet, when an humble Soul shall contemplate her own unworthiness, she shall meet with many doubts, and suddenly find how little we stand in need of the Precept of St. Paul, *Work out your salvation with fear and trembling.* That which is the cause of my Election, I hold to be the cause of my Salvation, which was the mercy and beneplacit of GOD, before I was, or the foundation of the World. *Before Abraham was, I am,* is the saying of CHRIST; yet is it true in some sense, if I say it of my self; for I was not

onely before my self, but Adam, that is, in the Idea of
GOD, and the decree of that Synod held from all Eternity.
And in this sense, I say, the World was before the Creation, and at an end before it had a beginning; and thus
was I dead before I was alive: though my grave be England, my dying place was Paradise: and Eve miscarried of
me before she conceiv'd of Cain.

Insolent zeals, that do decry good Works and rely
onely upon Faith, take not away merit: for, depending
upon the efficacy of their Faith, they enforce the condition of GOD, and in a more sophistical way do seem to
challenge Heaven. It was decreed by GOD, that only those
that lapt in the water like Dogs, should have the honour
to destroy the Midianites; yet could none of those justly
challenge, or imagine he deserved, that honour there-
upon. I do not deny but that true Faith, and such as
GOD requires, is not onely a mark or token, but also a
means, of our Salvation; but where to find this, is as
obscure to me as my last end. And if our Saviour could
object unto His own Disciples and Favourites, a Faith,
that, to the quantity of a grain of Mustard-seed, is able
to remove Mountains; surely, that which we boast of, is
not any thing, or at the most, but a remove from nothing.
This is the Tenor of my belief; wherein though there be
many things singular, and to the humour of my irregular
self, yet, if they square not with maturer Judgements, I
disclaim them, and do no further father them, than the
learned and best judgements shall authorize them.

THE SECOND PART

Now for that other Virtue of Charity, without which
Faith is a meer notion, and of no existence, I have ever
endeavoured to nourish the merciful disposition and
humane inclination I borrowed from my Parents, and

regulate it to the written and prescribed Laws of Charity. And if I hold the true Anatomy of my self, I am delineated and naturally framed to such a piece of virtue; for I am of a constitution so general, that it consorts and sympathiseth with all things. I have no antipathy, or rather Idiosyncrasie, in dyet, humour, air, any thing. I wonder not at the French for their dishes of Frogs, Snails and Toadstools, nor at the Jews for Locusts and Grasshoppers; but being amongst them, make them my common Viands, and I find they agree with my Stomach as well as theirs. I could digest a Salad gathered in a Church-yard, as well as in a Garden. I cannot start at the presence of a Serpent, Scorpion, Lizard, or Salamander: at the sight of a Toad or Viper, I find in me no desire to take up a stone to destroy them. I feel not in my self those common Antipathies that I can discover in others: those National repugnances do not touch me, nor do I behold with prejudice the French, Italian, Spaniard, or Dutch: but where I find their actions in balance with my Countrymen's, I honour, love, and embrace them in the same degree. I was born in the eighth Climate, but seem for to be framed and constellated unto all. I am no Plant that will not prosper out of a Garden. All places, all airs, make unto me one Countrey; I am in England every where, and under any Meridian. I have been shipwrackt, yet am not enemy with the Sea or Winds; I can study, play, or sleep in a Tempest. In brief, I am averse from nothing: my Conscience would give me the lye if I should say I absolutely detest or hate any essence but the Devil; or so at least abhor any thing, but that we might come to composition. If there be any among those common objects of hatred I do contemn and laugh at, it is that great enemy of Reason, Virtue and Religion, the Multitude: that numerous piece of monstrosity, which, taken asunder, seem men, and the reasonable creatures of GOD; but, confused together, make but one great beast, and a monstrosity more prodigious than Hydra. It is no breach of Charity to call these *Fools;* it is the style all holy Writers have afforded them, set down by Solomon in Canonical Scripture, and a point of our Faith to believe so. Neither in the name of *Multitude* do I onely include the base and minor sort of people; there is a rabble even amongst the Gentry, a sort of Plebeian heads, whose fancy moves with the same wheel as these; men in the same Level with Mechanicks, though their fortunes do somewhat guild their infirmities, and their purses compound for their follies. But as, in casting account, three or four men together come short in account of one man placed by himself below them; so neither are a troop of these ignorant *Doradoes* of that true esteem and value, as many a forlorn person, whose condition doth place him below their feet. Let us speak like Politicians: there is a Nobility without Heraldry, a natural dignity, whereby one man is ranked with another, another filed before him, according to the quality of his Desert, and preheminence of his good parts. Though the corruption of these times and the byas of present practice wheel another way, thus it was in the first and primitive Commonwealths, and is yet in the integrity and Cradle of well-order'd Polities, till corruption getteth ground; ruder desires labouring after that which wiser considerations contemn, every one having a liberty to amass and heap up riches, and they a licence or faculty to do or purchase any thing.

This general and indifferent temper of mine doth more neerly disposed me to this noble virtue. It is a happiness to be born and framed unto virtue, and to grow up from the seeds of nature, rather than the inoculation and forced graffs of education: yet if we are directed only by our particular Natures, and regulate our inclinations by no higher rule than that of our reasons, we are but Moralists; Divinity will still call us Heathens. Therefore this great work of charity must have other motives, ends, and impulsions. I give no alms only to satisfie the hunger of my Brother, but to fulfil and accomplish the Will and Command of my GOD: I draw not my purse for his sake that demands it, but His That enjoyned it: I relieve no man upon the Rhetorick of his miseries, nor to content mine own commiserating disposition; for this is still but moral charity, and an act that oweth more to passion than reason. He that relieves another upon the bare suggestion and bowels of pity, doth not this, so much for his sake as for his own; for by compassion we make others misery our own, and so, by relieving them, we relieve our selves also. It is as erroneous a conceit to redress other Mens misfortunes upon the common considerations of merciful natures, that it may be one day our own case; for this is a sinister and politick kind of charity, whereby we seem to bespeak the pities of men in the like occasions. And truly I have observed that those professed Eleemosynaries, though in a croud or multitude, do yet direct and place their petitions on a few and selected persons: there is surely a Physiognomy, which those experienced and Master Mendicants observe, whereby they instantly discover a merciful aspect, and will single out a face wherein they spy the signatures and marks of Mercy. For there are mystically in our faces certain Characters which carry in them the motto of our Souls, wherein he that cannot read A. B. C. may read our natures. I hold moreover that there is a Phytognomy, or Physiognomy, not only of Men, but of Plants and Vegetables; and in every one of them some outward figures which hang as signs or bushes of their inward forms. The Finger of GOD hath left an Inscription upon all His works, not graphical or composed of Letters, but of their several forms, constitutions, parts, and operations, which, aptly joyned together, do make one word that doth express their natures. By these Letters GOD calls the Stars by their names;

and by this Alphabet Adam assigned to every creature a name peculiar to its Nature. Now there are, besides these Characters in our Faces, certain mystical figures in our Hands, which I dare not call meer dashes, strokes á la volée, or at random, because delineated by a Pencil that never works in vain; and hereof I take more particular notice, because I carry that in mine own hand which I could never read of nor discover in another. Aristotle, I confess, in his acute and singular Book of *Physiognomy*, hath made no mention of Chiromancy; yet I believe the Egyptians, who were neerer addicted to those abstruse and mystical sciences, had a knowledge therein, to which those vagabond and counterfeit Egyptians did after pretend, and perhaps retained a few corrupted principles, which sometimes might verifie their prognosticks.

It is the common wonder of all men, how among so many millions of faces, there should be none alike: now contrary, I wonder as much how there should be any. He that shall consider how many thousand several words have been carelesly and without study composed out of twenty-four Letters; withal, how many hundred lines there are to be drawn in the Fabrick of one Man, shall easily find that this variety is necessary; and it will be very hard that they shall so concur as to make one portract like another. Let a Painter carelessly limb out a million of Faces, and you shall find them all different; yea, let him have his Copy before him, yet after all his art there will remain a sensible distinction; for the pattern or example of every thing is the perfectest in that kind, whereof we still come short, though we transcend or go beyond it, because herein it is wide, and agrees not in all points unto the copy. Nor doth the similitude of Creatures disparage the variety of Nature, nor any way confound the Works of GOD. For even in things alike there is diversity; and those that do seem to accord do manifestly disagree. And thus is man like GOD; for in the same

things that we resemble Him, we are utterly different
from Him. There was never anything so like another as
in all points to concur: there will ever some reserved
difference slip in, to prevent the identity; without which,
two several things would not be alike, but the same,
which is impossible.

But to return from Philosophy to Charity: I hold not
so narrow a conceit of this virtue, as to conceive that to
give Alms is onely to be Charitable, or think a piece of
Liberality can comprehend the Total of Charity. Divinity
hath wisely divided the act thereof into many branches,
and hath taught us in this narrow way many paths unto
goodness; as many ways as we may do good, so many ways
we may be charitable. There are infirmities not onely of
Body, but of Soul, and Fortunes, which do require the
merciful hand of our abilities. I cannot contemn a man
for ignorance, but behold him with as much pity as I do
Lazarus. It is no greater Charity to cloath his body,
than apparel the nakedness of his Soul. It is an honourable object to see the reasons of other men wear our
Liveries, and their borrowed understandings do homage
to the bounty of ours: it is the cheapest way of beneficence, and, like the natural charity of the Sun, illuminates
another without obscuring itself. To be reserved and
caitiff in this part of goodness, is the sordidest piece of
covetousness, and more contemptible than pecuniary
Avarice. To this (as calling my self a Scholar,) I am obliged by the duty of my condition: I make not therefore
my head a grave, but a treasure, of knowledge; I intend
no Monopoly, but a community, in learning; I study not
for my own sake only, but for theirs that study not for
themselves. I envy no man that knows more than my self,
but pity them that know less. I instruct no man as an exercise of my knowledge, or with an intent rather to nourish and keep it alive in mine own head then beget and
propagate it in his: and in the midst of all my endeavours

there is but one thought that dejects me, that my acquired parts must perish with my self, nor can be Lega-
cied among my honoured Friends. I cannot fall out or
contemn a man for an errour, or conceive why a difference in Opinion should divide an affection; for Controversies, Disputes, and Argumentations, both in Philosophy and in Divinity, if they meet with discreet and
peaceable natures, do not infringe the Laws of Charity.
In all disputes, so much as there is of passion, so much as
there is of nothing to the purpose; for then Reason, like
a bad Hound, spends upon a false Scent, and forsakes
the question first started. And this is one reason why
Controversies are never determined; for, though they be
amply proposed, they are scarce at all handled, they do so
swell with unnecessary Digressions; and the Parenthesis
on the party is often as large as the main discourse upon
the subject. The Foundations of Religion are already
established, and the Principles of Salvation subscribed
unto by all: there remains not many controversies worth
a Passion; and yet never any disputed without, not only
in Divinity, but in inferiour Arts. What a βατραχομυομαχία
and hot skirmish is betwixt S. and T. in Lucian! How do
Grammarians hack and slash for the Genitive case
in *Jupiter!* How do they break their own pates to salve
that of Priscian!

Si foret in terris, rideret Democritus.

Yea, even amongst wiser militants, how many wounds
have been given, and credits slain, for the poor victory
of an opinion, or beggarly conquest of a distinction!
Scholars are men of Peace, they bear no Arms, but their
tongues are sharper than Actius his razor; their Pens
carry farther, and give a louder report than Thunder: I had rather stand the shock of a Basilisco, than
the fury of a merciless Pen. It is not meer Zeal to Learning, or Devotion to the Muses, that wiser Princes Patron

the Arts, and carry an indulgent aspect unto Scholars; but a desire to have their names eternized by the memory of their writings, and a fear of the revengeful Pen of succeeding ages; for these are the men, that, when they have played their parts, and had their *exits,* must step out and give the moral of their Scenes, and deliver unto Posterity an Inventory of their Virtues and Vices. And surely there goes a great deal of Conscience to the compiling of an History: there is no reproach to the scandal of a Story; it is such an authentick kind of falshood that with authority belies our good names to all Nations and Posterity.

There is another offence unto Charity, which no Author hath ever written of, and few take notice of; and that's the reproach, not of whole professions, mysteries, and conditions, but of whole Nations, wherein by opprobious Epithets we miscall each other, and by an uncharitable Logick, from a disposition in a few, conclude a habit in all.

> *Le mutin Anglois, et le bravache Escossois,*
> *Et le fol François,*
> *Le poultron Romain, le larron de Gascongne,*
> *L'Espagnol superbe, et l'Aleman yvrongne.*

St. Paul, that calls the Cretians *lyars,* doth it but indirectly, and upon quotation of their own Poet. It is as bloody a thought in one way, as Nero's was in another; for by a word we wound a thousand, and at one blow assassine the honour of a Nation. It is as compleat a piece of madness to miscal and rave against the times, or think to recal men to reason by a fit of passion. Democritus, that thought to laugh the times into goodness, seems to me as deeply Hypochondriack as Heraclitus, that bewailed them. It moves not my spleen to behold the multitude in their proper humours, that is, in their fits of folly and madness; as well understanding that wisdom is not prophan'd unto the World, and 'tis the priviledge of a few to be Vertuous. They that endeavour to abolish Vice, destroy also Virtue; for contraries, though they destroy one another, are yet the life of one another. Thus Virtue (abolish vice,) is an Idea. Again, the community of sin doth not disparage goodness; for when Vice gains upon the major part, Virtue, in whom it remains, becomes more excellent; and being lost in some, multiplies its goodness in others which remain untouched and persist intire in the general inundation. I can therefore behold Vice without a Satyr, content only with an admonition, or instructive reprehension; for Noble Natures, and such as are capable of goodness, are railed into vice, that might as easily be admonished into virtue; and we should all be so far the Orators of goodness, as to protect her from the power of Vice, and maintain the cause of injured truth. No man can justly censure or condemn another, because indeed no man truly knows another. This I perceive in my self; for I am in the dark to all the world, and my nearest friends behold me but in a cloud. Those that know me but superficially, think less of me than I do of my self; those of my neer acquaintance think more; GOD, Who truly knows me, knows that I am nothing; for He only beholds me and all the world, Who looks not on us through a derived ray, or a trajection of a sensible species, but beholds the substance without the helps of accidents, and the forms of things as we their operations. Further, no man can judge another, because no man knows himself: for we censure others but as they disagree from that humour which we fancy laudable in our selves, and commend others but for that wherein they seem to quadrate and consent with us. So that, in conclusion, all is but that we all condemn, Self-love. 'Tis the general complaint of these times, and perhaps of those past, that charity grows cold; which I perceive most verified in those which most do manifest the fires and flame of zeal; for it is a virtue that best agrees with coldest na tures, and such as are complexioned for humility. But how shall we expect Charity towards others, when we are uncharitable to our selves? *Charity begins at home,* is the voice of the World; yet is every man his greatest enemy, and, as it were, his own Executioner. *Non occides,* is the Commandment of GOD, yet scarce observed by any man; for I perceive every man is his own *Atropos,* and lends a hand to cut the thred of his own days. Cain was not therefore the first Murtherer, but Adam, who brought in death; whereof he beheld the practice and example in his own son Abel, and saw that verified in the experience of another, which faith could not perswade him in the Theory of himself.

There is, I think, no man that apprehends his own miseries less than my self, and no man that so neerly apprehends anothers. I could lose an arm without a tear, and with few groans, methinks, be quartered into pieces; yet can I weep most seriously at a Play, and receive with true passion the counterfeit grief of those known and professed Impostures. It is a barbarous part of inhumanity to add unto any afflicted parties misery, or indeavour to multiply in any man a passion whose single nature is already above his patience. This was the greatest affliction of Job, and those oblique expostulations of his Friends a deeper injury than the down-right blows of the Devil. It is not the tears of our own eyes only, but of our friends also, that do exhaust the current of our sorrows; which, falling into many streams, runs more peaceably, and is contented with a narrower channel. It is an act within the power of charity, to translate a passion out of one breast into another, and to divide a sorrow almost out of it self; for an affliction, like a dimension, may be so divided, as, if not indivisible, at least to become insensible. Now with my friend I desire not to share or participate, but to engross, his sorrows; that, by making them mine own, I may more easily discuss them; for in mine own reason, and within my self, I can command that which I cannot intreat without my self, and within the circle of another. I have often thought those noble pairs and examples of friendship not so truly Histories of what had been, as fictions of what should be; but I now perceive nothing in them but possibilities, nor any thing in the Heroick examples of Damon and Pythias, Achilles and Patroclus, which methinks upon some grounds I could not perform within the narrow compass of my self. That a man should lay down his life for his Friend, seems strange to vulgar affections, and such as confine themselves within that Worldly principle, *Charity begins at home.* For mine own part I could never remember the relations that I held unto my self, nor the respect that I owe unto my own nature, in the cause of God, my Country, and my Friends. Next to these three, I do embrace my self. I confess I do not observe that order that the Schools ordain our affections, to love our Parents, Wives, Children, and then our Friends; for, excepting the injunctions of Religion, I do not find in my self such a necessary and indissoluble Sympathy to all those of my blood. I hope I do not break the fifth Commandment, if I conceive I may love my friend before the nearest of my blood, even those to whom I owe the principles of life. I never yet cast a true affection on a woman; but I have loved my friend as I do virtue, my soul, my God. From hence me thinks I do conceive how God loves man, what happiness there is in the love of God. Omitting all other, there are three most mystical unions: 1. two natures in one person; 2. three persons in one nature; 3. one soul in two bodies; for though indeed they be really divided, yet are they so united, as they seem but one, and make rather a duality than two distinct souls.

There are wonders in true affection: it is a body of *Enigma's,* mysteries, and riddles; wherein two so become one, as they both become two. I love my friend before my self, and yet methinks I do not love him enough: some few months hence my multiplied affection will make me believe I have not loved him at all. When I am from him, I am dead till I be with him; when I am with him, I am not satisfied, but would still be nearer him. United souls are not satisfied with imbraces, but desire to be truly each other; which being impossible, their desires are infinite, and must proceed without a possibility of satisfaction. Another misery there is in affection, that whom we truly love like our own selves, we forget their looks, nor can our memory retain the Idea of their faces; and it is no wonder, for they are our selves, and our affection makes their looks our own. This noble affection falls not on vulgar and common constitutions, but on such as are mark'd for virtue: he that can love his friend with this noble ardour, will in a competent degree affect all. Now, if we can bring our affections to look beyond the body, and cast an eye upon the soul, we have found out the true object, not only of friendship, but Charity; and the greatest happiness that we can bequeath the soul, is that wherein we all do place our last felicity, Salvation; which though it be not in our power to bestow, it is in our charity and pious invocations to desire, if not procure and further. I cannot contentedly frame a prayer for my self in particular, without a catalogue for my friends; nor request a happiness, wherein my sociable disposition doth not desire the fellowship of my neighbour. I never hear the Toll of a passing Bell, though in my mirth, without my prayers and best wishes for the departing spirit; I cannot go to cure the body of my patient, but I forget my profession, and call unto GOD for his soul; I cannot see one say his prayers, but, in stead of imitating him, I fall into a supplication for him, who perhaps is no more to me than a common nature: and if GOD hath vouchsafed an ear to my supplications, there are surely many happy that never saw me, and enjoy the blessing of mine unknown devotions. To pray for Enemies, that is, for their salvation, is no harsh precept, but the practice of our daily and ordinary devotions. I cannot believe the story of the Italian: our bad wishes and uncharitable desires proceed no further than this life; it is the Devil, and the uncharitable votes of Hell, that desire our misery in the World to come.

To do no injury, nor take none, was a principle, which to my former years and impatient affections seemed to contain enough of Morality; but my more setled years and Christian constitution have fallen upon severer resolutions. I can hold there is no such thing as injury; that, if there be, there is no such injury as revenge, and no such revenge as the contempt of an injury; that to hate another, is to malign himself; that the truest way to love another, is to despise our selves. I were unjust unto mine own Conscience, if I should say I am at variance with any thing like my self. I find there are many pieces in this one fabrick of man; this frame is raised upon a mass of Antipathies. I am one methinks, but as the World; wherein notwithstanding there are a swarm of distinct essences, and in them another World of contrarieties; we carry private and domestick enemies within, publick and more hostile adversaries without. The Devil, that did but buffet St. Paul, plays methinks at sharp with me. Let me be nothing, if within the compass of my self I do not find the battail of Lepanto, Passion against Reason, Reason against Faith, Faith against the Devil, and my Conscience against all. There is another man within me, that's angry with me, rebukes, commands, and dastards me. I have no Conscience of Marble to resist the hammer of more heavy offences; nor yet so soft and waxen, as to take the impression of each single peccadillo or scrape of infirmity. I am of a strange belief, that it is as easie to be forgiven some sins,

as to commit some others. For my Original sin, I hold
it to be washed away in my Baptism: for my actual transgressions, I compute and reckon with GOD but from my
last repentance, Sacrament, or general absolution; and
therefore am not terrified with the sins or madness of
my youth. I thank the goodness of GOD, I have no sins
that want a name; I am not singular in offences; my transgressions are Epidemical, and from the common breath
of our corruption. For there are certain tempers of body,
which, matcht with an humorous depravity of mind, do
hatch and produce vitiosities, whose newness and monstrosity of nature admits no name: this was the temper
of that Lecher that fell in love with a Statua, and the
constitution of Nero in his Spintrian recreations. For the
Heavens are not only fruitful in new and unheard-of
stars, the Earth in plants and animals, but mens minds
also in villainy and vices. Now the dulness of my reason,
and the vulgarity of my disposition, never prompted my
invention, nor solicited my affection unto any of these;
yet even those common and quotidian infirmities that so
necessarily attend me, and do seem to be my very nature,
have so dejected me, so broken the estimation that I
should have otherwise of my self, that I repute my self the
most abjectest piece of mortality. Divines prescribe a fit
of sorrow to repentance: there goes indignation, anger,
sorrow, hatred, into mine; passions of a contrary nature,
which neither seem to sute with this action, nor my
proper constitution. It is no breach of charity to our
selves, to be at variance with our Vices, nor to abhor that
part of us which is an enemy to the ground of charity,
our GOD; wherein we do but imitate our great selves, the
world, whose divided Antipathies and contrary faces do
yet carry a charitable regard unto the whole, by their
particular discords preserving the common harmony,
and keeping in fetters those powers, whose rebellions,
once Masters, might be the ruine of all.

I thank GOD, amongst those millions of Vices I do inherit and hold from Adam, I have escaped one, and that a mortal enemy to Charity, the first and father-sin, not onely of man, but of the devil, Pride: a vice whose name is comprehended in a Monosyllable, but in its nature not circumscribed with a World. I have escaped it in a condition that can hardly avoid it. Those petty acquisitions and reputed perfections that advance and elevate the conceits of other men, add no feathers unto mine. I have seen a Grammarian towr and plume himself over a single line in Horace, and shew more pride in the construction of one Ode, than the Author in the composure of the whole book. For my own part, besides the *Jargon* and *Patois* of several Provinces, I understand no less than six Languages; yet I protest I have no higher conceit of my self, than had our Fathers before the confusion of Babel, when there was but one Language in the World, and none to boast himself either Linguist or Critick. I have not onely seen several Countries, beheld the nature of their Climes, the Chorography of their Provinces, Topography of their Cities, but understood their several Laws, Customs, and Policies; yet cannot all this perswade the dulness of my spirit unto such an opinion of my self, as I behold in nimbler and conceited heads, that never looked a degree beyond their Nests. I know the names, and somewhat more, of all the constellations in my Horizon; yet I have seen a prating Mariner, that could onely name the pointers and the North Star, out-talk me, and conceit himself a whole Sphere above me. I know most of the Plants of my Countrey, and of those about me; yet methinks I do not know so many as when I did but know a hundred, and had scarcely ever Simpled further than *Cheapside*. For, indeed, heads of capacity, and such as are not full with a handful or easie measure of knowledge, think they know nothing till they know all; which being impossible, they fall upon the opinion of Socrates, and only know they know not any thing. I cannot think that Homer pin'd away upon the riddle of the fishermen; or that Aristotle, who understood the uncertainty of knowledge, and confessed so often the reason of man too weak for the works of nature, did ever drown himself upon the flux and reflux of Euripus. We do but learn to-day what our better advanced judgements will unteach to morrow; and Aristotle doth but instruct us, as Plato did him; that is, to confute himself. I have run through all sorts, yet find no rest in any: though our first studies and *junior* endeavours may style us Peripateticks, Stoicks, or Academicks; yet I perceive the wisest heads prove, at last, almost all Scepticks, and stand like Janus in the field of knowledge. I have therefore one common and authentick Philosophy I learned in the Schools, whereby I discourse and satisfy the reason of other men; another more reserved, and drawn from experience, whereby I content mine own. Solomon, that complained of ignorance in the height of knowledge, hath not only humbled my conceits, but discouraged my endeavours. There is yet another conceit that hath sometimes made me shut my books, which tells me it is a vanity to waste our days in the blind pursuit of knowledge; it is but attending a little longer, and we shall enjoy that by instinct and infusion, which we endeavour at here by labour and inquisition. It is better to sit down in a modest ignorance, and rest contented with the natural blessing of our own reasons, than buy the uncertain knowledge of this life with sweat and vexation, which Death gives every fool *gratis,* and is an accessary of our glorification.

I was never yet once, and commend their resolutions who never marry twice: not that I disallow of second marriage; as neither, in all cases, of Polygamy, which, considering some times, and the unequal number of both sexes, may be also necessary. The whole World was made

for man, but the twelfth part of man for woman: Man
is the whole World, and the Breath of GOD; Woman the
Rib and crooked piece of man. I could be content that we
might procreate like trees, without conjunction, or that
there were any way to perpetuate the World without this
trivial and vulgar way of union: it is the foolishest act a
wise man commits in all his life; nor is there any thing
that will more deject his cool'd imagination, when he
shall consider what an odd and unworthy piece of folly
he hath committed. I speak not in prejudice, nor am
averse from that sweet Sex, but naturally amorous of all
that is beautiful. I can look a whole day with delight
upon a handsome Picture, though it be but of an Horse.
It is my temper, and I like it the better, to affect all
harmony; and sure there is musick even in the beauty,
and the silent note which Cupid strikes, far sweeter
than the sound of an instrument. For there is a musick
where ever there is a harmony, order, or proportion:
and thus far we may maintain the music of the Sphears;
for those well-ordered motions, and regular paces, though
they give no sound unto the ear, yet to the understanding
they strike a note most full of harmony. Whosoever is
harmonically composed delights in harmony; which
makes me much distrust the symmetry of those heads
which declaim against all Church-Musick. For my self,
not only from my obedience, but my particular Genius,
I do embrace it: for even that vulgar and Tavern-
Musick, which makes one man merry, another mad,
strikes in me a deep fit of devotion, and a profound contemplation of the First Composer. There is something in
it of Divinity more than the ear discovers: it is an Hieroglyphical and shadowed lesson of the whole World,
and creatures of GOD; such a melody to the ear, as the
whole World, well understood, would afford the understanding. In brief, it is a sensible fit of that harmony
which intellectually sounds in the ears of GOD. I will not

say, with Plato, the soul is an harmony, but harmonical, and hath its nearest sympathy unto Musick: thus some, whose temper of body agrees, and humours the constitution of their souls, are born Poets, though indeed all are naturally inclined unto Rhythme. This made Tacitus, in the very first line of his Story, fall upon a verse; and Cicero, the worst of Poets, but declaiming for a Poet, falls in the very first sentence upon a perfect Hexameter. I feel not in me those sordid and unchristian desires of my profession; I do not secretly implore and wish for Plagues, rejoyce at Famines, revolve Ephemerides and Almanacks in expectation of malignant Aspects, fatal Conjunctions, and Eclipses. I rejoyce not at unwholesome Springs, nor unseasonable Winters: my Prayer goes with the Husbandman's; I desire every thing in its proper season, that neither men nor the times be put out of temper. Let me be sick my self, if sometimes the malady of my patient be not a disease unto me. I desire rather to cure his infirmities than my own necessities. Where I do him no good, methinks it is scarce honest gain; though I confess 'tis but the worthy salary of our well-intended endeavours. I am not only ashamed, but heartily sorry, that, besides death, there are diseases incurable: yet not for my own sake, or that they be beyond my Art, but for the general cause and sake of humanity, whose common cause I apprehend as mine own. And to speak more generally, those three Noble Professions which all civil Commonwealths do honour, are raised upon the fall of Adam, and are not any way exempt from their infirmities; there are not only diseases incurable in Physick, but cases indissolvable in Laws, Vices incorrigible in Divinity. If General Councils may err, I do not see why particular Courts should be infallible: their perfectest rules are raised upon the erroneous reasons of Man, and the Laws of one do but condemn the rules of another; as Aristotle oft-times the opinions of his Predecessours, because, though agreeable to reason, yet were not consonant to his own rules, and the Logick of his proper Principles. Again, (to speak nothing of the Sin against the HOLY GHOST, whose cure not onely, but whose nature is unknown,) I can cure the Gout or Stone in some, sooner than Divinity, Pride, or Avarice in others. I can cure Vices by Physick when they remain incurable by Divinity, and shall obey my Pills when they contemn their precepts. I boast nothing, but plainly say, we all labour against our own cure; for death is the cure of all diseases. There is no *Catholicon* or universal remedy I know, but this; which, though nauseous to queasie stomachs, yet to prepare appetites is Nectar, and a pleasant potion of immortality.

For my Conversation, it is like the Sun's, with all men, and with a friendly aspect to good and bad. Methinks there is no man bad, and the worst, best; that is, while they are kept within the circle of those qualities wherein they are good: there is no man's mind of such discordant and jarring a temper, to which a tunable disposition may not strike a harmony. *Magnæ virtutes, nec minora vitia;* it is the posie of the best natures, and may be inverted on the worst; there are in the most depraved and venemous dispositions, certain pieces that remain untoucht, which by an *Antiperistasis* become more excellent, or by the excellency of their antipathies are able to preserve themselves from the contagion of their enemy vices, and persist intire beyond the general corruption. For it is also thus in nature: the greatest Balsomes do lie enveloped in the bodies of most powerful Corrosives. I say, moreover, and I ground upon experience, that poisons contain within themselves their own Antidote, and that which preserves them from the venome of themselves, without which they were not deleterious to others onely, but to themselves also. But it is the corruption that I fear within me, not the contagion of commerce without me. 'Tis that unruly regiment within me, that will destroy me; 'tis I that do infect my self; the man without a Navel yet lives in me; I feel that original canker and corrode and devour me; and therefore *Defenda me Dios de me,* "LORD deliver me from my self," is a part of my Letany, and the first voice of my retired imaginations. There is no man alone, because every man is a Microcosm, and carries the whole World about him. *Nunquam minus solus quam cum solus,* though it be the Apothegme of a wise man, is yet true in the mouth of a fool. Indeed, though in a Wilderness, a man is never alone, not only because he is with himself and his own thoughts, but because he is with the Devil, who ever consorts with our solitude, and is that unruly rebel that musters up those disordered motions which accompany our sequestred imaginations. And to speak more narrowly, there is no such thing as solitude, nor any thing that can be said to be alone and by itself, but GOD, Who is His own circle, and can subsist by Himself; all others, besides their dissimilar and Heterogeneous parts, which in a manner multiply their natures, cannot subsist without the concourse of GOD, and the society of that hand which doth uphold their natures. In brief, there can be nothing truly alone and by it self, which is not truly one; and such is only GOD: all others do transcend an unity, and so by consequence are many.

Now for my life, it is a miracle of thirty years, which to relate, were not a History, but a piece of Poetry, and would sound to common ears like a Fable. For the World, I count it not an Inn, but an Hospital; and a place not to live, but to dye in. The world that I regard is my self; it is the Microcosm of my own frame that I cast mine eye on; for the other, I use it but like my Globe, and turn it round sometimes for my recreation. Men that look upon my outside, perusing only my condition and Fortunes, do err in my Altitude; for I am above Atlas his shoulders.

The earth is a point not only in respect of the Heavens above us, but of that heavenly and celestial part within us; that mass of Flesh that circumscribes me, limits not my mind: that surface that tells the Heavens it hath an end, cannot persuade me I have any: I take my circle to be above three hundred and sixty; though the number of the Ark do measure my body, it comprehendeth not my mind: whilst I study to find how I am a Microcosm, or little World, I find my self something more than the great. There is surely a piece of Divinity in us, something that was before the Elements, and owes no homage unto the Sun. Nature tells me I am the Image of GOD, as well as Scripture: he that understands not thus much, hath not his introduction or first lesson, and is yet to begin the Alphabet of man. Let me not injure the felicity of others, if I say I am as happy as any: *Ruat cœlum, fiat voluntas Tua,* salveth all; so that whatsoever happens, it is but what our daily prayers desire. In brief, I am content; and what should Providence add more? Surely this is it we call Happiness, and this do I enjoy; with this I am happy in a dream, and as content to enjoy a happiness in a fancy, as others in a more apparent truth and realty. There is surely a neerer apprehension of any thing that delights us in our dreams, than in our waked senses: without this I were unhappy; for my awaked judgment discontents me, ever whispering unto me, that I am from my friend; but my friendly dreams in the night requite me, and make me think I am within his arms. I thank GOD for my happy dreams, as I do for my good rest; for there is a satisfaction in them unto reasonable desires, and such as can be content with a fit of happiness: and surely it is not a melancholy conceit to think we are all asleep in this World, and that the conceits of this life are as meer dreams to those of the next; as the Phantasms of the night, to the conceits of the day. There is an equal delusion in both, and the one doth but seem to be the embleme or picture of the other: we are somewhat more than our selves in our sleeps, and the slumber of the body seems to be but the waking of the soul. It is the ligation of sense, but the liberty of reason; and our waking conceptions do not match the Fancies of our sleeps. At my Nativity my Ascendant was the watery sign of Scorpius; I was born in the Planetary hour of Saturn, and I think I have a piece of that Leaden Planet in me. I am no way facetious, nor disposed for the mirth and galliardize of company; yet in one dream I can compose a whole Comedy, behold the action, apprehend the jests, and laugh my self awake at the conceits thereof. Were my memory as faithful as my reason is then fruitful, I would never study but in my dreams; and this time also would I chuse for my devotions: but our grosser memories have then so little hold of our abstracted understandings, that they forget the story, and can only relate to our awaked souls, a confused and broken tale of that that hath passed. Aristotle, who hath written a singular Tract *Of Sleep,* hath not, methinks, throughly defined it; nor yet Galen, though he seem to have corrected it; for those Noctambuloes and night-walkers, though in their sleep, do yet injoy the action of their senses. We must therefore say that there is something in us that is not in the jurisdiction of Morpheus; and that those abstracted and ecstatick souls do walk about in their own corps, as spirits with the bodies they assume, wherein they seem to hear, see, and feel, though indeed the Organs are destitute of sense, and their natures of those faculties that should inform them. Thus it is observed, that men sometimes, upon the hour of their departure, do speak and reason above themselves; for then the soul, beginning to be freed from the ligaments of the body, begins to reason like her self, and to discourse in a strain above mortality.

We term sleep a death; and yet it is waking that kills

us, and destroys those spirits that are the house of life. 'Tis indeed a part of life that best expresseth death; for every man truely lives, so long as he acts his nature, or some way makes good the faculties of himself. Themistocles, therefore, that slew his Soldier in his sleep, was a merciful Executioner: 'tis a kind of punishment the mildness of no laws hath invented: I wonder the fancy of Lucan and Seneca did not discover it. It is that death by which we may be literally said to dye daily; a death which Adam dyed before his mortality; a death whereby we live a middle and moderating point between life and death: in fine, so like death, I dare not trust it without my prayers, and an half adieu unto the World, and take my farewel in a Colloquy with GOD.

> The night is come, like to the day,
> Depart not Thou, great GOD, away.
> Let not my sins, black as the night,
> Eclipse the lustre of Thy light:
> Keep still in my Horizon; for to me
> The Sun makes not the day, but Thee.
> Thou, Whose nature cannot sleep,
> On my temples Centry keep;
> Guard me 'gainst those watchful foes,
> Whose eyes are open while mine close.
> Let no dreams my head infest,
> But such as Jacob's temples blest.
> While I do rest, my Soul advance;
> Make my sleep a holy trance;
> That I may, my rest being wrought,
> Awake into some holy thought;
> And with as active vigour run
> My course, as doth the nimble Sun.
> Sleep is a death; O make me try,
> By sleeping, what it is to die;
> And as gently lay my head
> On my grave, as now my bed.
> Howere I rest, great GOD, let me
> Awake again at last with Thee;
> And thus assur'd, behold I lie
> Securely, or to awake or die.

These are my drowsie days; in vain
I do now wake to sleep again:
O come that hour, when I shall never
Sleep again, but wake for ever.

This is the Dormative I take to bedward; I need no other
Laudanum than this to make me sleep; after which I
close mine eyes in security, content to take my leave of
the Sun, and sleep unto the Resurrection.

The method I should use in distributive Justice, I often
observe in commutative; and keep a Geometrical proportion in both, whereby becoming equable to others, I become unjust to my self, and supererogate in that common
principle, *Do unto others as thou wouldst be done unto
thy self*. I was not born unto riches, neither is it, I think,
my Star to be wealthy; or, if it were, the freedom of my
mind, and frankness of my disposition, were able to contradict and cross my fates: for to me, avarice seems not
so much a vice, as a deplorable piece of madness; to conceive ourselves pipkins, or be perswaded that we are dead,
is not so ridiculous, nor so many degrees beyond the
power of Hellebore, as this. The opinions of Theory, and
positions of men, are not so void of reason as their practised conclusions. Some have held that Snow is black,
that the earth moves, that the Soul is air, fire, water; but
all this is Philosophy, and there is no delirium, if we do
but speculate the folly and indisputable dotage of avarice
to that subterraneous Idol, and God of the Earth. I do
confess I am an Atheist; I cannot perswade myself to honour that the World adores; whatsoever virtue its prepared
substance may have within my body, it hath no influence
nor operation without. I would not entertain a base design, or an action that should call me villain, for the
Indies; and for this only do I love and honour my own
soul, and have methinks two arms too few to embrace
myself. Aristotle is too severe, that will not allow us to
be truely liberal without wealth, and the bountiful hand

of Fortune. If this be true, I must confess I am charitable only in my liberal intentions, and bountiful well-wishes; but if the example of the Mite be not only an act of wonder, but an example of the noblest Charity, surely poor men may also build Hospitals, and the rich alone have not erected Cathedrals. I have a private method which others observe not; I take the opportunity of my self to do good; I borrow occasion of Charity from mine own necessities, and supply the wants of others, when I am in most need my self: for it is an honest stratagem to take advantage of our selves, and so to husband the acts of vertue, that, where they are defective in one circumstance, they may repay their want and multiply their goodness in another. I have not Peru in my desires, but a competence, and ability to perform those good works to which He hath inclined my nature. He is rich, who hath enough to be charitable; and it is hard to be so poor, that a noble mind may not find a way to this piece of goodness. *He that giveth to the poor, lendeth to the* LORD: there is more Rhetorick in that one sentence, than in a Library of Sermons; and indeed, if those Sentences were understood by the Reader, with the same Emphasis as they are delivered by the Author, we needed not those Volumes of instructions, but might be honest by an Epitome. Upon this motive only I cannot behold a Beggar without relieving his Necessities with my Purse, or his Soul with my Prayers; these scenical and accidental differences between us, cannot make me forget that common and untoucht part of us both: there is under these *Centoes* and miserable outsides, these mutilate and semibodies, a soul of the same alloy with our own, whose Genealogy is GOD as well as ours, and in as fair a way to Salvation as our selves. Statists that labour to contrive a Common-wealth without poverty, take away the object of charity, not understanding only the Common-wealth of a Christian, but forgetting the prophecie of CHRIST.

Now, there is another part of charity, which is the Basis and Pillar of this, and that is the love of GOD, for Whom we love our neighbour; for this I think charity, to love GOD for Himself, and our neighbour for GOD. All that is truly amiable is GOD, or as it were a divided piece of Him, that retains a reflex or shadow of Himself. Nor is it strange that we should place affection on that which is invisible: all that we truly love is thus; what we adore under affection of our senses, deserves not the honour of so pure a title. Thus we adore Virtue, though to the eyes of sense she be invisible: thus that part of our noble friends that we love, is not that part that we imbrace, but that insensible part that our arms cannot embrace. GOD, being all goodness, can love nothing but Himself; He loves us but for that part which is as it were Himself, and the traduction of His Holy Spirit. Let us call to assize the loves of our parents, the affection of our wives and children, and they are all dumb shows and dreams, without reality, truth, or constancy. For first there is a strong bond of affection between us and our Parents; yet how easily dissolved! We betake our selves to a woman, forget our mother in a wife, and the womb that bare us, in that that shall bear our Image. This woman blessing us with children, our affection leaves the level it held before, and sinks from our bed unto our issue and picture of Posterity, where affection holds no steady mansion. They, growing up in years, desire our ends; or applying themselves to a woman, take a lawful way to love another better than our selves. Thus I perceive a man may be buried alive, and behold his grave in his own issue.

I conclude therefore, and say, there is no happiness under (or, as Copernicus will have it, *above*) the Sun, nor any Crambe in that repeated verity and burthen of all the wisdom of Solomon, *All is vanity and vexation of Spirit*. There is no felicity in that the World adores. Aristotle, whilst he labours to refute the Idea's of Plato,

falls upon one himself; for his *summum bonum* is a
Chimæra, and there is no such thing as his Felicity.
That wherein GOD Himself is happy, the holy Angels are
happy, in whose defect the Devils are unhappy, that dare
I call happiness: whatsoever conduceth unto this, may
with an easy Metaphor deserve that name; whatsoever
else the World terms Happiness, is to me a story out of
Pliny, a tale of Boccace or Malizspini, an apparition, or
neat delusion, wherein there is no more of Happiness
than the name. Bless me in this life with but peace of my
Conscience, command of my affections, the love of Thy
self and my dearest friends, and I shall be happy enough
to pity Cæsar. These are, O LORD, the humble desires of
my most reasonable ambition, and all I dare call happiness on earth; wherein I set no rule or limit to Thy Hand
or Providence. Dispose of me according to the wisdom
of Thy pleasure: Thy will be done, though in my own
undoing.

FINIS

PSEUDODOXIA EPIDEMICA:
or, Enquiries into
Very many received Tenents,
And commonly presumed Truths.
1646

PSEUDODOXIA EPIDEMICA

BOOK II, CHAPTER 3

CONCERNING THE LOADSTONE, THEREIN OF SUNDRY COMMON OPINIONS, AND RECEIVED SEVERAL RELATIONS: NATURAL, HISTORICAL, MEDICAL, MAGICAL

AND first not only a simple Heterodox, but a very hard Paradox, it will seem, and of great absurdity unto obstinate ears, if we say, attraction is unjustly appropriated unto the Loadstone, and that perhaps we speak not properly, when we say vulgarly and appropriately the Loadstone draweth Iron; and yet herein we should not want experiment and great Authority. The words of Renatus des Cartes in his *Principles of Philosophy* are very plain: *Praeterea magnes trahet ferrum, sive potius magnes & ferrum ad invicem accedunt, neque enim ulla ibi tractio est.* The same is solemnly determined by Cabeus: *Nec magnes trahit proprie ferrum, nec ferrum ad se magnetem provocat, sed ambo pari conatu ad invicem confluunt.* Concordant hereto is the assertion of Doctor Ridley, Physitian unto the Emperour of Russia, in his Tract of Magnetical Bodies, defining Magnetical attraction to be a natural incitation and disposition conforming unto contiguity, an union of one Magnetical Body with another, and no violent haling of the weak unto the stronger. And this is also the Doctrine of Gilbertus, by whom this motion is termed Coition, and that not made by any faculty attractive of one, but a Syndrome and concourse of each; a Coition alway of their vigours, and also of their bodies, if bulk or impediment prevent not. And therefore those contrary actions which flow from opposite Poles or Faces, are not so properly expulsion and attraction, as *Sequela* and *Fuga,* a mutual flight and following. Consonant whereto are also the determinations of Helmontius, Kircherus, and Licetus.

The same is also confirmed by experiment; for if a piece of Iron be fastened in the side of a bowl or bason of water, a Loadstone swimming freely in a Boat of Cork, will presently make unto it. So if a Steel or Knife untouched, be offered toward the Needle that is touched, the Needle nimbly moveth toward it, and conformeth unto union with the Steel that moveth not. Again, If a Loadstone be finely filed, the Atoms or dust thereof will adhere unto Iron that was never touched, even as the powder of Iron doth also unto the Loadstone. And lastly, if in two Skiffs of Cork, a Loadstone and Steel be placed within the Orb of their activities, the one doth not move, the other standing still, but both hoise sail and steer unto each other. So that if the Loadstone attract, the Steel hath also its attraction; for in this action the Alliciency is reciprocal, which joyntly felt, they mutually approach and run into each other's arms.

And therefore surely more moderate expressions become this action, then what the Ancients have used; which some have delivered in the most violent terms of their language; so Austin calls it, *Mirabilem ferri raptorem:* Hippocrates, λίθος ὅ τι τὸν σίδηρον ἀρπάζει, *Lapis qui ferrum rapit.* Galen disputing against Epicurus useth the term ἕλκειν, but this also is too violent: among the Ancients Aristotle spake most warily, λίθος ὅστις τὸν σίδηρον κινεῖ, *Lapis qui ferrum movet:* and in some tolerable acception do run the expressions of Aquinas, Scaliger and Cusanus.

Many relations are made, and great expectations are raised from the *Magnes Carneus,* or a Loadstone, that hath a faculty to attract not only iron but flesh, but this upon enquiry, and as Cabeus also observed, is nothing else but a weak and inanimate kind of Loadstone, veined here and there with a few magnetical and ferreous lines, but consisting of a bolary and clammy substance, whereby it adheres like *Hæmatites,* or *Terra Lemnia,* unto the Lips. And this is that stone which is to be understood, when Physitians joyn it with *Ætites,* or the Eagle stone, and promise therein a vertue against abortion.

There is sometime a mistake concerning the variation of the Compass, and therein one point is taken for another. For beyond the Equator some men account its variation by the diversion of the Northern point, whereas beyond that Circle the Southern point is Soveraign, and the North submits his preheminency. For in the Southern coast either of America or Africa; the Southern point deflects and varieth toward the Land, as being disposed and spirited that way by the Meridional and proper Hemisphere. And therefore on that side of the Earth the varying point is best accounted by the South. And therefore also the writings of some, and Maps of others, are to be enquired, that make the Needle decline unto the East twelve degrees at Capo Frio; and six at the straits of Magellan; accounting hereby one point for another, and preferring the North in the Liberties and Province of the South.

But certainly false it is what is commonly affirmed and believed, that Garlick doth hinder the attraction of the Loadstone, which is notwithstanding delivered by grave and worthy Writers, by Pliny, Solinus, Ptolomy, Plutarch,

Albertus, Mathiolus, Rueus, Langius, and many more. An effect as strange as that of Homer's Moly, and the Garlick that Mercury bestowed upon Ulysses. But that it is evidently false, many experiments declare. For an Iron wire heated red hot and quenched in the juice of Garlick, doth notwithstanding contract a verticity from the Earth, and attracteth the Southern point of the Needle. If also the tooth of a Loadstone be covered or stuck in Garlick, it will notwithstanding attract; and Needles excited and fixed in Garlick until they begin to rust, do yet retain their attractive and polary respects.

Of the same stamp is that which is obtruded upon us by Authors ancient and modern, that an Adamant or Diamond prevents or suspends the attraction of the Loadstone: as is in open terms delivered by Pliny. *Adamas dissidet cum Magnete lapide, ut juxta positus ferrum non patiatur abstrahi, aut si admotus magnes apprehenderit, rapiat atque auferat.* For if a Diamond be placed between a Needle and a Loadstone, there will nevertheless ensue a Coition even over the body of the Diamond. And an easie matter it is to touch or excite a Needle through a Diamond, by placing it at the tooth of a Loadstone; and therefore the relation is false, or our estimation of these gemms untrue; nor are they Diamonds which carry that name amongst us.

It is not suddenly to be received what Paracelsus[1] affirmeth, that if a Loadstone be anointed with Mercurial oyl, or onely put into Quicksilver, it omitteth its attraction for ever. For we have found that Loadstones and touched Needles which have laid long time in Quicksilver have not amitted their attraction. And we also find that red hot Needles or wires extinguished in Quicksilver, do yet acquire a verticity according to the Laws of position in extinction. Of greater repugnancy unto reason is that

[1] *De generatione rerum.*

which he delivers concerning its graduation, that heated in fire and often extinguished in oyl of Mars or Iron, it acquires an ability to extract or draw forth a nail fastened in a wall; for, as we have declared before, the vigour of the Loadstone is destroyed by fire, nor will it be re-impregnated by any other Magnete then the Earth.

Nor is it to be made out what seemeth very plausible, and formerly hath deceived us, that a Loadstone will not attract an Iron or Steel red hot. The falsity hereof discovered first by Kircherus, we can confirm by iterated experiment; very sensibly in armed Loadstones, and obscurely in any other.

True it is, that besides fire some other wayes there are of its destruction, as Age, Rust; and what is least dreamt on, an unnatural or contrary situation. For being impolarily adjoyned unto a more vigorous Loadstone, it will in a short time enchange its Poles; or being kept in undue position, that is, not lying on the Meridian, or else with its poles inverted, it receives in longer time impair in activity, exchange of Faces; and is more powerfully preserved by position then by the dust of Steel. But the sudden and surest way is fire; that is, fire not onely actual but potential; the one surely and suddenly, the other slowly and imperfectly; the one changing, the other destroying the figure. For if distilled Vinegar or *Aqua fortis* be poured upon the powder of Loadstone, the subsiding powder dryed, retains some Magnetical vertue, and will be attracted by the Loadstone: but if the menstruum or dissolvent be evaporated to a consistence, and afterward doth shoot into Icycles or Crystals, the Loadstone hath no power upon them; and if in a full dissolution of Steel a separation of parts be made by precipitation or exhaltation, the exsiccated powder hath lost its wings and ascends not unto the Loadstone. And though a Loadstone fired doth presently omit its proper vertue, and according to the position in cooling contracts a new verticity from the Earth; yet if the same be laid awhile in *aqua fortis* or other corrosive water, and taken out before a considerable corrosion, it still reserves its attraction, and will convert the Needle according to former polarity. And that duly preserved from violent corrosion, or the natural disease of rust, it may long conserve its vertue, beside the Magnetical vertue of the Earth, which hath lasted since the Creation, a great example we have from the observation of our learned friend Mr. Graves,[1] in an Ægyptian Idol cut out of Loadstone, and found among the Mummies; which still retains its attraction, though probably taken out of the Mine about two thousand years ago.

It is improbable what Pliny affirmeth concerning the object of its attraction, that it attracts not only ferreous bodies, but also *liquorem vitri;* for in the body of Glass there is no ferreous or magnetical nature which might occasion attraction. For of the Glass we use, the purest is made of the finest sand and the ashes of Chali or Glaswort, and the courser or green sort of the ashes of Brake or other plants. True it is that in the making of Glass, it hath been an ancient practice to cast in pieces of magnet, or perhaps manganes: conceiving it carried away all ferreous and earthy parts, from the pure and running portion of Glass, which the Loadstone would not respect; and therefore if that attraction were not rather Electrical then Magnetical, it was a wondrous effect what Helmont delivereth concerning a Glass wherein the Magistery of Loadstone was prepared, which after retained an attractive quality.

But whether the Magnet attracteth more then common Iron, may be tried in other bodies. It seems to attract the Smyris or Emery in powder; It draweth the shining or glassie powder brought from the Indies, and usually implied in writing-dust. There is also in Smiths' Cinders

---

[1] In his learned *Pyramidography.*

by some adhesion of Iron whereby they appear as it were glazed, sometime to be found a magnetical operation; for some thereof applied have power to move the Needle. But whether the ashes of vegetables which grow over Iron Mines contract a magnetical quality, as containing some mineral particles, which by sublimation ascend unto their Roots, and are attracted together with their nourishment; according as some affirm from the like observations upon the Mines of Silver, Quick silver, and Gold; we must refer unto further experiment.

It is also improbable and something singular what some conceive, and Eusebius Nierembergius, a learned Jesuit of Spain delivers, that the body of man is magnetical, and being placed in a Boat, the Vessel will never rest untill the head respecteth the North. If this be true, the bodies of Christians do lye unnaturally in their Graves. King Cheops in his Tomb, and the Jews in their beds have fallen upon the natural position: who reverentially declining the situation of their Temple, nor willing to lye as that stood, do place their Beds from North to South, and delight to sleep Meridionally. This Opinion confirmed would much advance the Microcosmical conceit, and commend the Geography of Paracelsus, who according to the Cardinal points of the World, divideth the body of man; and therefore working upon humane ordure, and by long preparation rendring it odiferous, he terms it *Zibeta Occidentalis,* Western Civet; making the face the East, but the posteriours the America or Western part of his Microcosm. The verity hereof might easily be tried in Wales, where there are portable Boats, and made of Leather, which would convert upon the impulsion of any verticity; and seem to be the same whereof in his description of Britain Cæsar hath left some mention.

Another kind of verticity, is that which *Angelus doce mihi jus,*[1] *alia*s, Michael Sundevogis, in a Tract *De Sul-*

[1] Anagrammatically.

phure, discovereth in Vegetables, from sticks let fall or depressed under water; which equally framed and permitted unto themselves, will ascend at the upper end, or that which was vertical in their vegetation; wherein notwithstanding, as yet, we have not found satisfaction. Although perhaps too greedy of Magnalities, we are apt to make but favourable experiments concerning welcom Truths, and such desired verities.

It is also wondrous strange what Lælius Bisciola reporteth, that if unto ten ounces of Loadstone one of Iron be added, it encreaseth not unto eleven, but weighs ten ounces still. A relation inexcusable in a work of leisurable hours:[1] the examination being as ready as the relation, and the falsity tried as easily as delivered. Nor is it to be omitted what is taken up by the Cæsius Bernardus a late Mineralogist, and originally confirmed by Porta, that Needles touched with a Diamond contract a verticity, even as they do with a Loadstone, which will not consist with experiment. And therefore, as Gilbertus observeth, he might be deceived, in touching such Needles with Diamonds, which had a verticity before, as we have declared most Needles to have; and so had he touched them with Gold or Silver, he might have concluded a magnetical vertue therein.

In the same form may we place Fracastorius his attraction of silver, Philostratus his Pantarbes; Apollodorus and Beda his relation of the Loadstone that attracted onely in the night. But most inexcusable is Franciscus Rueus, a man of our own profession; who in his discourse of Gemms mentioned in the Apocalyps, undertakes a Chapter of the Loadstone. Wherein substantially and upon experiment he scarce delivereth any thing: making long enumeration of its traditional qualities, whereof he seemeth to believe many, and some above convicted by

[1] *Horae subsecivae.*

experience, he is fain to salve as impostures of the Devil. But Boetius de Boot, Physitian unto Rodulphus the second, hath recompenced this defect; and in his Tract, *De Lapidibus & Gemmis,* speaks very materially hereof; and his Discourse is consonant unto Experience and Reason.

As for Relations Historical, though many there be of less account, yet two alone deserve consideration; The first concerneth magnetical Rocks, and attractive Mountains in several parts of the Earth. The other the Tomb of Mahomet and bodies suspended in the air. Of Rocks magnetical there are likewise two relations; for some are delivered to be in the Indies, and some in the extremity of the North, and about the very Pole. The Northern account is commonly ascribed unto Olaus Magnus, Archbishop of Upsale, who out of his Predecessor Joannes, Saxo, and others, compiled a History of some Northern Nations; but this assertion we have not discovered in that Work of his which commonly passeth amongst us, and should believe his Geography herein no more then that in the first line of his Book; when he affirmeth that Biarmia (which is not seventy degrees in latitude) hath the Pole for its Zenith, and Equinoctial for the Horizon.

Now upon this foundation, how uncertain soever men have erected mighty illations, ascribing thereto the cause of the Needle's direction, and conceiving the effluctions from these Mountains and Rocks invite the Lilly toward the North. Which conceit though countenanced by learned men, is not made out either by experience or reason, for no man hath yet attained or given a sensible account of the Pole by some degrees. It is also observed the Needle doth very much vary as it approacheth the Pole; whereas were there such direction from the Rocks, upon a nearer approachment it would more directly respect them. Beside, were there such magnetical Rocks under the Pole, yet being so far removed they would produce no such effect. For they that sail by the Isle of Ilua, now called Elba, in the Thuscan Sea which abounds in veins of Loadstone, observe no variation or inclination of the Needle; much less may they expect a direction from Rocks at the end of the Earth. And lastly, men that ascribe thus much unto Rocks of the North, must presume or discover the like magneticals at the South: For in the Southern Seas and far beyond the Equator, variations are large, and declinations as constant as in the Northern Ocean.

The other relation of Loadstone Mines and Rocks, in the shore of India is delivered of old by Pliny; wherein, saith he, they are so placed both in abundance and vigour, that it proves an adventure of hazard to pass those Coasts in a Ship with Iron nails. Serapion the Moor, an Author of good esteem and reasonable Antiquity, confirmeth the same, whose expression in the word *magnes* is this. The Mine of this Stone is in the Sea-coast of India, whereto when Ships approach, there is no Iron in them which flies not like a Bird unto those Mountains; and therefore their Ships are fastened not with Iron but Wood, for otherwise they would be torn to pieces. But this assertion, how positive soever, is contradicted [1] by all Navigators that pass that way; which are now many, and of our own Nation, and might surely have been controlled by Nearchus the Admiral of Alexander; who not knowing the Compass, was fain to coast that shore.

For the relation concerning Mahomet, it is generally believed his Tomb at Medina Talnabi, in Arabia, without any visible supporters hangeth in the air between two Loadstones artificially contrived both above and below; which conceit is fabulous and evidently false from the testimony of Ocular Testators, who affirm his Tomb is made of Stone, and lyeth upon the ground; as besides others the learned Vossius observeth from Gabriel Sionita, and Joannes Hesronita, two Maronites in their relations

---

[1] (Probably) There be no magnetical rocks.

hereof. Of such intentions and attempt by Mahometans we read in some Relators, and that might be the occasion of the Fable, which by tradition of time and distance of place enlarged into the Story of being accomplished. And this hath been promoted by attempts of the like nature; for we read in Pliny that one Dinocrates began to Arch the Temple of Arsinoe in Alexandria with Loadstone, that so her Stature might be suspended in the air to the amazement of the beholders. And to lead on our crudelity herein, confirmation may be drawn from History and Writers of good authority. So is it reported by Ruffinus, that in the Temple of Serapis there was an Iron Chariot suspended by Loadstones in the air; which stones re- moved, the Chariot fell and dashed into pieces. The like doth Beda report of Bellerophon's Horse, which framed of Iron, was placed between two Loadstones, with wings expansed, pendulous in the air.

The verity of these Stories we shall not further dispute, their possibility we may in some way determine; if we conceive what no man will deny, that bodies suspended in the air have this suspension from one or many Load- stones placed both above and below it; or else by one or many placed only above it. Likewise the body to be sus- pended in respect of the Loadstone above, is either placed first at a pendulous distance in the medium, or else at- tracted unto that site by the vigour of the Loadstone. And so we first affirm that possible it is a body may be suspended between two Loadstones; that is, it being so equally attracted unto both, that it determineth it self unto neither. But surely this position will be of no dura- tion; for if the air be agitated or the body waved either way, it omits the equilibration, and disposeth it self unto the nearest attractor. Again, It is not impossible (though hardly feasible) by a single Loadstone to suspend an Iron in the air, the Iron being artificially placed and at a distance guided toward the stone, until it find the neutral point, wherein its gravity just equals the magnetical quality, the one exactly extolling as much as the other depresseth. And lastly, Impossible it is that if an Iron rest upon the ground, and a Loadstone be placed over it, it should ever so arise as to hang in the way or medium; for that vigour which at a distance is able to overcome the resistance of its gravity and to lift up it from the Earth, will as it approacheth nearer be still more able to attract it; never remaining in the middle that could not abide in the extreams. Now the way of *Baptista Porta* that by a thred fastneth a Needle to a Table, and then so guides and orders the same, that by the attraction of the Load-stone it abideth in the air, infringeth not this reason; for this is a violent retention, and if the thred be loosened, the Needle ascends and adheres unto the Attractor.

The third consideration concerneth Medical relations; wherein what ever effects are delivered, they are either derived from its mineral and ferreous condition, or else magnetical operation. Unto the ferreous and mineral quality pertaineth what Dioscorides, an ancient Writer and Souldier under Anthony and Cleopatra, affirmeth, that half a dram of Loadstone given with Honey and Water, proves a purgative medicine, and evacuateth gross humours. But this is a quality of great incertainty; for omitting the vehicle of Water and Honey, which is of a laxative power it self, the powder of some Loadstones in this dose doth rather constipate and binde, then purge and loosen the belly. And if sometimes it cause any laxity, it is probably in the same way with Iron and Steel un-prepared, which will disturb some bodies, and work by Purge and Vomit. And therefore, whereas it is delivered in a Book ascribed unto Galen, that it is a good medicine in dropsies, and evacuates the waters of persons so af-fected: It may I confess by siccity and astriction afford a confirmation unto parts relaxed, and such as be hydropi-cally disposed; and by these qualities it may be useful in

Hernias or Ruptures, and for these it is commended by Ætius, Ægineta, and Oribasius; who only affirm that it contains the vertue of Hæmatites, and being burnt was sometimes vended for it. Wherein notwithstanding there is an higher vertue; and in the same prepared, or in rich veins thereof, though crude, we have observed the effects of Chalybeat Medicines; and the benefits of Iron and Steel in strong obstructions. And therefore that was probably a different vein of Loadstone, or infected with other mineral mixture, which the Ancients commended for a purgative medicine, and ranked the same with the violentest kinds thereof: with Hippophae, Cneoron, and Thymelæa, as we find it in Hippocrates;[1] and might be somewhat doubtful, whether by the magnesian stone, he understood the Loadstone, did not Achilles Statius define the same, the Stone that loveth Iron.

To this mineral condition belongeth what is delivered by some, that wounds which are made with weapons excited by the Loadstone, contract a malignity, and become of more difficult cure; which nevertheless is not to be found in the incision of Chyrurgions with knives and lancets touched; which leave no such effect behind them. Hither we also refer that affirmative, which sayes the Loadstone is poison; and therefore in the lists of poisons we find it in many Authors. But this our experience cannot confirm, and the practice of the King of Zeilan clearly contradicteth; who as Garcias ab Horto, Physitian unto the Spanish Viceroy delivereth, hath all his meat served up in dishes of Loadstone, and conceives thereby he preserveth the vigour of youth.

But surely from a magnetical activity must be made out what is let fall by Ætius, that a Loadstone held in the hand of one that is podagrical, doth either cure or give great ease in the Gout. Or what Marcellus Empericus

---

[1] *De morbis internis.*

affirmeth, that as an amulet, it also cureth the headach; which are but additions unto its proper nature, and hopeful enlargements of its allowed attraction. For perceiving its secret power to draw magnetical bodies, men have invented a new attraction, to draw out the dolour and pain of any part. And from such grounds it surely became a philter, and was conceived a medicine of some venereal attraction; and therefore upon this stone they graved the Image of Venus, according unto that of Claudian, *Venerem magnetica gemma figurat.* Hither must we also refer what is delivered concerning its power to draw out of the body bullets and heads of arrows, and for the like intention is mixed up in plaisters. Which course, although as vain and ineffectual it be rejected by many good Authors, yet is it not methinks so readily to be denied, nor the Practice of many Physicians which have thus compounded plaisters, thus suddenly to be condemned, as may be observed in the *Emplastrum divinum Nicolai,* the *Emplastrum nigrum* of Augspurg, the *Opodeldoch* and *Attractium* of Paracelsus, with several more in the Dispensatory of Wecker, and practice of Sennertus. The cure also of Hernias, or Ruptures in Pareus: and the method also of curation lately delivered by Daniel Beckherus,[1] and approved by the Professors of Leyden, that is, of a young man of Spruceland that casually swallowed a knife about ten inches long, which was cut out of his stomach, and the wound healed up. In which cure to attract the knife to a convenient situation, there was applied a plaister made up with the powder of Loadstone. Now this kind of practice Libavius, Gilbertus, and lately Swickardus[2] condemn, as vain, and altogether unuseful; because a Loadstone in powder hath no attractive power; for in that form it omits his polary respects, and loseth those parts which are the rule of attraction.

---

[1] *De cultrivoro Prussiaco,* 1636.
[2] In his *Ars Magnetica.*

Wherein to speak compendiously, if experiment hath not deceived us, we first affirm that a Loadstone in powder omits not all attraction. For if the powder of a rich vein be in a reasonable quantity presented toward the Needle freely placed, it will not appear to be void of all activity, but will be able to stir it. Nor hath it only a power to move the Needle in powder and by it self, but this will it also do, if incorporated and mixed with plaisters; as we have made trial in the *Emplastrum de Minio;* with half an ounce of the mass, mixing a dram of Loadstone. For applying the magdaleon or roal unto the Needle, it would both stir and attract it; not equally in all parts, but more vigorously in some, according unto the Mine of the Stone, more plentifully dispersed in the mass. And lastly, In the Loadstone powdered, the polary respects are not wholly destroyed. For those diminutive particles are not atomical or meerly indivisible, but consist of dimensions sufficient for their operations, though in obscurer effects. Thus if unto the powder of Loadstone or Iron we admove the North Pole of the Loadstone, the Powders or small divisions will erect and conform themselves thereto: but if the South pole approach, they will subside, and inverting their bodies, respect the Loadstone with the other extream. And this will happen not only in a body of powder together, but in any particle or dust divided from it.

Now though we disavow not these plaisters, yet shall we not omit two cautions in their use, that therein the Stone be not too subtilly powdered, for it will better manifest its attraction in a more sensible dimension. That where is desired a speedy effect, it may be considered whether it were not better to relinquish the powdered plaisters, and to apply an entire Loadstone unto the part: And though the other be not wholly ineffectual, whether this way be not more powerful, and so might have been in the cure of the young man delivered by Beckerus.

The last consideration concerneth Magical relations; in which account we comprehend effects derived and fathered upon hidden qualities, specifical forms, Antipathies, and Sympathies, whereof from received grounds of Art, no reasons are derived. Herein relations are strange and numerous; men being apt in all Ages to multiply wonders, and Philosophers dealing with admirable bodies, as Historians have done with excellent men, upon the strength of their great atcheivements, ascribing acts unto them not only false but impossible; and exceeding truth as much in their relations, as they have others in their actions. Hereof we shall briefly mention some delivered by Authors of good esteem: whereby we may discover the fabulous inventions of some, the credulous supinity of others, and the great disservice unto truth by both: multiplying obscurities in Nature, and authorising hidden qualities that are false: whereas wise men are ashamed there are so many true.

And first, Dioscorides puts a shrewd quality upon it, and such as men are apt enough to experiment, who therewith discovers the incontinency of a wife, by placing the Loadstone under her pillow, whereupon she will not be able to remain in bed with her husband. The same he also makes a help unto thievery. For Thieves saith he, having a design upon a house, do make a fire at the four corners thereof, and cast therein the fragments of Loadstone: whence ariseth a fume that so disturbeth the inhabitants, that they forsake the house and leave it to the spoil of the Robbers. This relation, how ridiculous soever, hath Albertus taken up above a thousand years after, and Marbodeus the Frenchman hath continued the same in Latine Verse, which with the Notes of Pictorius is currant unto our dayes. As strange must be the Lithomancy or divination from this Stone, whereby as Tzetzes delivers, Helenus the Prophet foretold the destruction of Troy: and the Magick thereof not safely to be believed, which was delivered by Orpheus, that sprinkled with water it will upon a question emit a voice not much unlike an Infant. But surely the Loadstone of Laurentius Guascus the Physitian, is never to be matched; wherewith, as Cardan delivereth, whatsoever Needles or Bodies were touched, the wounds and punctures made thereby, were never felt at all. And yet as strange is that which is delivered by some, that a Loadstone preserved in the salt of a Remora, acquires a power to attract gold out of the deepest Wells. Certainly a studied absurdity, not casually cast out, but plotted for perpetuity: for the strangeness of the effect ever to be admired, and the difficulty of the trail never to be convicted.

These conceits are of that monstrosity that they refute themselves in their recitements. There is another of better notice, and whispered thorow the World with some attention; credulous and vulgar auditors readily believing it, and more judicious and distinctive heads, not altogether rejecting it. The conceit is excellent, and if the effect would follow, somewhat divine; whereby we might communicate like spirits, and confer on earth with Menippus in the Moon. And this is pretended from the sympathy of two Needles touched with the same Loadstone, and placed in the center of two Abecedary circles or rings, with letters described round about them, one friend keeping one, and another the other, and agreeing upon an hour wherein they will communicate. For then, saith Tradition, at what distance of place soever, when one Needle shall be removed unto any letter; the other by a wonderful sympathy will move unto the same. But herein I confess my experience can find no truth; for having expressly framed two circles of Wood, and according to the number of the Latine letters divided each into twenty three parts, placing therein two stiles or Needles composed of the same steel, touched with the same Loadstone, and at the same point: of these two, whensoever, I removed the one, al-

though but at the distance of half a span, the other would
stand like Hercules' pillars, and if the Earth stand still,
have surely no motion at all. Now as it is not possible
that any body should have no boundaries, or Sphear of
its activity, so it is improbable it should effect that at distance, which nearer hand it cannot at all perform.

Again, The conceit is ill contrived, and one effect in-
ferred, whereas the contrary will ensue. For if the remov-
ing of one of the Needles from *A* to *B,* should have any
action or influence on the other, it would not intice it
from *A* to *B,* but repell it from *A* to *Z:* for Needles excited
by the same point of the stone, do not attract, but avoid
each other, even as these also do, when their invigorated
extreams approach unto one other.

Lastly, Were this conceit assuredly true, yet were it not
a conclusion at every distance to be tried by every head:
it being no ordinary or Almanack business, but a Problem
Mathematical, to finde out the difference of hours in different places; nor do the wisest exactly satisfie themselve
in all. For the hours of several places anticipate each
other, according unto their Longitudes, which are not
exactly discovered of every place; and therefore the trial
hereof at a considerable interval, is best performed at the
distance of the Antœci; that is, such habitations as have
the same Meridian and equal parallel, on different sides
of the Æquator; or more plainly the same Longitude and
the same Latitude unto the South, which we have in the
North. For unto such situations it is noon and midnight
at the very same time.

And therefore the Sympathy of these Needles is much
of the same mould with that intelligence which is pre
tended from the flesh of one body transmuted by insitior
into another. For if by the Art of Taliacotius,[1] a permu
tation of flesh, or transmutation be made from one man's
body into another, as if a piece of flesh be exchanged from

[1] *De curtorum Chyrurgia.*

the bicipital muscle of either partie's arm, and about them both, an Alphabet circumscribed; upon a time appointed as some conceptions affirm, they may communicate at what distance soever. For if the one shall prick himself in *A,* the other at the same time will have a sense thereof in the same part: and upon inspection of his arm perceive what letters the other points out in his. Which is a way of intelligence very strange: and would requite the lost Art of Pythagoras, who could read a reverse in the Moon.

Now this magnetical conceit how strange soever, might have some original in Reason; for men observing no solid body, whatsoever did interrupt its action, might be induced to believe no distance would terminate the same; and most conceiving it pointed unto the Pole of Heaven, might also opinion that nothing between could restrain it. Whosoever was the Author, the Æolus that blew it about, was Famianus Strada, that elegant Jesuit, in his Rhetorical prolusions, who chose out this subject to express the stile of Lucretius. But neither Baptista Porta, *De Furtivis literarum notis;* Trithemius in his *Stenography,* Selenus in his *Cryptography,* or *Nuncius inanimatus*[1] make any consideration hereof, although they deliver many ways to communicate thoughts at distance. And this we will not deny may in some manner be effected by the Loadstone; that is, from one room into another; by placing a table in the wall common unto both, and writing thereon the same letters one against another: for upon the approach of a vigorous Loadstone unto a letter on this side, the Needle will move unto the same on the other. But this is a very different way from ours at present; and hereof there are many ways delivered, and more may be discovered which contradict not the rule of its operations.

As for *Unguentum Armarium,* called also *Magneticum,* it belongs not to this discourse, it neither having the

---

[1] By D. Godwin, Bishop of Hereford.

Loadstone for its ingredient, nor any one of its actions: but supposeth other principles, as common and universal spirits, which convey the action of the remedy unto the part, and conjoins the vertue of bodies far disjoyned. But perhaps the cures it doth, are not worth so mighty principles; it commonly healing but simple wounds, and such as mundified and kept clean, do need no other hand then that of Nature, and the Balsam of the proper part. Unto which effect there being fields of Medicines, it may be a hazardous curiosity to rely on this; and because men say the effect doth generally follow, it might be worth the experiment to try, whether the same will not ensue, upon the same Method of cure, by ordinary Balsams, or common vulnerary plaisters.

Many other Magnetisms may be pretended, and the like attractions through all the creatures of Nature. Whether the same be verified in the action of the Sun upon inferiour bodies, whether there be Æolian Magnets, whether the flux and reflux of the Sea be caused by any Magnetism from the Moon; whether the like be really made out, or rather Metaphorically verified in the sympathies of Plant and Animals, might afford a large dispute; and Kircheru in his *Catena Magnetica* hath excellently discussed the same; which work came late unto our hand, but migh have much advantaged this Discourse.

Other Discourses there might be made of the Loadstone: as Moral, Mystical, Theological; and some hav handsomely done them; as Ambrose, Austine, Gulielmu Parisiensis, and many more, but these fall under no Rule and are as boundless as men's inventions. And thoug honest minds do glorifie God hereby; yet do they mos powerfully magnfie him, and are to be looked on wit another eye, who demonstratively set forth its Magnali ties; who not from postulated or precarious inferences entreat a courteous assent; but from experiments an undeniable effects, enforce the wonder of its Maker.

A LETTER TO A FRIEND,

UPON OCCASION OF THE DEATH OF HIS
INTIMATE FRIEND

1690

A LETTER TO A FRIEND

GIVE me leave to wonder that News of this nature should have such heavy Wings, that you should hear so little concerning your dearest Friend, and that I must make that unwilling Repetition to tell you, *Ad portam rigidos calces extendit,* that he is Dead and Buried, and by this time no Puny among the mighty Nations of the Dead; for tho he left this World not very many days past, yet every hour you know largely addeth unto that dark Society; and considering the incessant Mortality of Mankind, you cannot conceive there dieth in the whole Earth so few as a thousand an hour.

Altho at this distance you had no early Account or Particular of his Death; yet your Affection may cease to wonder that you had not some secret Sense or Intimation thereof by Dreams, thoughtful Whisperings, Mercurisms, Airy Nuncios or sympathetical Insinuations, which many seem to have had at the Death of their dearest Friends: for since we find in that famous Story, that Spirits themselves were fain to tell their Fellows at a distance, that the great Antonio was dead, we have a sufficient Excuse for our Ignorance in such Particulars, and must rest content with the common Road, and Appian way of Knowledge by Information. Tho the uncertainty of the End of this World hath confounded all Humane Predictions; yet they who shall live to see the Sun and Moon darkned, and the Stars to fall from Heaven, will hardly be deceived in the Advent of the last Day; and therefore strange it is, that the common Fallacy of consumptive Persons, who feel not themselves dying, and therefore still hope to live, should also reach their Friends in perfect Health and Judgment. That you should be so little acquainted with Plautus's sick Complexion, or that almost an Hippocratical Face should not alarum you to higher fears, or rather despair of his Continuation in such an emaciated State, wherein medical Predictions fail not, as sometimes in acute Diseases, and wherein 'tis as dangerous to be sentenced by a Physician as a Judge.

Upon my first Visit I was bold to tell them who had not let fall all hopes of his Recovery, That in my sad Opinion he was not like to behold a Grashopper, much less to pluck another Fig; and in no long time after seemed to discover that odd mortal Symptom in him not mention'd by Hippocrates, that is, to lose his own Face and look like some of his near Relations; for he maintained not his proper Countenance, but looked like his Uncle, the Lines of whose Face lay deep and invisible in his healthful Visage before: for as from our beginning we run through variety of Looks, before we come to consistent and settled Faces; so before our End, by sick and languishing Alterations, we put on new Visages: and in our Retreat to Earth, may fall upon such Looks which from community of seminal Originals were before latent in us.

He was fruitlessly put in hope of advantage by change of Air, and imbibing the pure Aerial Nitre of these Parts; and therefore being so far spent, he quickly found Sardinia in Tivoli,[1] and the most healthful Air of little effect, where Death had set her Broad Arrow;[2] for he lived not unto the middle of May, and confirmed the

---

[1] *Cum mors venerit, in medio Tibure Sardinia est.*
[2] In the King's Forests they set the Figure of a broad Arrow upon Trees that are to be cut down.

Observation of Hippocrates[1] of that mortal time of the
Year when the Leaves of the Fig-tree resemble a Daw's
Claw. He is happily seated who lives in Places whose
Air, Earth, and Water, promote not the Infirmities of his
weaker Parts, or is early removed into Regions that cor-
rect them. He that is tabidly inclined, were unwise to
pass his days in Portugal: Cholical Persons will find little
Comfort in Austria or Vienna: He that is Weak-legg'd
must not be in Love with Rome, nor an infirm Head
with Venice or Paris. Death hath not only particular Stars
in Heaven, but malevolent Places on Earth, which single
out our Infirmities, and strike at our weaker Parts; in
which Concern, passager and migrant Birds have the
great Advantages; who are naturally constituted for distant Habitations, whom no Seas nor Places limit, but
in their appointed Seasons will visit us from Greenland
and Mount Atlas, and as some think, even from the
Antipodes.[2]

Tho we could not have his Life, yet we missed not our
desires in his soft Departure, which was scarce an Expira-
tion; and his End not unlike his Beginning, when the
salient Point scarce affords a sensible motion, and his
Departure so like unto Sleep, that he scarce needed the
civil Ceremony of closing his Eyes; contrary unto the
common way wherein Death draws up, Sleep lets fall
the Eye-lids. With what strife and pains we came into the
World we know not; but 'tis commonly no easie matter
to get out of it: yet if it could be made out, that such
who have easie Nativities have commonly hard Deaths,
and contrarily; his Departure was so easie, that we might
justly suspect his Birth was of another nature, and that
some Juno sat cross-legg'd at his Nativity.

Besides his soft Death, the incurable state of his Disease might somewhat extenuate your Sorrow, who know

---

[1] Hippoc. *Epidem.*
[2] Bellonius *de Avibus.*

that Monsters but seldom happen, Miracles more rarely, in physick,[1] *Angelus Victorious* gives a serious Account of a Consumptive, Hectical, Pthysical Woman, who was suddenly cured by the Intercession of Ignatius.[2] We read not of any in Scripture who in this case applied unto our Saviour, though some may be contained in that large Expression, *that He went about Galilee healing all manner of Sickness, and all manner of Diseases.*[3] Amulets, Spells, Sigils, and Incantations, practised in other Diseases, are seldom pretended in this; and we find no Sigil in the *Archidoxis* of Paracelsus to cure an extreme Consumption or marasmus, which, if other Diseases fail, will put a period unto long Livers, and at last make dust of all. And therefore the Stoicks could not but think that the firy Principle would wear out all the rest, and at last make an end of the World, which notwithstanding without such a lingering period the Creator may effect at his Pleasure: and to make an end of all things on Earth, and our Planetical System of the World, he need but put out the Sun.

I was not so curious to entitle the Stars unto any concern of his Death, yet could not but take notice that he died when the Moon was in motion from the Meridian; at which time, an old Italian long ago would persuade me, that the greatest part of Men died; but herein I confess I could never satisfy my Curiosity; although from the time of Tides in Places upon or near the Sea, there may be considerable Deductions; and Pliny[4] hath an odd and remarkable Passage concerning the Death of Men and Animals upon the Recess or Ebb of the Sea. However,

[1] *Monstra contingunt in medicina.* Hippoc.—"Strange and rare Escapes there happen sometimes in Physick."

[2] *Angeli Victorii Consultationes.*

[3] Matt. iv. 25.

[4] *Aristoteles nullum animal nisi æstu recedente expirare affirmat; observatum id multum in Gallico Oceano et duntaxat in homine compertum.* Lib. 2, cap. 101.

certain it is he died in the dead and deep part of the Night, when *Nox* might be most apprehensibly said to be the Daughter of *Chaos,* the Mother of *Sleep* and *Death,* according to old Genealogy; and so went out of this World about that hour when our blessed Saviour entered it, and about what time many conceive he will return again unto it. Cardan hath a peculiar and no hard Observation from a Man's Hand, to know whether he was born in the day or night, which I confess holdeth in my own. And Scaliger to that purpose hath another from the tip of the Ear:[1] most men are begotten in the night, most animals in the day; but whether more Persons have been born in the Night or the Day, were a Curiosity undecidable, tho more have perished by violent Deaths in the Day; yet in natural Dissolutions both Times may hold an Indifferency, at least but contingent Inequality. The whole course of Time runs out in the Nativity and Death of Things; which whether they happen by Succession or Coincidence, are best computed by the natural, not artificial Day.

That Charles the Fifth was Crowned upon the Day of his Nativity, it being in his own power so to order it, makes no singular Animadversion; but that he should also take King Francis Prisoner upon that day, was an unexpected Coincidence, which made the same remarkable. Antipater who had an Anniversary Feast every Year upon his Birth-day, needed no Astrological Revolution to know what day he should dye on. When the fixed stars have made a Revolution unto the points from whence they first set out, some of the Ancients thought the World would have an end; which was a kind of dying upon the day of its Nativity. Now the disease prevailing and swiftly advancing about the time of his Nativity, some were of

[1] *Auris pars pendula Lobus dicitur, non omnibus ea pars est auribus; non enim iis qui noctu nati sunt, sed qui interdiu, maxima ex parte.*—*Com. in Aristot. de Animal.* Lib. 1.

Opinion, that he would leave the World on the day
he entred into it; but this being a lingring Disease,
and creeping softly on, nothing critical was found or expected, and he died not before fifteen days after. Nothing
is more common with Infants than to dye on the day of
their Nativity, to behold the worldly Hours and but the
Fractions thereof; and even to perish before their Nativity in the hidden World of the Womb, and before their
good Angel is conceived to undertake them. But in Persons who out-live many Years, and when there are no less
than three hundred and sixty-five days to determine their
Lives in every Year; that the first day should make the
last, that the Tail of the Snake should return into its
Mouth precisely at that time, and they should wind up
upon the day of their Nativity,[1] is indeed a remarkable
Coincidence, which tho Astrology had taken witty pains
to salve, yet hath it been very wary in making Predictions
of it.

In this consumptive Condition and remarkable Extenuation he came to be almost half himself, and left a great
part behind him which he carried not to the Grave. And
tho that story of Duke John Ernestus Mansfield [2] be not
so easily swallowed, that at his Death his Heart was
found not to be so big as a Nut; yet if the Bones of a good
Sceleton weigh little more than twenty pounds, his In-
wards and Flesh remaining could make no Bouffage, but
a light bit for the Grave. I never more lively beheld
the starved Characters of Dante[3] in any living Face; an
Aruspex might have read a Lecture upon him without
Exenteration, his Flesh being so consumed that he might,
in a manner, have discerned his Bowels without opening
of him: so that to be carried *sextâ cervice* to the Grave,
was but a civil unnecessity; and the Complements of the
Coffin might outweigh the Subject of it.

[1] According to the Egyptian Hieroglyphic.
[2] *Turkish history*.
[3] In the Poet Dante's Description.

Omnibonus Ferrarius[1] in mortal Dysenteries of Children looks for a Spot behind the Ear; in consumptive Diseases some eye the Complexion of Moals; Cardan eagerly views the Nails, some the Lines of the Hand, the Thenar or Muscle of the Thumb; some are so curious as to observe the depth of the Throatpit, how the proportion varieth of the Small of the Legs unto the Calf, or the compass of the Neck unto the Circumference of the Head: but all these, with many more, were so drowned in a mortal Visage and last Face of Hippocrates, that a weak Physiognomist might say at first eye, This was a Face of Earth, and that *Morta*[2] had set her Hard-Seal upon his Temples, easily perceiving what *caricatura*[3] Draughts Death makes upon pined Faces, and unto what an unknown degree a Man may live backward.

Tho the beard be only made a distinction of Sex and sign of masculine Heat by *Ulmus*,[4] yet the Precocity and early growth thereof in him, was not to be liked in reference unto long life. Lewis, that virtuous but unfortunate king of Hungary, who lost his Life at the Battle of Mohacz, was said to be born without a Skin, to have bearded at Fifteen, and to have shewn some gray Hairs about Twenty; from whence the Diviners conjectured that he would be spoiled of his Kingdom, and have but a short Life: but hairs make fallible Predictions, and many temples early gray have out-lived the Psalmist's Period.[5] Hairs which have most amused me have not been in the Face or Head but on the Back, and not in Men but Children, as I long ago observed in that Endemial Distemper of little children in Languedock, called the *Morgellons*,[6] wherein they critically break out

[1] *De Morbis Puerorum.*
[2] Morta, the Deity of Death or Fate.
[3] When Men's Faces are drawn with resemblance to some other Animals, the Italians call it, to be drawn in Caricatura.
[4] *Ulmus de usu barbæ humanæ.*
[5] The Life of a Man is Threescore and Ten.
[6] See Picotus *de Rheumatismo.*

with harsh Hairs on their Backs, which takes off the unquiet Symptoms of the Disease, and delivers them from
Coughs and Convulsions.

The Egyptian Mummies that I have seen, have had
their Mouths open, and somewhat gaping, which affordeth a good opportunity to view and observe their Teeth,
wherein 'tis not easie to find any wanting or decayed:
and therefore in Egypt, where one Man practised but one
Operation, or the Diseases but of single Parts, it must
needs be a barren Profession to confine unto that of
drawing of Teeth, and little better than to have been
Tooth-drawer unto King Pyrrhus,[1] who had but two
in his Head. How the Bannyans of India maintain the
Integrity of those parts, I find not particularly observed;
who notwithstanding have an Advantage of their Preservation by abstaining from all Flesh, and employing
their Teeth in such Food unto which they may seem at
first framed, from their Figure and Conformation: but
sharp and corroding Rheums had so early mouldred
those Rocks and hardest part of his Fabrick, that a Man
might well conceive that his Years were never like to
double or twice tell over his Teeth.[2] Corruption had
dealt more severely with them, than sepulchral Fires and
smart Flames with those of burnt Bodies of old; for in
the burnt Fragments of Urns which I have enquired into,
although I seem to find few Incisors or Shearers, yet the
Dog Teeth and Grinders do notably resist these Fires.[3]

---

[1] His upper and lower Jaw being solid, and without distinct rows
of teeth.

[2] Twice tell over his teeth, never live to threescore years.

[3] In the *MS. Sloan.* 1862, occurs the following paragraph:—
"Affection had so blinded some of his nearest relations, as to
retain some hope of a postliminious life, and that he might come
to life again, and therefore would not have him coffined before
the third day. Some such verbiasses [so in MS.], I confess, we find
in story, and one or two I remember myself, but they lived not long
after. Some contingent reanimations are to be hoped in diseases
wherein the lamp of life is but puffed out and seemingly choaked,

In the Years of his Childhood he had languished under
the Disease of his Country, the Rickets; after which notwithstanding many have become strong and active Men;
but whether any have attained unto very great Years the
Disease is scarce so old as to afford good Observation.
Whether the Children of the English Plantations be subject unto the same Infirmity, may be worth the observing.
Whether Lameness and Halting do still increase among
the Inhabitants of Rovigno in Istria, I know not; yet
scarce twenty Years ago Monsieur du Loyr observed, that
a third part of that People halted: but too certain it
is, that the Rickets encreaseth among us; the Small-pox
grows more pernicious than the Great: the King's Purse
knows that the King's Evil grows more common. Quartan
Agues are become no Strangers in Ireland; more common
and mortal in England: and though the Ancients gave
that Disease[1] very good Words, yet now that Bell makes
no strange sound which rings out for the Effects thereof.[2]

Some think there were few Consumptions in the Old

and not where the oil is quite spent and exhausted. Though Nonnus
will have it a fever, yet of what diseases Lazarus first died, is uncertain from the text, as his second death from good authentic history; but since some persons conceived to be dead do sometimes
return again unto evidence of life, that miracle was wisely managed
by our Saviour; for had he not been dead four days and under
corruption, there had not wanted enough who would have cavilled
[at] the same, which the scripture now puts out of doubt: and tradition also confirmeth, that he lived thirty years after, and being
pursued by the Jews, came by sea into Provence, by Marseilles, with
Mary Magdalen, Maximinus, and others; where remarkable places
carry their names unto this day. But to arise from the grave to
return again into it, is but an uncomfortable reviction. Few men
would be content to cradle it once again; except a man can lead
his second life better than the first, a man may be doubly condemned for living evilly twice, which were but to make the second
death in scripture the third, and to accumulate in the punishment
of two bad livers at the last day. To have performed the duty of
corruption in the grave, to live again as far from sin as death, and
arise like our Saviour for ever, are the only satisfactions of well-
weighed expectations."

[1] Ἀσφαλέστατος καὶ ῥῄιστος, securissima et facillima.—Hippoc.
[2] Pro febre quartana raro sonat compana.

World, when Men lived much upon Milk; and that the ancient Inhabitants of this Island were less troubled with Coughs when they went naked, and slept in Caves and Woods, than Men now in Chambers and Feather-beds. Plato will tell us, that there was no such Disease as a catarrh in Homer's time, and that it was but new in Greece in his Age. Polydore Virgil delivereth that Pleurisies were rare in England, who lived but in the days of Henry the Eighth. Some will allow no Diseases to be new, others think that many old ones are ceased; and that such which are esteemed new, will have but their time: However, the Mercy of God hath scattered the great heap of Diseases, and not loaded any one Country with all: some may be new in one Country which have been old in another. New discoveries of the Earth discover new Diseases: for besides the common swarm, there are endemial and local Infirmities proper unto certain Regions, which in the whole Earth make no small number: and if Asia, Africa, and America should bring in their List, Pandora's Box would swell, and there must be a strange Pathology.

Most Men expected to find a consumed kell, empty and bladder-like Guts, livid and marbled Lungs, and a withered Pericardium in this exuccous Corps: but some seemed too much to wonder that two Lobes of his Lungs adhered unto his side; for the like I have often found in Bodies of no suspected Consumptions or difficulty of Respiration. And the same more often happeneth in Men than other Animals: and some think, in Women than in Men: but the most remarkable I have met with, was in a Man, after a Cough of almost fifty Years, in whom all the Lobes adhered unto the Pleura,[1] and each Lobe unto another; who having also been much troubled with the

[1] So A. F.

Gout, brake the Rule of Cardan,[1] and died of the Stone
in the Bladder. Aristotle makes a query, Why some animals cough as Man, some not, as Oxen. If coughing be
taken as it consisteth of a natural and voluntary motion,
including expectoration and spitting out, it may be as
proper unto Man as bleeding at the Nose; otherwise we
find that Vegetius and Rural Writers have not left so
many Medicines in vain against the Coughs of Cattel;
and men who perish by Coughs dye the Death of Sheep,
Cats, and Lyons: and though Birds have no Midriff, yet
we meet with divers Remedies in Arrianus against the
Coughs of Hawks. And tho it might be thought, that
all Animals who have Lungs do cough; yet in cetaceous
Fishes, who have large and strong Lungs, the same is not
observed; nor yet in oviparous Quadrupeds: and in the
greatest thereof, the Crocodile, although we read much
of their Tears, we find nothing of that motion.

From the Thoughts of Sleep, when the Soul was conceived nearest unto Divinity, the Ancients erected an
Art of Divination, wherein while they too widely ex-
piated in loose and inconsequent Conjectures, Hippocrates[2] wisely considered Dreams as they presaged Alterations in the Body, and so afforded hints toward the
preservation of Health, and prevention of Diseases; and
therein was so serious as to advise Alteration of Diet,
Exercise, Sweating, Bathing, and Vomiting; and also so
religious, as to order Prayers and Supplications unto
respective Deities, in good dreams unto *Sol, Jupiter
cœlestis, Jupiter opulentus, Minerva, Mercurius,* and
Apollo; in bad unto *Tellus* and the Heroes.

And therefore I could not but take notice how his
Female Friends were irrationally curious so strictly to

---

[1] Cardan in his *Encomium Podagræ* reckoneth this among the
Dona Podagræ, that they are delivered thereby from the Pthysis
and Stone in the Bladder.
[2] Hippoc. *de Insomniis.*

examine his Dreams, and in this low state to hope for the Fantasms of Health. He was now past the healthful Dreams, of the Sun, Moon, and Stars in their Clarity and proper Courses. 'Twas too late to dream of Flying, of Limpid Fountains, smooth Waters, white Vestments, and fruitful green Trees, which are the Visions of healthful Sleeps, and at good distance from the Grave.

And they were also too deeply dejected that he should dream of his dead Friends, inconsequently divining, that he would not be long from them; for strange it was not that he should sometimes dream of the dead whose Thoughts run always upon Death; beside, to dream of the dead, so they appear not in dark Habits, and take nothing away from us, in Hippocrates[1] his Sense was of good signification: for we live by the dead, and every thing is or must be so before it becomes our Nourishment. And Cardan, who dream'd that he discoursed with his dead Father in the Moon, made thereof no mortal Interpretation: and even to dream that we are dead, was no condemnable Fantasm in old oneirocriticism, as having a signification of Liberty, vacuity from Cares, exemption and freedom from Troubles, unknown unto the dead.

Some Dreams I confess may admit of easie and feminine Exposition: he who dreamed that he could not see his right Shoulder, might easily fear to lose the sight of his right Eye; he that before a Journey dreamed that his Feet were cut off, had a plain warning not to undertake his intended Journey. But why to dream of Lettuce should presage some ensuing disease, why to eat figs should signify foolish Talk, why to eat Eggs great Trouble, and to dream of Blindness should be so highly commended, according to the oneirocritical Verses of Astrampsychus and Nicephorus, I shall leave unto your Divination.

[1] Hippoc. *de Insomniis.*

He was willing to quit the World alone and altogether, leaving no Earnest behind him for Corruption or
Aftergrave, having small content in that common satisfaction to survive or live in another, but amply satisfied
that his Disease should dye with himself, nor revive
in a Posterity to puzzle Physick, and make sad mementos
of their Parent hereditary. Leprosy awakes not sometimes before Forty, the Gout and Stone often later; but
consumptive and tabid [1] Roots sprout more early, and
at the fairest make seventeen Years of our Life doubtful
before that Age. They that enter the World with original
Diseases as well as Sin, have not only common Mortality
but sick Traductions to destroy them, make commonly
short Courses, and live not at length but in Figures; so
that a sound Cæsarean Nativity[2] may out-last a natural
Birth, and a Knife may sometimes make way for a more
lasting fruit than a Midwife; which makes so few Infants now able to endure the old Test of the River,[3] and
many to have feeble Children who could scarce have
been married at Sparta, and those provident States who
studied strong and healthful Generations; which happen but contingently in mere *pecuniary* Matches, or
Marriages, made by the Candle, wherein notwithstanding there is little redress to be hoped from an Astrologer
or a Lawyer, and a good discerning physician were like
to prove the most successful Counsellor.

Julius Scaliger, who in a sleepless Fit of the Gout
could make two hundred Verses in a Night, would have
but five plain Words upon his Tomb.[4] And this serious
Person, though no minor Wit, left the Poetry of his
Epitaph unto others; either unwilling to commend him-

---

[1] *Tabes maxime contingunt ab anno decimo octavo ad trigesimum
quintum.*—Hippoc.

[2] A sound Child cut out of the Body of the Mother.

[3] *Natos ad flumina primum deferimus sævoque gelu duramus et
undis.*

[4] *Julii Cæsaris Scaligeri quod fuit.*—Joseph Scaliger in vita patris.

self, or to be judged by a Distich, and perhaps considering how unhappy great Poets have been in versifying their own Epitaphs; wherein Petrarca, Dante, and Ariosto, have so unhappily failed, that if their Tombs should out-last their Works, Posterity would find so little of Apollo on them, as to mistake them for Ciceronian Poets.

In this deliberate and creeping progress unto the Grave, he was somewhat too young, and of too noble a mind, to fall upon that stupid Symptom observable in divers Persons near their Journey's end, and which may be reckoned among the mortal Symptoms of their last Disease; that is, to become more narrow-minded, miserable and tenacious, unready to part with anything when they are ready to part with all, and afraid to want when they have no time to spend; meanwhile Physicians, who know that many are mad but in a single depraved Imagination, and one prevalent Deciepiency; and that beside and out of such single Deliriums a Man may meet with sober Actions and good Sense in Bedlam; cannot but smile to see the Heirs and concerned Relations, gratulating themselves on the sober departure of their Friends; and though they behold such mad covetous Passages, content to think they dye in good Understanding, and in their sober Senses.

Avarice, which is not only Infidelity but Idolatry, either from covetous Progeny or questuary Education, had no root in his Breast, who made good Works the Expression of his Faith, and was big with desires unto public and lasting Charities; and surely where good Wishes and charitable Intentions exceed Abilities, Theorical Beneficency may be more than a Dream. They build not Castles in the Air who would build Churches on Earth: and tho they leave no such Structures here, may lay good Foundations in Heaven. In brief, his Life and Death were such, that I could not blame them who wished the like, and almost to have been himself; almost, I say; for tho we may wish the prosperous Appurtenances of others, or to be another in his happy Accidents, yet so intrinsical is every Man unto himself, that some doubt may be made, whether any would exchange his Being, or substantially become another Man.

He had wisely seen the World at home and abroad, and thereby observed under what variety Men are deluded in the pursuit of that which is not here to be found. And altho he had no Opinion of reputed Felicities below, and apprehended Men widely out in the estimate of such Happiness, yet his sober contempt of the World wrought no Democratism or Cynicism, no laughing or snarling at it, as well understanding there are not Felicities in this World to satisfy a serious Mind; and therefore to soften the stream of our Lives, we are fain to take in the reputed Contentations of this World, to unite with the Crowd in their Beatitudes, and to make ourselves happy by Consortion, Opinion, or Coexistimation: for strictly to separate from received and customary Felicities, and to confine unto the rigour of Realities, were to contract the Consolation of our Beings unto too uncomfortable Circumscriptions.

Not to fear Death,[1] nor desire it, was short of his Resolution: to be dissolved, and be with Christ, was his dying ditty. He conceived his Thred long, in no long course of Years, and when he had scarce out-lived the second Life of Lazarus;[2] esteeming it enough to approach the Years of his Saviour, who so ordered his own humane State, as not to be old upon Earth.

But to be content with Death may be better than to desire it: a miserable Life may make us wish for Death, but a virtuous one to rest in it; which is the Advantage of those resolved Christians, who looking on Death not

---

[1] *Summum nec metuas diem nec optes.*
[2] Who upon some Accounts, and Tradition, is said to have lived thirty Years after he was raised by our Saviour.—*Baronius.*

only as the sting, but the period and end of Sin, the Horizon and Isthmus between this Life and a better, and the Death of this World but as a Nativity of another, do contentedly submit unto the common Necessity, and envy not Enoch or Elias.

Not to be content with Life is the unsatisfactory state of those who destroy themselves;[1] who being afraid to live, run blindly upon their own Death, which no Man fears by Experience: and the Stoicks had a notable Doctrine to take away the fear thereof; that is, In such Extremities, to desire that which is not to be avoided, and wish what might be feared; and so made Evils voluntary, and to suit with their own Desires, which took off the terror of them.

But the ancient Martyrs were not encouraged by such Fallacies; who, though they feared not Death, were afraid to be their own Executioners; and therefore thought it more Wisdom to crucify their Lusts than their Bodies, to circumcise than stab their Hearts, and to mortify than kill themselves.

His willingness to leave this World about that Age when most Men think they may best enjoy it, though paradoxical unto worldly Ears, was not strange unto mine, who have so often observed, that many, though old, oft stick fast unto the World, and seem to be drawn like Cacus's Oxen, backward with great struggling and reluctancy unto the Grave. The long habit of Living makes meer Men more hardly to part with Life, and all to be nothing, but what is to come. To live at the rate of the old World, when some could scarce remember themselves young, may afford no better digested Death than a more moderate period. Many would have thought it an Happiness to have had their lot of Life in some

---

[1] In the speech of Vulteius in Lucan, animating his Soldiers in a great struggle to kill one another.—"Decernite Lethum, et metus omnis abest, cupias quodcunque necesse est." "All fear is over, do but resolve to die, and make your Desires meet Necessity."

notable Conjunctures of Ages past; but the uncertainty
of future Times hath tempted few to make a part in Ages
to come. And surely, he that hath taken the true Altitude of Things, and rightly calculated the degenerate
state of this Age, is not like to envy those that shall live
in the next, much less three or four hundred Years
hence, when no Man can comfortably imagine what
Face this World will carry: and therefore since every Age
makes a step unto the end of all things, and the scripture
affords so hard a Character of the last Times; quiet Minds
will be content with their Generations, and rather bless
Ages past than be ambitious of those to come.

Tho Age had set no Seal upon his Face, yet a dim Eye
might clearly discover Fifty in his Actions; and therefore
since Wisdom is the gray Hair, and an unspotted Life
old Age; altho his Years came short, he might have
been said to have held up with longer Livers, and to
have been Solomon's[1] Old Man. And surely if we deduct
all those days of our Life which we might wish unlived,
and which abate the comfort of those we now live; if
we reckon up only those days which God hath accepted
of our Lives, a Life of good Years will hardly be a span
long: the Son in this sense may out-live the Father, and
none be climaterically old. He that early arriveth unto
the Parts and Prudence of Age, is happily old without
the uncomfortable Attendants of it; and 'tis superfluous
to live unto gray Hairs, when in a precocious Temper we
anticipate the Virtues of them. In brief, he cannot be
accounted young who out-liveth the old Man. He that
hath early arrived unto the measure of a perfect Stature in Christ, hath already fulfilled the prime and longest Intention of his Being: and one day lived after the
perfect Rule of Piety, is to be preferred before sinning
Immortality.

Although he attained not unto the Years of his Pre-

[1] Wisdom, cap. iv.

decessors, yet he wanted not those preserving Virtues
which confirm the thread of weaker Constitutions. Cautelous Chastity and crafty sobriety were far from him;
those Jewels were Paragon, without Flaw, Hair, Ice,
or Cloud in him: which affords me a hint to proceed in
these good Wishes and few *Mementos* unto you.

. . . The remainder of this letter was included, with few alterations, in "Christian Morals."

HYDRIOTAPHIA,
Urne-Buriall,
or,
A Discourse of the Sepulchrall Urnes
lately found in Norfolk.
1658

THOMAS LE GROS, of CROSTWICK, ESQUIRE

WHEN the Funerall pyre was out, and the last valediction
over, men took a lasting adieu of their interred Friends,
little expecting the curiosity of future ages should comment upon their ashes, and, having no old experience
of the duration of their Reliques, held no opinion of such
after-considerations.

But who knows the fate of his bones, or how often he
is to be buried? who hath the Oracle of his ashes, or
whither they are to be scattered? The Reliques of many
lie like the ruines of Pompeys,[1] in all parts of the earth;
And when they arrive at your hands, these may seem to
have wandred far, who in a direct[2] and *Meridian* Travel,
have but few miles of known Earth between yourself
and the Pole.

That the bones of *Theseus* should be seen again in
Athens[3] was not beyond conjecture, and hopeful expectation; but that these should arise so opportunely to serve
your self, was an hit of fate and honour beyond prediction.

We cannot but wish these Urnes might have the effect
of Theatrical vessels, and great *Hippodrome* Urnes[4] in
Rome; to resound the acclamations and honour due unto
you. But these are sad and sepulchral Pitchers, which

[1] *Pompeios juvenes Asia, atque Europa, sed ipsum terrâ tegit
Lybies.*
[2] Little directly, but Sea between your house and Greenland.
[3] Brought back by Cimon. Plutarch.
[4] The great Urnes in the Hippodrome at Rome conceived to resound the voices of people at their shows.

have no joyful voices; silently expressing old mortality, the ruines of forgotten times, and can only speak with life, how long in this corruptible frame, some parts may be uncorrupted; yet able to outlast bones long unborn, and noblest pyle among us.[1]

We present not these as any strange sight or spectacle unknown to your eyes, who have beheld the best of Urnes and noblest variety of Ashes; Who are yourself no slender master of Antiquities, and can daily command the view of so many Imperiall faces; Which raiseth your thoughts unto old things, and consideration of times before you, when even living men were Antiquities; when the living might exceed the dead, and to depart this world, could not be properly said, to go unto the greater number.[2] And so run up your thoughts upon the ancient of dayes, the Antiquaries truest object, unto whom the eldest parcels are young, and earth itself an Infant; and without Ægyptian[3] account makes but small noise in thousands.

We were hinted by the occasion, not catched the opportunity to write of old things, or intrude upon the Antiquary. We are coldly drawn unto discourses of Antiquities, who have scarce time before us to comprehend new things, or make out learned Novelties. But seeing they arose as they lay, almost in silence among us, at least in short account suddenly passed over; we were very unwilling they should die again, and be buried twice among us.

Beside, to preserve the living, and make the dead to live, to keep men out of their Urnes, and discourse of humane fragments in them, is not impertinent unto our profession; whose study is life and death, who daily behold examples of mortality, and of all men least need

---

[1] Worthily possessed by that true Gentleman, Sir Horatio Townshend, my honored Friend.

[2] *Abiit ad plures.*

[3] Which makes the world so many years old.

artificial *mementos,* or coffins by our bedside, to minde us of our graves.

'Tis time to observe Occurrences, and let nothing remarkable escape us; The Supinity of elder dayes hath left so much in silence, or time hath so martyred the Records, that the most industrious heads[1] do find no easie work to erect a new *Britannia.*

'Tis opportune to look back upon old times, and contemplate our Forefathers. Great examples grow thin, and to be fetched from the passed world. Simplicity flies away, and iniquity comes at long strides upon us. We have enough to do to make up ourselves from present and passed times, and the whole stage of things scarce serveth for our instruction. A compleat peece of vertue must be made from the *Centos* of all ages, as all the beauties of *Greece* could make but one handsome *Venus.*

When the bones of King *Arthur* were digged up,[2] the old Race might think, they beheld therein some Originals of themselves; Unto these of our Urnes none here can pretend relation, and can only behold the Reliques of those persons who in their life giving the Laws unto their predecessors, after long obscurity, now lye at their mercies. But, remembring the early civility they brought upon these Countreys, and forgetting long passed mischiefs; We mercifully preserve their bones, and pisse not upon their ashes.

In the offer of these Antiquities we drive not at ancient Families, so long out-lasted by them; We are farre from erecting your worth upon the pillars of your Fore-fathers, whose merits you illustrate. We honour your old Virtues, conformable unto times before you, which are the Noblest Armoury. And, having long experience of your friendly conversation, void of empty Formality, full of freedome,

---

[1] Wherein Mr. Dugdale hath excellently well endeavoured, and worthy to be countenanced by ingenuous and noble persons.

[2] In the time of Henry the second. Cambden.

constant and Generous Honesty. I look upon you as a Gemme of the Old Rock,[1] and must professe myself even to Urne and Ashes,

Your ever faithful Friend and Servant,

THOMAS BROWNE.

Norwich, May 1.

[1] *Adamas de rupe veteri præstantissimus.*

HYDRIOTAPHIA

IN THE deep discovery of the Subterranean world, a shallow part would satisfie some enquirers; who, if two or three yards were open about the surface, would not care to rake the bowels of *Potosi*,[1] and regions towards the Centre. Nature hath furnished one part of the Earth, and man another. The treasures of time lie high, in Urnes, Coynes, and Monuments, scarce below the roots of some vegetables. Time hath endlesse rarities, and shows of all varieties; which reveals old things in heaven, makes new discoveries in earth, and even earth itself a discovery. That great Antiquity *America* lay buried for a thousand years; and a large part of the earth is still in the Urne unto us.

Though if *Adam* were made out of an extract of the Earth, all parts might challenge a restitution, yet few have returned their bones farre lower than they might receive them; not affecting the graves of Giants, under hilly and heavy coverings, but content with lesse than their owne depth, have wished their bones might lie soft, and the earth be light upon them; Even such as hope to rise again, would not be content with centrall interrment, or so desperately to place their reliques as to lie beyond discovery, and in no way to be seen again; which happy contrivance hath made communication with our fore-

[1] The rich mountain of Peru.

fathers, and left unto our view some parts, which they never beheld themselves.

Though earth hath engrossed the name yet water hath proved the smartest grave; which in forty dayes swallowed almost mankinde, and the living creation; Fishes not wholly escaping, except the Salt Ocean were handsomely contempered by a mixture of the fresh Element.

Many have taken voluminous pains to determine the state of the soul upon disunion; but men have been most phantasticall in the singular contrivances of their corporall dissolution: whilst the sobrest Nations have rested in two wayes, of simple inhumation and burning.

That carnall interment or burying was of the elder date, the old examples of *Abraham* and the Patriarchs are sufficient to illustrate; And were without competition, if it could be made out, that *Adam* was buried near *Damascus,* or Mount *Calvary,* according to some Tradition. God himself, that buried but one, was pleased to make choice of this way, collectible from Scripture-expression, and the hot contest between Satan and the Arch-Angel, about discovering the body of Moses. But the practice of Burning was also of great Antiquity, and of no slender extent. For (not to derive the same from *Hercules*) noble descriptions there are hereof in the Grecian Funerals of *Homer,* in the formall Obsequies of *Patroclus,* and *Achilles;* and somewhat elder in the *Theban* warre, and solemn combustion of *Meneceus,* and *Archemorus,* contemporary unto *Jair* the Eighth Judge of *Israel.* Confirmable also among the *Trojans,* from the Funerall Pyre of *Hector,* burnt before the gates of *Troy,* And the burning of *Penthesilea,*[1] the *Amazonean Queen:* and long continuance of that practice, in the inward Countries of *Asia;* while as low as the Reign of *Julian,* we find that the King of *Chionia*[2] burnt the

[1] Q. Calaber. lib. i.
[2] Gumbrates king of Chionia a Countrey near Persia.—Ammianus Marcellinus.

body of his Son, and interred the ashes in a silver Urne.

The same practice extended also farre West,[1] and besides *Herulians, Getes,* and *Thracians,* was in use with most of the *Celtæ, Sarmatians, Germans, Gauls, Danes, Swedes, Norwegians;* not to omit some use thereof among *Carthaginians* and *Americans:* Of greater Antiquity among the *Romans* then most opinion, or *Pliny* seems to allow. For (beside the old Table Laws of burning or burying within the City,[2] of making the Funerall fire with plained wood, or quenching the fire with wine), *Manilus* the Consul burnt the body of his Son: *Numa* by special clause of his Will, was not burnt but buried; and *Remus* was solemnly buried, according to the description of *Ovid.*[3]

Cornelius Sylla was not the first whose body was burned in *Rome,* but of the *Cornelian* family; which, being indifferently, not frequently used before; from that time spread, and became the prevalent practice. Not totally pursued in the highest runne of Cremation; For when even Crows were funerally burnt, *Poppæa* the wife of *Nero* found a peculiar grave enterment. Now as all customes were founded upon some bottome of Reason, so there wanted not grounds for this; according to severall apprehensions of the most rationall dissolution. Some being of the opinion of *Thales,* that water was the originall of all things, thought it most equall to submit unto the principle of putrefaction, and conclude in a moist relentment. Others conceived it most natural to end in fire, as due unto the master principle in the composition, according to the doctrine of *Heraclitus.* And

---

[1] Arnoldi Montani *not. in* Cæs. *Commentar.* L. Gyraldus Kirkmannus.

[2] 12 *Tabul. part* i. *de jure sacro. Hominem mortuum in urbe ne sepilito, neve urito, tom.* 2. *Rogum asciâ ne polito, tom.* 4. *Item Vigeneri Annotat. in Livium, et* Alex. ab Alex. *cum* Tiraquello. Roscinus *cum* Dempstero.

[3] *Ultimo plorato subdita flamma rogo. De Fast. lib.* iv. *cum* Car. Neapol. *Anaptyxi.*

therefore heaped up large piles, more actively to waft them toward that Element, whereby they also declined a visible degeneration into worms, and left a lasting parcell of their composition.

Some apprehended a purifying virtue in fire, refining the grosser commixture, and firing out the Æthereall particles so deeply immersed in it. And such as by tradition or rationall conjecture held any hint of the finall pyre of all things; or that this Element at last must be too hard for all the rest; might conceive most naturally of the fiery dissolution. Others pretending no natural grounds, politickly declined the malice of enemies upon their buried bodies. Which consideration led *Sylla* unto this practise; who having thus served the body of *Marius,* could not but fear a retaliation upon his own; entertained after in the Civill wars, and revengeful contentions of *Rome.*

But as many Nations embraced, and many left it indifferent, so others too much affected, or strictly declined this practice. The *Indian Brachmans* seemed too great friends unto fire, who burnt themselves alive, and thought it the noblest way to end their dayes in fire; according to the expression of the Indian, burning himself at *Athens,*[1] in his last words upon the pyre unto the amazed spectators, *Thus I make my-selfe immortall.*

But the *Chaldeans,* the great Idolaters of fire, abhorred the burning of their carcasses, as a pollution of that Deity. The *Persian magi* declined it upon the like scruple, and being only solicitous about their bones, exposed their flesh to the prey of Birds and Dogges. And the *Persees* now in *India,* which expose their bodies unto Vultures, and endure not so much as *feretra* or Beers of Wood, the proper fuell of fire, are led on with such niceties. But

---

[1] And therefore the Inscription of his Tomb was made accordingly. —Nic. Damas.

whether the ancient *Germans,* who burned their dead, held any such fear to pollute their Deity of *Herthus,* or the earth, we have no Authentick conjecture.

The Ægyptians were afraid of fire, not as a Deity, but a devouring Element, mercilessly consuming their bodies, and leaving too little of them; and therefore by precious Embalments, depositure in dry earths, or handsome inclosure in glasses, contrived the notablest wayes of integrall conservation. And from such Ægyptian scruples imbibed by *Pythagoras,* it may be conjectured that *Numa* and the Pythagoricall Sect first waved the fiery solution.

The *Scythians* who swore by winde and sword, that is, by life and death, were so farre from burning their bodies, that they declined all interrment, and made their graves in the ayr: and the *Ichthyophagi* or fish-eating Nations about Ægypt, affected the Sea for their grave: Thereby declining visible corruption, and restoring the debt of their bodies. Whereas the old Heroes in *Homer,* dreaded nothing more than water or drowning; probably upon the old opinion of the fiery substance of the soul, only extinguishable by that Element; And therefore the Poet emphatically implieth the totall destruction in this kinde of death, which happened to *Ajax Oileus.*[1]

The old *Balearians*[2] had a peculiar mode, for they used great Urnes and much wood, but no fire in their burials, while they bruised the flesh and bones of the dead, crowded them into Urnes, and laid heapes of wood upon them. And the *Chinois*[3] without cremation or urnall interrment of their bodies, make use of trees and much burning, while they plant a Pine-tree by their grave, and burn great numbers of printed draughts of slaves and horses over it, civilly content with their companies in effigie which barbarous Nations exact unto reality.

[1] Which Magius reades ἐξαπόλωλε.
[2] Diodorus Siculus.
[3] Ramusius in *Navigat.*

Christians abhorred this way of obsequies, and though they stickt not to give their bodies to be burnt in their lives, detested that mode after death; affecting rather a depositure than absumption, and properly submitting unto the sentence of God, to return not unto ashes but unto dust againe, conformable unto the practice of the Patriarchs, the interrment of our Saviour, of *Peter*, *Paul* and the ancient Martyrs. And so farre at last declining promiscuous interrment with Pagans, that some have suffered Ecclesiastical censures for making no scruple thereof.[1]

The *Musselman* beleevers will never admit this fiery resolution. For they hold a present trial from their black and white Angels in the grave; which they must have made so hollow, that they may rise upon their knees.

The Jewish Nation, though they entertained the old way of inhumation, yet sometimes admitted this practice. For the men of *Jabesh* burnt the body of *Saul*. And by no prohibited practice to avoid contagion or pollution, in time of pestilence, burnt the bodies of their friends.[2] And when they burnt not their dead bodies, yet sometimes used great burnings neare and about them, deducible from the expressions concerning *Jehoram, Sedechias,* and the sumptuous pyre of Asa: And were so little averse from Pagan burning, that the Jews lamenting the death of *Cæsar* their friend, and revenger on *Pompey,* frequented the place where his body was burnt for many nights together.[3] And as they raised noble Monuments and *Mausolæums* for their own Nation,[4] so they were not scrupulous in erecting some for others, according to the

---

[1] Martialis the Bishop. Ciprian.
[2] Amos vi. 10.
[3] Sueton. *in vita Jul. Cæs.*
[4] As that magnificent sepulchral Monument erected by Simon. Macc. i. 13.

practice of *Daniel,* who left that lasting sepulchrall pyle in *Echbatana,* for the *Medean* and *Persian* Kings.[1]

But even in times of subjection and hottest use, they conformed not unto the *Romane* practice of burning; whereby the Prophecy was secured concerning the body of Christ, that it should not see corruption, or a bone should not be broken; which we beleeve was also providentially prevented, from the Souldier's spear and nails that past by the little bones both in his hands and feet: Nor of ordinary contrivance, that it should not corrupt on the Crosse, according to the Laws of *Romane* crucifixion, or an hair of his head perish, though observable in Jewish customes, to cut the hairs of Malefactors.

Nor in their long co-habitation with Ægyptians, crept into a custome of their exact embalming, wherein deeply slashing the muscles, and taking out the brains and entrails, they had broken the subject of so entire a Resurrection, nor fully answered the types of *Enoch, Elijah,* or *Jonah,* which yet to prevent or restore, was of equall facility unto that rising power, able to break the fasciations and bands of death, to get clear out of the Cerecloth, and an hundred pounds of oyntment, and out of the Sepulchre before the stone was rolled from it.

But though they embraced not this practice of burning, yet entertained they many ceremonies agreeable unto *Greeke* and *Romane* obsequies. And he that observeth their funerall Feasts, their Lamentations at the grave, their musick and weeping mourners; how they closed the eyes of their friends, how they washed, anointed, and kissed the dead; may easily conclude these were not meere Pagan-Civilities. But whether that mournfull burthen, and treble calling out after *Absalom,*[2] had any refer-

---

[1] Κατασκεύασμα θαυμασίως πεποιημένον, whereof a Jewish Priest had always the custody, unto Josephus his dayes.—*Jos. Antiq.* lib. x.

[2] *O Absalom, my son, my son!* Sam. II. 18.

ence unto the last conclamation, and triple valediction, used by other Nations, we hold but a wavering conjecture.

Civilians make sepulture but of the Law of Nations, others doe naturally found it and discover it also in animals. They that are so thick skinned as still to credit the story of the *Phœnix*, may say something for animall burning: More serious conjectures finde some examples of sepulture in *elephants, cranes,* the *sepulchrall* Cells of Pismires, and practice of Bees; which civill society carrieth out their dead, and hath exequies, if not interrments.

CHAPTER II

THE Solemnities, Ceremonies, Rites of their Cremation or enterrment, so solemnly delivered by Authours, we shall not disparage our Reader to repeat. Only the last and lasting part in their Urns, collected bones and Ashes, we cannot wholly omit or decline that Subject, which occasion lately presented, in some discovered among us.

In a Field of old *Walsingham,* not many moneths past, were digged up between fourty and fifty Urnes, deposited in a dry and sandy soil, not a yard deep, nor farre from one another: Not all strictly of one figure, but most answering these described: some containing two pounds of bones, distinguishable in skulls, ribs, jawes, thigh-bones, and teeth, with fresh impressions of their combustion. Besides the extraneous substances, like peeces of small boxes, or combes handsomely wrought, handles of small brasse instruments, brazen nippers, and in one some kinde of Opale.[1]

Near the same plot of ground, for about six yards compasse, were digged up coals and incinerated substances,

[1] In one sent me by my worthy friend, Dr. Thomas Witherley of Walsingham.

which begat conjecture that this was the *Ustrina* or place of burning their bodies, or some sacrificing place unto the *Manes,* which was properly below the surface of the ground, as the *Aræ* and Altars unto the gods and *Heroes* above it.

That these were the urnes of *Romanes* from the common custome and place where they were found, is no obscure conjecture, not farre from a *Romane* Garrison, and but five Miles from *Brancaster,* set down by ancient Record under the name of *Brannodunum.* And where the adjoyning Towne, containing seven Parishes, in no very different sound, but Saxon Termination, still retains the name of *Burnham,* which being an early station, it is not improbable the neighbour parts were filled with habitations, either of *Romanes* themselves, or *Brittains Romanised,* which observed the *Romane* customs.

Nor is it improbable, that the *Romanes* early possessed this Countrey; for though we meet not with such strict particulars of these parts before the new Institution of *Constantine,* and military charge of the Count of the *Saxon* shore, and that about the *Saxon* Invasions, the *Dalmatian* Horsemen were in the Garrison of *Brancaster:* Yet in the time of *Claudius, Vespasian,* and *Severus,* we finde no less than three Legions dispersed through the Province of *Brittain.*[1] And as high as the Reign of *Claudius* a great overthrow was given unto the *Iceni,* by the *Romane* Lieutenant *Ostorius.* Not long after, the Countrey was so molested, that, in hope of a better state, *Prastaagus* bequeathed his Kingdome unto *Nero* and his Daughters; and *Boadicea,* his Queen fought the last decisive Battle with *Paulinus.* After which time and Conquest of *Agricola,* the Lieutenant of *Vespasian,* probable it is they wholly possessed this countrey, ordering it into Garrisons or Habitations best suitable with their securities. And so some Romane Habitations, not improbable in

[1] In Omphrius.

these parts, as high as the time of *Vespasian,* where
the *Saxons* after seated, in those thin-fill'd Mappes we
yet finde the Name of *Walsingham.* Now if the *Iceni*
were but *Gammadims, Anconians,* or men that lived
in an angle, wedge, or Elbow of *Brittain,* according to
the Originall Etymologie, this countrey will challenge the
Emphaticall appellation, as most properly making the
Elbow or Iken of *Icenia.*

That *Britain* was notably populous is undeniable, from
that expression of Cæsar.[1] That the *Romans* themselves
were early in no small Numbers Seventy Thousand, with
their associats slain by *Boadicea,* affords a sure account.
And though many *Roman* habitations are now knowne,
yet some by old works, Rampiers, Coyns, and Urnes, doe
testifie their Possessions. Some Urnes have been found
at *Castor,* some also about *Southcreake,* and not many
years past, no lesse than ten in a Field at *Buxton,*[2] not
near any recorded Garison. Nor is it strange to find
Romane Coynes of Copper and Silver among us; of *Vespasian, Trajan, Adrian, Commodus, Antoninus, Severus,*
&c. But the greater number of *Dioclesian, Constantine,
Constans, Valens,* with many of *Victorinus Posthumius,
Tetricus,* and the thirty Tyrants in the Reigne of *Gal-
lienus;* and some as high as *Adrianus* have been found
about *Thetford,* or *Sitomagus,* mentioned in the itinerary
of *Antoninus,* as the way from *Venta* or *Castor* unto
London.[3] But the most frequent discovery is made at the

---

[1] *Hominum infinita multitudo est, creberrimaque ædificia ferè
Gallicis consimilia.*—Cæs. *de Bello Gall.* l. v.

[2] In the ground of my worthy Friend Rob. Jegon, Esq. wherein
some things contained were preserved by the most worthy Sir
William Paston, Bart.

[3] From Castor to Thetford the Romanes accounted thirty-two
miles, and from thence observed not our common road to London,
but passed by Combretonium ad Ansam, Canonium, Caesaromagus,
etc. by Bretenham, Coggeshall, Chelmeford, Burntwood, etc.

two *Casters* by *Norwich* and *Yarmouth*,[1] at Burghcastle,
and *Brancaster*.[2]

Besides the *Norman, Saxon,* and *Danish* peeces of
Cuthred, Canutus, William, Matilda,[3] and others, some
Brittish Coynes of gold have been dispersedly found; and
no small number of silver peeces near *Norwich;*[4] with a
rude head upon the obverse, and an ill formed horse
on the reverse, with inscriptions *Ic. Duro. T.;* whether
implying *Iceni, Durotriges, Tascia,* or *Trinobantes,* we
leave to higher conjecture. Vulgar Chronology will have
Norwich Castle as old as *Julius Cæsar;* but his distance
from these parts, and its *Gothick* form of structure,
abridgeth such Antiquity. The *British* Coyns afford conjecture of early habitation in these parts, though the City
of *Norwich* arose from the ruines of *Venta,* and though
perhaps not without some habitation before, was enlarged, builded, and nominated by the *Saxons.* In what
bulk or populosity it stood in the old East-Angle Monarchy tradition and history are silent. Considerable it was
in the *Danish* Eruptions, when *Sueno* burnt *Thetford*
and *Norwich,*[5] and *Ulfketel,* the Governour thereof, was
able to make some resistance, and after endeavoured to
burn the *Danish* navy.

How the *Romanes* left so many Coynes in Countreys of
their Conquests, seems of hard resolution, except we consider how they buried them under ground when upon

[1] Most at Caster by Yarmouth, found in a place called East-bloudy-
burgh furlong, belonging to Mr. Thomas Wood, a person of
civility, industry and knowledge in this way, who hath made observation of remarkable things about him, and from whom we have received divers Silver and Copper Coynes.

[2] Belonging to that Noble Gentleman, and true example of worth,
Sir Ralph Hare, Baronet, my honoured Friend.

[3] A peece of Maud, the Empresse, said to be found in Buckenham
Castle, with this Inscription, *Elle n' a elle.*

[4] At Thorpe.

[5] Brampton Abbas Jorvalensis.

barbarous invasions they were fain to desert their habitations in most part of their Empire, and the strictness of
their laws forbidding to transfer them to any other uses;
wherein the *Spartans*[1] were singular, who, to make their
Copper money uselesse, contempered it with vinegar.
That the *Brittains* left any, some wonder; since their
money was iron and Iron rings before *Cæsar;* and those
of after stamp by permission, and but small in bulk and
bigness; that so few of the *Saxons* remain, because, overcome by succeeding Conquerours upon the place, their
Coynes, by degrees, passed into other stamps and the
marks of after-ages.

Than the time of these Urnes deposited, or precise
Antiquity of these Reliques, nothing of more uncertainty. For since the Lieutenant of *Claudius* seems to
have made the first progresse into these parts, since
Boadicea was overthrown by the Forces of *Nero,* and
Agricola put a full end to these Conquests; it is not
probable the Countrey was fully garrison'd or planted
before; and therefore however these Urnes might be of
later date, not likely of higher Antiquity.

And the succeeding Emperours desisted not from their
Conquests in these and other parts; as testified by history
and medall inscription yet extant; The Province of *Brittain* in so divided a distance from *Rome,* beholding the
faces of many Imperiall persons, and in large account
no fewer than *Cæsar, Claudius, Britannicus, Vespasian,
Titus, Adrian, Severus, Commodus, Geta,* and *Caracalla.*

A great obscurity herein, because no medall or Emperours Coyne enclosed, which might denote the date of
their interrments, observable in many Urnes, and found
in those of Spittle Fields, by *London,*[2] which contained
the Coynes of *Claudius, Vespasian, Commodus, Antoninus,* attended with Lacrymatories, Lamps, Bottles of

[1] Plut. in *Vita Lycurg.*
[2] Stowe's *Survey of London.*

Liquor, and other appurtenances of affectionate superstition, which in these rurall interrments were wanting.

Some uncertainty there is from the period or term of
burning, or the cessation of that practise. *Macrobius*
affirmeth it was disused in his days. But most agree,
though without authentick record, that it ceased with
the Antonini. Most safely to be understood after the
Reigne of those Emperours, which assumed the name
of *Antoninus*, extending unto *Heliogabalus*. Not strictly
after *Marcus;* For about fifty years later we find the
magnificent burning, and consecration of *Severus;* and
if we so fix this period or cessation, these Urnes will challenge above thirteen hundred years.

But whether this practise was onely then left by Emperours and great persons, or generally about *Rome*, and
not in other Provinces, we hold no authentick account.
For after *Tertullian*, in the dayes of *Minucius* it was obviously objected upon Christians, that they condemned
the practise of burning.[1] And we find a passage in *Sido-
nius*,[2] which asserteth that practise in *France* unto a
lower account. And perhaps not fully disused till Christianity fully established, which gave the finall extinction
to these sepulchrall Bonefires.

Whether they were the bones of men or women or children, no authentick decision from ancient custome in
distincte places of buriall. Although not improbably conjectured, that the double Sepulture or burying place of
Abraham, had in it such intention. But from exility of
bones, thinnesse of skulls, smallnesse of teeth, ribbes,
and thigh-bones; not improbable that many thereof were
persons of *minor* age, or women. Confirmable also from
things contained in them: In most were found substances
resembling Combes, Plates like Boxes, fastened with
Iron pins, and handsomely overwrought like the necks

---

[1] *Execrantur rogos, et damnant ignium sepulturam.*—Min. *in Oct.*
[2] Sidon. Apollinaris.

or Bridges of Musicall Instruments, long brasse plates
overwrought like the handles of neat implements, brazen
nippers to pull away hair, and in one a kinde of Opale,
yet maintaining a blewish colour.

Now that they accustomed to burn or bury with them,
things wherein they excelled, delighted, or which were
dear unto them, either as farewells unto all pleasure, or
vain apprehension that they might use them in the other
world, is testified by all Antiquity. Observable from the
Gemme or Berill Ring upon the finger of *Cynthia*, the
Mistresse of *Propertius*, when after her Funerall Pyre
her Ghost appeared unto him. And notably illustrated
from the Contents of that *Romane* Urne preserved by
Cardinal *Farnese*,[1] wherein besides great number of
Gemmes with heads of Gods and Goddesses, were found
an Ape of *Agath*, a Grasshopper, an Elephant of Ambre,
a Crystall Ball, three glasses, two Spoones, and six Nuts
of Crystall, and beyond the content of Urnes, in the
Monument of *Childerick*, the first,[2] and fourth King from
Pharamond, casually discovered three years past at *Tour-
nay*, restoring unto the world much gold richly adorning
his Sword, two hundred rubies, many hundred Imperial
Coyns, three hundred golden Bees, the bones and horse
shoe of his horse interred with him, according to the
barbarous magnificence of those dayes in their sepulchral
Obsequies. Although if we steer by the conjecture of
many and Septuagint expression; some trace thereof may
be found even with the ancient Hebrews, not only from
the Sepulchrall treasure of *David*, but the circumcision
knives which *Joshua* also buried.

Some men considering the contents of these Urnes,
lasting peeces and toyes included in them, and the custome of burning with many other Nations, might somewhat doubt whether all Urnes found among us, were

[1] Vigeneri *Annot. in* 4 *Liv.*
[2] Chifflet in *Anast. Childer.*

properly *Romane* Reliques, or some not belonging unto our *Brittish, Saxon,* or *Danish* Forefathers.

In the form of Buriall among the ancient *Brittains,* the large Discourses of *Cæsar, Tacitus,* and *Strabo* are silent: For the discovery whereof, with other particulars, we much deplore the losse of that Letter which *Cicero* expected or received from his Brother *Quintus,* as a resolution of *Brittish* customes; or the account which might have been made by *Scribonius Largus,* the Physician, accompanying the Emperour *Claudius,* who might have also discovered that frugall Bit of the Old *Brittains,* which in the bignesse of a Bean could satisfie their thirst and hunger.[1]

But that the *Druids* and ruling Priests used to burn and bury, is expressed by *Pomponius;* That *Bellinus,* the Brother of *Brennus,* and King of the *Brittains,* was burnt, is acknowledged by *Polydorus,* as also by *Amandus Zierexensis* in *Historia,* and *Pineda* in his *Universa historia* Spanish That they held that practise in *Gallia, Cæsar* expressly delivereth. Whether the *Brittains* (probably descended from them, of like Religion, Language and Manners) did not sometimes make use of burning; or whether at least such as were after civilized unto the *Romane* life and manners, conformed not unto this practise, we have no historicall assertion or deniall. But since, from the account of *Tacitus* the *Romanes* early wrought so much civility upon the British stock, that they brought them to build Temples, to wear the Gowne, and study the *Romane* Laws and language, that they conformed also unto their religious rites and customes in burials, seems no improbable conjecture.

That burning the dead was used in *Sarmatia,* is affirmed by *Gaguinus,* that the *Sueons* and *Gothlanders* used to burne their Princes and great persons, is delivered by *Saxo* and *Olaus;* that this was the old *Germane*

---

[1] *Dionis excerpta per Xiphilin. in Severo.*

practise, is also asserted by *Tacitus*. And though we are bare in historical particulars of such obsequies in this Island, or that the *Saxons, Jutes,* and *Angles* burnt their dead, yet came they from parts where 'twas of ancient practise; the *Germanes* using it, from whom they were descended. And even in *Jutland* and *Sleswick* in *Anglia Cymbrica,* Urnes with bones were found not many years before us.[1]

But the *Danish* and Northern Nations have raised an *Æra* or point of compute from their Custome of burning their dead:[2] Some deriving it from *Unguinus,* some from *Frotho* the great; who ordained by Law, that Princes and Chief Commanders should be committed unto the fire, though the common sort had the common grave interrment. So *Starkatterus,* that old *Heroe,* was burnt, and *Ringo* royally burnt the body of *Harald* the King slain by him.

What time this custome generally expired in that Nation, we discern no assured period; whether it ceased before Christianity, or upon their Conversion, by *Ausgurius* the Gaul, in the time of *Ludovicus Pius* the Sonne of *Charles* the Great, according to good computes; or whether it might not be used by some persons, while for a hundred and eighty years Paganisme and Christianity were promiscuously embraced among them, there is no assured conclusion. About which time the *Danes* were busie in *England,* and particularly infested this Countrey; Where many Castles and strongholds, were built by them, or against them, and great number of names and Families still derived from them. But since this custome was probably disused before their Invasion or Conquest, and the *Romanes* confessedly practised the same, since their possession of this Island, the most assured

[1] Roisold.
[2] *Brendetyde Ild tyde.*

account will fall upon the *Romanes,* or *Brittains Romanized.*

However, certain it is, that Urnes conceived of no *Romane* Originall, are often digged up both in *Norway,* and *Denmark,* handsomely described, and graphically represented by the Learned Physician *Wormius.*[1] And in some parts of *Denmark* in no ordinary number, as stands delivered by Authours exactly describing those Countreys.[2] And they contained not only bones, but many other substances in them, as Knives, peeces of Iron, Brasse and Wood, and one of *Norwaye* a brasse gilded Jewesharp.

Nor were they confused or carelesse in disposing the noblest sort, while they placed large stones in circle about the Urnes, or bodies which they interred: Somewhat answerable unto the monument of *Rollrich* stones in *England,*[3] or sepulcrall Monument probably erected by *Rollo,* who after conquered *Normandy,* Where 'tis not improbable somewhat might be discovered. Mean while to what Nation or person belonged that large Urne found at *Ashburie,*[4] containing mighty bones, and a Buckler; What those large Urnes found at Little *Massingham;*[5] or why the *Anglesea* Urnes are placed with their mouths downward, remains yet undiscovered.

CHAPTER III

PLAYSTERED and whited Sepulchres were anciently affected in cadaverous, and corruptive Burials; and the rigid Jews were wont to garnish the Sepulchres of the

[1] *Olai Wormii Monumenta et Antiquitat. Dan.*

[2] Adolphus Cyprius in *Annal. Sleswic., urnis adeo abundabat collis; &c.*

[3] In Oxfordshire, Cambden.

[4] In Cheshire, Twinus *de rebus Albionicis.*

[5] In Norfolk, Hollingshead.

righteous;[1] *Ulysses* in *Hecuba*[2] cared not how meanly
he lived, so he might finde a noble Tomb after death.
Great Princes affected great Monuments, And the fair
and larger Urnes contained no vulgar ashes, which makes
that disparity in those which time discovereth among us.
The present Urnes were not of one capacity, the largest
containing above a gallon, Some not much above half
that measure; nor all of one figure, wherein there is no
strict conformity, in the same or different Countreys;
Observable from those represented by *Casalius, Bosio,*
and others, though all found in *Italy;* While many have
handles, ears, and long necks, but most imitate a circular
figure, in a sphericall and round composure; whether
from any mystery, best duration or capacity, were but
a conjecture. But the common form with necks was a
proper figure, making our last bed like our first; nor
much unlike the Urnes of our Nativity, while we lay in
the nether part of the Earth,[3] and inward vault of our
Microcosme, Many Urnes are red, these but of a black
colour, somewhat smooth, and dully sounding, which begat some doubt, whether they were burnt, or only baked
in Oven or Sunne: According to the ancient way, in many
bricks, tiles, pots, and testaceous works; and as the word
testa is properly to be taken, when occurring without
addition: And chiefly intended by *Pliny,* when he commendeth bricks and tiles of two years old, and to make
them in the spring. Nor only these concealed peeces, but
the open magnificence of Antiquity, ran much in the
Artifice of Clay. Hereof the house of *Mausolus* was built,
thus old *Jupiter* stood in the Capitoll and the *Statua* of
Hercules, made in the Reign of *Tarquinius Priscus,* was
extant in *Plinies* dayes. And such as declined burning or
Funeral Urnes, affected Coffins of Clay, according to the

[1] Matt. xxiii.
[2] Euripides.
[3] Psal. lxiii.

mode of *Pythagoras,* a way preferred by *Varro.* But the
spirit of great ones was above these circumscriptions,
affecting copper, silver, gold, and *Porphyrie* Urnes,
wherein *Severus* lay, after a serious view and sentence
on that which should contain him.[1] Some of these Urnes
were thought to have been silvered over, from sparklings
in several pots, with small Tinsell parcels; uncertain
whether from the earth, or the first mixture in them.

Among these Urnes we could obtain no good account
of their coverings; only one seemed arched over with
some kinde of brickwork. Of those found at *Buxton,*
some were covered with flints, some, in other parts, with
tiles, those at *Yarmouth Caster* were closed with *Romane*
bricks, and some have proper earthen covers adapted
and fitted to them. But in the *Homericall* Urne of *Patroclus,* whatever was the solid Tegument, we finde the im-
mediate covering to be a purple peece of silk: and such
as had no covers might have the earth closely pressed into
them, after which disposure were probably some of these,
wherein we found the bones and ashes half mortered
unto the sand and sides of the Urne, and some long roots
of Quich, or Dog's-grass, wreathed about the bones.

No Lamps, included Liquors, Lacrymatories, or Tear-
bottles, attended these rurall Urnes, either as sacred unto
the *Manes,* or passionate expressions of their surviving
friends. While with rich flames, and hired tears they
solemnized their Obsequies, and in the most lamented
Monuments made one part of their Inscriptions.[2] Some
finde sepulchrall Vessels containing liquors, which time
hath incrassated into gellies. For besides these Lacrymatories, notable Lamps, with Vessels of Oyles, and aromaticall Liquors attended noble Ossuaries. And some yet
retaining a Vinosity,[3] and spirit in them, which if any

---

[1] Χωρήσεις τὸν ἄνθρωπον, ὃν ἡ οἰκουμένη οὐκ ἐχώρησεν.—Dion.
[2] *Cum lacrymis posuêre.*
[3] Lazius.

have tasted they have farre exceeded the Palats of Antiquity. Liquors not to be computed by years of annuall
Magistrates, but by great conjunctions and the fatall
periods of kingdomes.[1] The draughts of Consulary date,
were but crude unto these, and *Opimian* wine[2] but in the
must unto them.

In sundry Graves and Sepulchres, we meet with Rings,
Coynes, and Chalices. Ancient frugality was so severe,
that they allowed no gold to attend the corps, but only
that which served to fasten their teeth.[3] Whether the
Opaline stone in this Urne were burnt upon the finger
of the dead, or cast into the fire by some affectionate
friend, it will consist with either custome. But other incinerable substances were found so fresh, that they could
feel no sindge from fire. These upon view were judged
to be wood, but sinking in water and tried by the fire,
we found them to be bone or Ivory. In their hardnesse
and yellow colour they most resembled Box, which, in
old expressions found the Epithete of Eternall,[4] and perhaps in such conservatories might have passed uncorrupted.

That Bay-leaves were found green in the Tomb of
S. *Humbert,*[5] after an hundred and fifty years, was looked
upon as miraculous. Remarkable it was unto old Spectators, that the Cypresse of the temple of *Diana,* lasted so
many hundred years: The wood of the Ark and Olive
Rod of *Aaron,* were older at the Captivity. But the
Cypresse of the Ark of *Noah,* was the greatest vegetable
Antiquity, if *Josephus* were not deceived, by some fragments of it in his dayes. To omit the Moore-logs and firre-
trees found under-ground in many parts of *England;* the

[1] About five hundred years.—Plato.

[2] *Vinum Opiminianum annorum centum.*—Petron.

[3] 12. Tabul. 1. xi. *De Jure Sacro. Neve aurum addito, quoi auro
dentes vincti escunt, ast im cum illo sepelire urereve, se fraude esto.*

[4] Plin. 1. xvi. *Inter ξύλα ἀσαπῆ numerat Theophrastus.*

[5] Surius.

undated ruines of windes, flouds, or earthquakes; and which in *Flanders* still shew from what quarter they fell, as generally lying in a North-East position.[1]

But though we found not these peeces to be Wood, according to first apprehension, yet we missed not altogether of some woody substance; For the bones were not so clearly pickt but some coals were found amongst them; A way to make wood perpetuall, and a fit associat for metall whereon was laid the foundation of the great *Ephesian* Temple, and which were made the lasting tests of old boundaries and Landmarks. Whilest we look on these, we admire not Observations of Coals found fresh, after four hundred years.[2] In a long deserted habitation[3] even egg-shells have been found fresh, not tending to corruption.

In the Monument of King *Childerick* the Iron Reliques were found all rusty and crumbling into peeces. But our little Iron pins which fastened the Ivory works, held well together, and lost not their Magneticall quality, though wanting a tenacious moisture for the firmer union of parts, although it be hardly drawn into fusion, yet that metall soon submitteth unto rust and dissolution. In the brazen peeces we admired not the duration, but the freedome from rust, and ill savour; upon the hardest attrition, but now exposed unto the piercing atomes of ayre; in the space of a few moneths, they begin to spot and betray their green entrals. We conceive not these Urnes to have descended thus naked as they appear, or to have entred their graves without the old habit of flowers. The Urne of *Philopœmen* was so laden with flowers and ribbons, that it afforded no sight of itself. The rigid *Lycurgus* allowed Olive and Myrtle. The *Athenians* might fairly except against the practise of *Democritus*, to be buried

---

[1] Gorop. Becanus in *Niloscopio*.
[2] Of Beringuccio *nella pyrotechnia*.
[3] At Elmeham.

up in honey; as fearing to embezzle a great commodity of their Countrey, and the best of that kinde in Europe. But *Plato* seemed too frugally politick, who allowed no larger Monument than would contain for Heroick Verses, and designed the most barren ground for sepulture: Though we cannot commend the goodnesse of that sepulchrall ground which was set at no higher rate then the mean salary of *Judas*. Though the earth had confounded the ashes of these Ossuaries, yet the bones were so smartly burnt, that some thin plates of brasse were found half melted among them: whereby we apprehend they were not of the meanest carcasses, perfunctorily fired as sometimes in military, and commonly in pestilence, burnings; or after the manner of abject corps, hudled forth and carelessly burnt, without the Esquiline Port at *Rome;* which was an affront continued upon *Tiberius,* while they but half burnt his body,[1] and in the *amphitheatre,* according to the custome in notable Malefactors; whereas *Nero* seemed not so much to feare his death as that his head should be cut off, and his body not burnt entire.

Some finding many fragments of sculs in these Urnes, suspected a mixture of bones; in none we searched was there cause of such conjecture, though sometimes they declined not that practise. The ashes of *Domitian*[2] were mingled with those of *Julia,* of *Achilles* with those of *Patroclus:* All Urnes contained not single ashes; Without confused burnings they affectionately compounded their bones; passionately endeavouring to continue their living Unions. And when distance of death denied such conjunctions, unsatisfied affections, conceived some satisfaction to be neighbours in the grave, to lye Urne by Urne, and touch but in their names. And many were so curious to continue their living relations, that they contrived

---

[1] Sueton. in *vitâ Tib. Et in Amphitheatro semiustulandum,* not. Casaub.

[2] Sueton. in *vitâ Domitian.*

large, and family Urnes, wherein the Ashes of their nearest friends and kindred might successively be received,[1]
at least some parcels thereof, while their collaterall memorials lay in *minor* vessels about them.

Antiquity held too light thoughts from Objects of
mortality, while some drew provocatives of mirth from
Anatomies,[2] and Jugglers showed tricks with Skeletons.
When Fidlers made not so pleasant mirth as Fencers, and
men could sit with quiet stomacks, while hanging was
plaied before them.[3] Old considerations made few *memento's* by sculs and bones upon their monuments. In the
Ægyptian Obelisks and Hieroglyphicall figures is not
easie to meet with bones. The sepulchrall Lamps speak
nothing lesse then sepulture; and in their literall
draughts prove often obscene and antick peeces: Where
we finde *D. M.*[4] it is obvious to meet with sacrificing
patera's and vessels of libation, upon old sepulchrall
Monuments. In the Jewish *Hypogæum*[5] and subterranean
Cell at *Rome,* was little observable beside the variety of
Lamps, and frequent draughts of the holy Candlestick.
In authentick draughts of *Anthony* and *Jerome* we meet
with thigh-bones and deaths-heads; but the cemeterial
Cels of ancient Christians and Martyrs, were filled with
draughts of Scripture Stories; not declining the flourishes
of Cypresse, Palmes, and Olive; and the mysticall Figures
of Peacocks, Doves and Cocks. But iterately affecting the
pourtraits of *Enoch, Lazarus, Jonas,* and the Vision of
Ezechiel, as hopefull draughts, and hinting imagery of

---

[1] See the most learned and worthy Mr. M. Casaubon upon
Antoninus.

[2] *Sic erimus cuncti, &c. Ergo dum vivimus vivamus.*

[3] Ἀγώνον παίζειν. A barbarous pastime at Feasts, when men stood
upon a rolling Globe, with their necks in a Rope, fastened to a
beame, and a knife in their hands, ready to cut it when the stone was
rolled away, wherein if they failed, they lost their lives to the laughter of their spectators.—Athenaeus.

[4] *Diis manibus.*

[5] Bosio.

the Resurrection; which is the life of the grave, and
sweetens our habitations in the Land of Moles and Pismires.

Gentile Inscriptions precisely delivered the extent of
mens lives, seldome the manner of their deaths, which
history itself so often leaves obscure in the records of
memorable persons. There is scarce any Philosopher but
dies twice or thrice in *Laertius;* Nor almost any life without two or three deaths in *Plutarch;* which makes the
tragicall ends of noble persons more favourably resented
by compassionate Readers, who finde some relief in the
Election of such differences.

The certainty of death is attended with uncertainties,
in time, manner, places. The variety of Monuments hath
often obscured true graves; and *cenotaphs* confounded
Sepulchres. For beside their reall Tombs, many have
found honorary and empty Sepulchres. The variety of
Homers Monuments made him of various Countreys.
Euripides[1] had his Tomb in *Africa,* but his sepulture in
Macedonia. And *Severus*[2] found his real Sepulchre in
Rome, but his empty grave in *Gallia.*

He that lay in a golden Urne,[3] eminently above the
Earth, was not like to finde the quiet of these bones.
Many of these Urnes were broke by a vulgar discoverer
in hope of inclosed treasure. The ashes of Marcellus[4]
were lost above ground, upon the like account. Where
profit hath prompted, no age hath wanted such miners.
For which the most barbarous Expilators found the most
civill Rhetorick. Gold once out of the earth is no more
due unto it; What was unreasonably committed to the
ground is reasonably resumed from it: Let Monuments
and rich Fabricks, not Riches adorn mens ashes. The

[1] Pausan. *in Atticis.*
[2] Lamprid. in *vit. Alexand. Severi.*
[3] Trajanus.—Dion.
[4] Plut. in *vit. Marcelli.* The commission of the Gothish King
Theodoric for finding out sepulchrall treasure.—Cassiodor. Var. 1. 4.

commerce of the living is not to be transferred unto the dead; It is not injustice to take that which none complains to lose, and no man is wronged where no man is possessor.

What virtue yet sleeps in this *terra damnata* and aged cinders, were petty magick to experiment; These crumbling reliques and long-fired particles superannate such expectations; Bones, hairs, nails, and teeth of the dead, were the treasures of old Sorcerers. In vain we revive such practices; present superstition too visibly perpetuates the folly of our Fore-fathers, wherein unto old Observation[1] this Island was so complete, that it might have instructed *Persia*.

Plato's historian of the other world, lies twelve dayes incorrupted, while his soul was viewing the large stations of the dead. How to keep the corps seven dayes from corruption by anointing and washing, without exenteration, were an hazardable peece of art, in our choicest practise. How they made distinct separation of bones and ashes from fiery admixture, hath found no historicall solution. Though they seemed to make a distinct collection, and overlooked not *Pyrrhus* his toe. Some provision they might make by fictile Vessels, Coverings, Tiles, or flat stones, upon and about the body. And in the same Field, not farre from these Urnes, many stones were found under ground, as also by carefull separation of extraneous matter, composing and raking up the burnt bones with forks, observable in that notable lamp of *Galvanus*.[2] *Martianus*, who had the sight of the *Vas Ustrinum*[3] or vessell wherein they burnt the dead, found in the Esquiline Field at *Rome*, might have afforded clearer solution. But their insatisfaction herein begat that remarkable

---

[1] *Britannia hodie eam attonitè celebrat tantis ceremoniis, ut dedisse Persis videri possit.*—Plin. 1. 30.

[2] To be seen in Licet. *de reconditis veterum lucernis.*

[3] *Typographia. Roma ex Martiano. Erat et vas ustrinum appellatum, quod in eo cadavera comburerentur.* Cap. *de Campo Esquilino.*

invention in the Funerall Pyres of some Princes, by incombustible sheets made with a texture of *Asbestos,* incremable flax, or Salamander's wool, which preserved their bones and ashes incommixed.

How the bulk of a man should sink into so few pounds of bones and ashes, may seem strange unto any who considers not its constitution, and how slender a masse will remain upon an open and urging fire of the carnall composition. Even bones themselves reduced into ashes, do abate a notable proportion. And consisting much of a volatile salt, when that is fired out, make a light kind of cinders. Although their bulk be disproportionable to their weight, when the heavy principle of Salt is fired out, and the Earth almost only remaineth; Observable in sallow, which makes more Ashes than Oake; and discovers the common fraud of selling Ashes by measure, and not by ponderation.

Some bones make best Skeletons,[1] some bodies quick and speediest ashes. Who would expect a quick flame from Hydropicall *Heraclitus?* The poysoned Souldier, when his Belly brake, put out two pyres in *Plutarch.*[2] But in the plague of *Athens,*[3] one private pyre served two or three Intruders; and the *Saracens* burnt in large heaps, by the King of *Castile,*[4] shewed how little Fuell sufficeth. Though the Funerall pyre of *Patroclus* took up an hundred foot,[5] a peece of an old boat burnt *Pompey;* And if the burthen of *Isaac* were sufficient for an holocaust, a man may carry his owne pyre.

From animals are drawn good burning lights, and good medicines against burning;[6] Though the seminall

---

[1] Old bones according to *Lyserus.* Those of young persons not tall nor fat according to Columbus.

[2] In *vitâ Gracc.*

[3] Thucydides.

[4] Laurent. Valla.

[5] Ἑκατόμπεδον ἔνθα ἤ ἔνθα.

[6] Sperm. ranarum, Alb. Ovor.

humour seems of a contrary nature to fire, yet the body compleated proves a combustible lump, wherein fire findes flame even from bones, and some fuell almost from all parts. Though the *Metropolis* of humidity[1] seems least disposed unto it, which might render the sculls of these Urnes lesse burned than other bones. But all flies or sinks before fire almost in all bodies: when the common ligament is dissolved, the attenuable parts ascend, the rest subside in coal, calx or ashes.

To burn the bones of the King of Edom for lime,[2] seems no irrationall ferity; But to drink of the ashes of dead relations,[3] a passionate prodigality. He that hath the ashes of his friend, hath an everlasting treasure; where fire taketh leave, corruption slowly enters; In bones well burnt, fire makes a wall against itself; experimented in copels, and tests of metals, which consist of such ingredients. What the Sun compoundeth, fire analyseth, not transmuteth. That devouring agent leaves almost always a morsell for the Earth, whereof all things are but a colonie; and which, if time permits, the mother Element will have in their primitive masse again.

He that looks for Urnes and old sepulchrall reliques, must not seek them in the ruines of Temples: where no Religion anciently placed them. These were found in a Field, according to ancient custome, in noble or private buriall; the old practise of the *Canaanites*, the Family of *Abraham*, and the burying-place of *Josua*, in the borders of his possessions; and also agreeable unto *Roman* practice to bury by highwayes, whereby their Monuments were under eye; Memorials of themselves, and *memento's* of mortality unto living passengers; whom the Epitaphs of great ones were fain to beg to stay and look upon them; A language though sometimes used, not so proper

[1] The brain. Hippocrates.
[2] Amos ii. 1.
[3] As Artemisia of her Husband Mausolus.

in Church-Inscriptions.[1] The sensible Rhetorick of the
dead, to exemplarity of good life, first admitted the bones
of pious men, and Martyrs within Church wals; which
in succeeding ages crept into promiscuous practise. While
Constantine was peculiarly favoured to be admitted into
the Church Porch; and the first thus buried in *England*
was in the dayes of *Cuthred*.

Christians dispute how their bodies should lye in the
grave.[2] In urnall interrment they clearly escaped this
controversie; though we decline the Religious consideration, yet in cemiteriall and narrower burying-places, to
avoid confusion and crosse position, a certain posture
were to be admitted; which even Pagan civility observed.
The *Persians* lay North and South, the *Megarians* and
Phœnicians placed their heads to the East; The *Athenians,* some think, towards the West, which Christians still
retain. And *Beda* will have it to be the posture of our
Saviour. That he was crucified with his face toward the
West, we will not contend with tradition and probable
account; But we applaud not the hand of the Painter,
in exalting his Crosse so high above those on either side;
since hereof we finde no authentick account in history,
and even the crosses found by *Helena,* pretend no such
distinction from longitude or dimension.

To be knav'd out of our graves, to have our sculs made
drinking-bowls, and our bones turned into Pipes, to
delight and sport our Enemies, are Tragicall abominations escaped in burning Burials.

Urnall interrments and burnt Reliques lye not in fear
of worms, or to be an heritage for Serpents; In carnall
sepulture, corruptions seem peculiar unto parts, and
some speak of snakes out of the spinall marrow. But
while we suppose common wormes in graves, 'tis not easie
to finde any there; few in Churchyards above a foot deep,

[1] *Siste viator.*
[2] Kirkmannus *de funer.*

fewer or none in Churches, though in fresh decayed bodies. Teeth, bones, and hair, give the most lasting defiance to corruption. In an Hydropicall body, ten years buried in the Churchyard, we met with a fat concretion, where the nitre of the Earth, and the salt and lixivious liquor of the body, had coagulated large lumps of fat, into the consistence of the hardest castle-soap; whereof part remaineth with us. After a battle with the *Persians,* the *Roman* Corps decayed in few dayes, while the *Persian* bodies remained dry and uncorrupted. Bodies in the same ground do not uniformly dissolve, nor bones equally moulder; whereof in the opprobrious disease we expect no long duration. The body of the Marquesse of *Dorset* seemed sound and handsomely cereclothed, that after seventy-eight years was found uncorrupted.[1] Common Tombs preserve not beyond powder: A firmer consistence and compage of parts might be expected from Arefaction, deep buriall or charcoal. The greatest Antiquities of mortall bodies may remain in putrefied bones, whereof, though we take not in the pillar of *Lot's* wife, or Metamorphosis of *Ortelius,*[2] some may be older than Pyramids, in the putrefied Reliques of the generall inundation. When *Alexander* opened the Tomb of *Cyrus,* the remaining bones discovered his proportion, whereof urnall fragments afford but a bad conjecture, and have this disadvantage of grave enterrments, that they leave us ignorant of most personal discoveries. For since bones afford not only rectitude and stability, but figure unto the body; it is no impossible Physiognomy to conjecture at fleshy appendencies; and after what shape the muscles and carnous parts might hang in their full consistences.

[1] Of Thomas, Marquesse of Dorset, whose body being buried 1530, was 1608, upon the cutting open of the Cerecloth, found perfect and nothing corrupted, the flesh not hardened, but in colour, proportion, and softnesse like an ordinary corps newly to be interred.— Burton's *descript. of Leicestershire.*

[2] In his Map of Russia.

A full-spread *Cariola*[1] shows a well-shaped horse behinde handsome formed sculls give some analogy to fleshy resemblance. A criticall view of bones makes a good distinction of sexes. Even colour is not beyond conjecture; since it is hard to be deceived in the distinction of *Negro's* sculls.[2] *Dante's*[3] Characters are to be found in sculls as well as faces. *Hercules* is not only known by his foot. Other parts make out their comproportions and inferences upon whole or parts. And since the dimensions of the head measure the whole body, and the figure thereof gives conjecture of the principall faculties; Physiognomy outlives ourselves, and ends not in our graves.

Severe contemplators observing these lasting reliques, may think them good monuments of persons past, little advantage to future beings. And considering that power which subdueth all things unto itself, that can resume the scattered Atomes, or identifie out of any thing, conceive it superfluous to expect a resurrection out of Reliques. But the soul subsisting, other matter, clothed with due accidents, may salve the individuality: Yet the Saints we observe arose from graves and monuments, about the holy City. Some think the ancient Patriarchs so earnestly desired to lay their bones in *Canaan,* as hoping to make a part of that Resurrection, and, though thirty miles from Mount Calvary, at least to lie in that Region which should produce the first-fruits of the dead. And if accord-

[1] That part in the Skeleton of a Horse, which is made by the haunch-bones.

[2] For their extraordinary thickness.

[3] The Poet Dante in his view of Purgatory, found gluttons so meagre, and extenuated, that he conceited them to have been in the Siege of Jerusalem, and that it was easie to have discovered *Homo* or *Omo* in their faces: M being made by the two lines of their cheeks, arching over the Eye-brows to the nose, and their sunk eyes making O O which makes up *Omo.*

Parean l'occhiaie anella senza gemme:
Chi, nel viso degli uomini legge OMO,
*Ben avria quivi conosciuto l'*EMME.—*Purgat.* xxiii. 31.

ing to learned conjecture, the bodies of men shall rise
where their greatest Reliques remain, many are not like
to erre in the Topography of their Resurrection, though
their bones or bodies be after translated by Angels into
the field of *Ezechiel's* vision, or as some will order it, into
the Valley of Judgement, or *Jehosaphat*.[1]

CHAPTER IV

CHRISTIANS have handsomely glossed the deformity of
death, by careful consideration of the body, and civil rites
which take off brutall terminations. And though they
conceived all reparable by a resurrection, cast not off all
care of enterrment. And since the ashes of Sacrifices burnt
upon the Altar of God were carefully carried out by the
Priests, and deposed in a clean field; since they acknowledged their bodies to be the lodging of Christ, and temples of the holy Ghost, they devolved not all upon the
sufficiency of soul-existence; and therefore with long serv-
ices and full solemnities concluded their last Exequies,
wherein to all distinctions the Greek devotion seems most
pathetically ceremonious.[2]

Christian invention hath chiefly driven at Rites, which
speak hopes of another life, and hints of a Resurrection. And if the ancient Gentiles held not the immortality of their better part, and some subsistence after
death; in severall rites, customes, actions and expressions,
they contradicted their own opinions: wherein *Democritus* went high, even to the thought of a resurrection, as
scoffingly recorded by *Pliny*.[3] What can be more expresse
than the expression of *Phocyllides*?[4] Or who would ex-

[1] Tirin. in Ezek.

[2] *Rituale Græcum, operâ J. Goar, in officio exequiarum.*

[3] *Similis * * * * reviviscendi promissa a Democrito vanitas, qui non
revixit ipse. Quæ (malum) ista dementia est, iterari vitam morte?*—
Plin. l. vii. c. 55.

[4] Καὶ τάχα δ' ἐκ γαίης ἐλπίζομεν ἐς φάος ἐλθεῖν λείψαν ἀποιχομένων,
et deinceps.

pect from *Lucretius*[1] a sentence of *Ecclesiastes?* Before
Plato could speak, the soul had wings in *Homer*, which
fell not, but flew out of the body into the mansions of the
dead; who also observed that handsome distinction of
Demas and *Soma*, for the body conjoyned to the soul,
and body separated from it. *Lucian* spoke much truth
in jest, when he said that part of *Hercules* which proceeded from *Alchmena* perished, that from *Jupiter* remained immortall. Thus *Socrates*[2] was content that his
friends should bury his body, so they would not think
they buried *Socrates*, and regarding only his immortall
part, was indifferent to be burnt or buried. From such
Considerations, *Diogenes* might contemn Sepulture. And
being satisfied that the soul could not perish, grow carelesse of corporall enterrment. The *Stoicks* who thought
the souls of wise men their habitation about the *moon*,
might make slight account of subterraneous deposition;
whereas the *Pythagoreans* and transcorporating Philosophers, who were to be often buried, held great care
of their enterrment. And the Platonicks rejected not a
due care of the grave, though they put their ashes to un-
reasonable expectations, in their tedious term of return
and long set revolution.

Men have lost their reason in nothing so much as their
religion, wherein stones and clouts make martyrs; and,
since the religion of one seems madnesse unto another, to
afford an account or rationall of old Rites requires no
rigid Reader. That they kindled the pyre aversely, or
turning their face from it, was an handsome Symbole
of unwilling ministration; That they washed their bones
with wine and milk, that the mother wrapped them in
linnen and dryed them in her bosome, the first fostering
part, and place of their nourishment; that they opened

---

[1] *Cedit enim retro de terrâ quod fuit ante in terram, etc.*—Lucret.
[2] Plato in *Phæd.*

their eyes towards heaven, before they kindled the fire,
as the place of their hopes or originall, were no improper
Ceremonies. Their last valediction,[1] thrice uttered by the
attendants, was also very solemn, and somewhat answered
by Christians, who thought it too little, if they threw not
the earth thrice upon the enterred body. That in strew-
ing their Tombs the *Romans* affected the Rose, the
Greeks *Amaranthus* and myrtle; that the Funerall pyre
consisted of sweet fuell Cypresse, Firre, Larix, Yewe, and
Trees perpetually verdant, lay silent expressions of their
surviving hopes. Wherein Christians, who deck their
Coffins with Bays, have found a more elegant Embleme.
For that he seeming dead, will restore itself from the
root, and its dry and exuccous leaves resume their verdure again; which, if we mistake not, we have also observed in furze. Whether the planting of yewe in Churchyards hold not its original from ancient Funerall rites, or
as an Embleme of Resurrection, from its perpetual verdure, may also admit conjecture.

They made use of Musick to excite or quiet the affections of their friends, according to different harmonies.
But the secret and symbolicall hint was the harmonical
nature of the soul; which delivered from the body, went
again to enjoy the primitive harmony of heaven, from
whence it first descended; which according to its progresse
traced by antiquity, came down by *Cancer,* and ascended
by *Capricornus.*

They burnt not children before their teeth appeared,
as apprehending their bodies too tender a morsell for
fire, and that their gristly bones would scarce leave
separable reliques after the pyrall combustion. That they
kindled not fire in their houses for some dayes after was
a strict memoriall of the late afflicting fire. And mourning without hope, they had an happy fraud against ex-

[1] *Vale, vale, vale, nos te ordine quo natura permittet sequamur.*

cessive lamentation, by a common opinion that deep sorrows disturb their ghosts.[1]

That they buried their dead on their backs, or in a supine position, seems agreeable unto profound sleep, and common posture of dying; contrary to the most naturall way of birth; Nor unlike our pendulous posture, in the doubtful state of the womb. *Diogenes* was singular, who preferred a prone situation in the grave, and some Christians[2] like neither, who decline the figure of rest, and make choice of an erect posture.

That they carried them out of the world with their feet forward, not inconsonant unto reason: As contrary unto the native posture of man, and his production first into it. And also agreeable unto their opinions, while they bid adieu unto the world, not to look again upon it; whereas *Mahometans* who think to return to a delightfull life again, are carried forth with their heads forward, and looking toward their houses.

They closed their eyes as parts which first die or first discover the sad effects of death. But their iterated clamations to excite their dying or dead friends, or revoke them unto life again, was a vanity of affection; as not presumably ignorant of the criticall tests of death, by apposition of feathers, glasses, and reflection of figures, which dead eyes represent not; which however not strictly verifiable in fresh and warm *cadavers,* could hardly elude the test, in corps of four or five dayes.[3]

That they suck'd in the last breath of their expiring friends, was surely a practice of no medical institution, but a loose opinion that the soul passed out that way, and a fondnesse of affection from some *Pythagoricall* foundation,[4] that the spirit of one body passed into another; which they wished might be their own.

[1] *Tu manes ne læde meos.*
[2] Russians, &c.
[3] At least by some difference from living eyes.
[4] Francesco Perucci, *Pompe funebri.*

That they powred oyle upon the pyre, was a tolerable practise, while the intention rested in facilitating the accension; But to place good *Omens* in the quick and speedy burning, to sacrifice unto the windes for a dispatch in this office, was a low form of superstition.

The *Archimime,* or *Jester,* attending the Funerall train, and imitating the speeches, gesture, and manners of the deceased, was too light for such solemnities, contradicting their Funerall Orations and dolefull rites of the grave.

That they buried a peece of money with them as a Fee of the *Elysian Ferriman,* was a practise full of folly. But the ancient custome of placing coynes in considerable Urnes, and the present practise of burying medals in the Noble Foundations of *Europe,* are laudable wayes of historicall discoveries, in actions, persons, Chronologies; and posterity will applaud them.

We examine not the old Laws of Sepulture, exempting certain persons from buriall or burning. But hereby we apprehend that these were not the bones of persons planet-struck or burnt with fire from Heaven; No reliques of Traitors to their Countrey, Self-killers, or Sacrilegious Malefactors; Persons in old apprehension unworthy of the *earth;* condemned unto the *Tartaras* of Hell, and bottomlesse pit of *Pluto,* from whence there was no redemption.

Nor were only many customes questionable in order to their Obsequies, but also sundry practises, fictions, and conceptions, discordant or obscure, of their state and future beings; whether unto eight or ten bodies of men to adde one of a woman, as being more inflammable, and unctuously constituted for the better pyrall combustion, were any rationall practise; Or whether the complaint of *Perianders* Wife be tolerable, that wanting her Funerall burning, she suffered intolerable cold in Hell, according to the constitution of the infernall house of

Pluto, wherein cold makes a great part of their tortures; it cannot passe without some question.

Why the Female Ghosts appear unto *Ulysses,* before the *Heroes* and masculine spirits? Why the *Psyche* or soul of *Tiresias* is of the masculine gender,[1] who being blinde on earth, sees more than all the rest in hell; Why the Funerall Suppers consisted of Egges, Beans, Smallage, and Lettuce, since the dead are made to eat Asphodels[2] about the *Elyzian* medows? Why since there is no Sacrifice acceptable, nor any propitiation for the Covenant of the grave; men set up the Deity of *Morta,* and fruitlessly adored Divinities without ears? it cannot escape some doubt.

The dead seem all alive in the human *Hades* of *Homer,* yet cannot well speak, prophesie, or know the living, except they drink bloud, wherein is the life of man. And therefore the souls of *Penelope's* Paramours, conducted by *Mercury,* chirped like bats, and those which followed *Hercules,* made a noise but like a flock of birds.

The departed spirits know things past and to come, yet are ignorant of things present. *Agamemnon* foretels what should happen unto *Ulysses,* yet ignorantly enquires what is become of his own Son. The Ghosts are afraid of swords in *Homer,* yet *Sibylla* tells *Æneas* in *Virgil,* the thin habit of spirits was beyond the force of weapons. The spirits put off their malice with their bodies, and *Cæsar* and *Pompey* accord in Latine Hell, yet *Ajax* in *Homer* endures not a conference with *Ulysses;* And *Deiphobus* appears all mangled in *Virgils* Ghosts, yet we meet with perfect shadows among the wounded ghosts of *Homer.*

Since *Charon* in *Lucian* applauds his condition among the dead, whether it be handsomely said of *Achilles,* that living contemner of death, that he had rather be a plowman's servant, than Emperour of the dead? How *Hercu-*

---

[1] In Homer:—Ψυχὴ Θηβαίου Τειρεσίαο σκῆπτρον ἔχων.
[2] In Lucian.

les his soul is in hell, and yet in heaven, and *Julius* his soul in a Starre, yet seen by *Æneas* in hell, except the Ghosts were but Images and shadows of the soul, received in higher mansions, according to the ancient division of body, soul, and image, or *simulachrum* of them both. The particulars of future beings must needs be dark unto ancient Theories, which Christian Philosophy yet determines but in a Cloud of opinions. A Dialogue between two Infants in the womb concerning the state of this world, might handsomely illustrate our ignorance of the next, whereof methinks we yet discourse in *Platoes* denne, and are but *Embryon* Philosophers.

Pythagoras escapes in the fabulous hell of *Dante*,[1] among that swarm of Philosophers, wherein whilest we meet with *Plato* and *Socrates, Cato* is to be found in no lower place than Purgatory. Among all the set, *Epicurus* is most considerable, whom men make honest without an Elyzium, who contemned life without encouragement of immortality, and making nothing after death, yet made nothing of the King of terrours.

Were the happiness of the next world as closely apprehended as the felicities of this, it were a martyrdome to live; and unto such as consider none hereafter, it must be more than death to dye, which makes us amazed at those audacities, that durst nothing, and return into their *Chaos* again. Certainly such spirits as could contemn death, when they expected no better being after, would have scorned to live, had they known any. And therefore we applaud not the judgment of *Machiavel*, that Christianity makes men cowards, or that with the confidence of but half dying, the despised virtues of patience and humility, have abased the spirits of men, which Pagan principles exalted, but rather regulated the wildenesse of audacities, in the attempts, grounds, and eternall sequels of death; wherein men of the bold-

[1] *Del Inferno*, cant. 4.

est spirits are often prodigiously temerarious. Nor can we extenuate the valour of ancient Martyrs, who contemned death in the uncomfortable scene of their lives, and in their decrepit Martyrdomes did probably lose not many moneths of their dayes, or parted with life when it was scarce worth the living. For (beside that long time past holds no consideration unto a slender time to come) they had no small disadvantage from the constitution of old age, which naturally makes men fearfull; And complexionally superannuated from the bold and courageous thoughts of youth and fervent years. But the contempt of death from corporall animosity, promoteth not our felicity. They may sit in the *Orchestra*, and noblest Seats of Heaven, who have held up shaking hands in the fire, and humanely contended for glory.

Meanwhile *Epicurus* lyes deep in *Dante's* hell, wherein we meet with Tombs enclosing souls which denied their immortalities. But whether the virtuous heathen, who lived better than he spake, or erring in the principles of himself, yet lived above Philosophers of more specious Maximes, lye so deep as he is placed; at least so low as not to rise against Christians, who beleeving or knowing that truth, have lastingly denied it in their practise and conversation, were a quæry too sad to insist on.

But all or most apprehensions rested in Opinions of some future being, which, ignorantly or coldly beleeved, begat those perverted conceptions, Ceremonies, Sayings, which Christians pity or laugh at. Happy are they, which live not in that disadvantage of time, when men could say little for futurity, but from reason. Whereby the noblest minds fell often upon doubtfull deaths, and melancholly dissolutions; With these hopes *Socrates* warmed his doubtfull spirits against that cold potion, and *Cato* before he durst give the fatall stroak, spent part of the night in reading the immortality of

Plato, thereby confirming his wavering hand unto the animosity of that attempt.

It is the heaviest stone that melancholy can throw at a man, to tell him he is at the end of his nature; or that there is no further state to come, unto which this seems progressionall, and otherwise made in vaine; Without this accomplishment the naturall expectation and desire of such state, were but a fallacy in nature, unsatisfied Considerators; would quarrell the justice of their constitutions, and rest content that *Adam* had fallen lower, whereby by knowing no other Originall, and deeper ignorance of themselves, they might have enjoyed the happinesse of inferiour creatures, who in tranquillity possesse their Constitutions, as having not the apprehension to deplore their own natures, And being framed below the circumference of these hopes, or cognition of better being, the wisedom of God hath necessitated their Contentment; But the superior ingredient and obscured part of our selves, whereto all present felicities afford no resting contentment, will be able at last to tell us, we are more than our present selves; and evacuate such hopes in the fruition of their own accomplishments.

CHAPTER V

Now since these dead bones have already out-lasted the living ones of *Methuselah,* and in a yard under ground, and thin walls of clay, out-worn all the strong and specious buildings above it; and quietly rested under the drums and tramplings of three conquests; what Prince can promise such diuturnity unto his Reliques, or might not gladly say,

Sic ego componi versus in ossa velim.[1]

[1] *Tibullus.*

Time which antiquates Antiquities, and hath an art to make dust of all things, hath yet spared these *minor* Monuments.

In vain we hope to be known by open and visible conservatories, when to be unknown was the means of their continuation and obscurity their protection: If they dyed by violent hands, and were thrust into their Urnes, these bones become considerable, and some old Philosophers would honour them,[1] whose souls they conceived most pure, which were thus snatched from their bodies; and to retain a stranger propension unto them: whereas they weariedly left a languishing corps, and with faint desires of re-union. If they fell by long and aged decay, yet wrapt up in the bundle of time, they fall into indistinction, and make but one blot with Infants. If we begin to die when we live, and long life be but a prolongation of death; our life is a sad composition; We live with death, and die not in a moment. How many pulses made up the life of *Methuselah,* were work for *Archimedes:* Common Counters summe up the life of *Moses* his man.[2] Our dayes become considerable like petty sums by minute accumulations; where numerous fractions make up but small round numbers; and our dayes of a span long make not one little finger.[3]

If the nearnesse of our last necessity, brought a nearer conformity into it, there were a happinesse in hoary hairs, and no calamity in half senses. But the long habit of living indisposeth us for dying; when Avarice makes us the sport of death; When even *David* grew politickly cruell; and *Solomon* could hardly be said to be the wisest of men. But many are too early old, and before the date of age.

---

[1] *Oracula Chaldaica cum scholiis Pselli et Plethonis.* βίῃ λιπόντων σῶμα ψυχαὶ καθαρώταται. *Vi corpus relinquentium animæ purissimæ.*
[2] In the Psalme of Moses.
[3] According to the ancient Arithmetick of the hand, wherein the little finger of the right hand contracted, signified an hundred.— Pierius in *Hieroglyph.*

Adversity stretcheth our dayes, misery makes *Alcmenas* nights,[1] and time hath no wings unto it. But the most tedious being is that which can unwish itself, content to be nothing, or never to have been, which was beyond the *male*content of *Job,* who cursed not the day of his life, but his Nativity: Content to have so farre been, as to have a Title to future being; Although he had lived here but in an hidden state of life, and as it were an abortion.

What Song the *Syrens* sang, or what name *Achilles* assumed when he hid himself among women, though puzling Questions,[2] are not beyond all conjecture. What time the persons of these Ossuaries entred the famous Nations of the dead,[3] and slept with Princes and Counsellours,[4] might admit a wide solution. But who were the proprietaries of these bones, or what bodies these ashes made up, were a question above Antiquarism. Not to be resolved by man, nor easily perhaps by spirits, except we consult the Provinciall Guardians, or tutellary Observators. Had they made as good provision for their names, as they have done for their Reliques, they had not so grosly erred in the art of perpetuation. But to subsist in bones, and be but Pyramidally extant, is a fallacy in duration. Vain ashes, which in the oblivion of names, persons, times, and sexes, have found unto themselves, a fruitless continuation, and only arise unto late posterity, as Emblemes of mortall vanities; Antidotes against pride, vain-glory, and madding vices. Pagan vain-glories which thought the world might last for ever, had encouragement for ambition, and, finding no *Atropos* unto the immortality of their Names, were never dampt with the necessity of oblivion. Even old ambitions had the

---

[1] One night as long as three.
[2] The puzzling questions of Tiberius unto Grammarians.—Marcel. Donatus in Suet.
[3] Κλυτὰ ἔθνεα νεκρῶν.—Hom.
[4] Job.

advantage of ours, in the attempts of their vain-glories, who acting early, and before the probable Meridian of time, have by this time found great accomplishment of their designes, whereby the ancient *Heroes* have already out-lasted their Monuments, and Mechanicall preservations. But in this latter Scene of time, we cannot expect such mummies unto our memories, when ambition may fear the Prophecy of *Elias,*[1] and *Charles* the fifth can never hope to live within two *Methuselas* of *Hector.*[2]

And therefore restlesse inquietude for the diuturnity of our memories unto present considerations, seems a vanity almost out of date, and superannuated peece of folly. We cannot hope to live so long in our names, as some have done in their persons, one face of *Janus* holds no proportion unto the other. 'Tis too late to be ambitious. The great mutations of the world are acted, or time may be too short for our designes. To extend our memories by Monuments, whose death we daily pray for, and whose duration we cannot hope, without injury to our expectations, in the advent of the last day, were a contradiction to our beliefs. We whose generations are ordained in this setting part of time, are providentially taken off from such imaginations; And being necessitated to eye the remaining particle of futurity, are naturally constituted unto thoughts of the next world, and cannot excusably decline the consideration of that duration, which maketh Pyramids pillars of snow, and all that's past a moment.

Circles and right lines limit and close all bodies, and the mortall right-lined circle[3] must conclude and shut up all. There is no antidote against the *Opium* of time, which temporally considereth all things; Our Fathers

---

[1] That the world may last but six thousand years.

[2] Hector's fame lasting above two lives of Methuselah, before that famous Prince was extant.

[3] Θ The Character of death.

finde their graves in our short memories, and sadly tell us
how we may be buried in our Survivors. Grave-stones tell
truth scarce fourty years.[1] Generations passe while some
trees stand, and old families last not three oaks. To be
read by bare Inscriptions like many in *Gruter*,[2] to hope
for Eternity by Ænigmaticall Epithetes or first letters of
our names, to be studied by Antiquaries, who we were,
and have new Names given us like many of the Mummies,[3] are cold consolations unto the Students of perpetuity, even by everlasting Languages.

To be content that times to come should only know
there was such a man, not caring whether they knew
more of him, was a frigid ambition in *Cardan:*[4] dispar-
aging his horoscopal inclination and judgement of himself, who cares to subsist like *Hippocrates* Patients, or
Achilles horses in *Homer,* under naked nominations,
without deserts and noble acts, which are the balsame
of our memories, the *Entelechia* and soul of our subsist-
ences. To be namelesse in worthy deeds exceeds an infamous history. The *Canaanitish* woman lives more happily without a name, than *Herodias* with one. And who
had not rather have been the good theef, then *Pilate?*

But the iniquity of oblivion blindely scattereth her
poppy, and deals with the memory of men without distinction to merit of perpetuity. Who can but pity the
founder of the Pyramids? *Herostratus* lives that burnt
the Temple of *Diana,* he is almost lost that built it; Time
hath spared the Epitaph of Adrians horse, confounded
that of himself. In vain we compute our felicities by the
advantage of our good names, since bad have equall

---

[1] Old ones being taken up, and other bodies laid under them.

[2] *Gruteri Inscriptiones Antiquæ.*

[3] Which men show in several Countries, giving them what names
they please; and unto some the names of the old Egyptian Kings, out
of Herodotus.

[4] *Cuperem notum esse quod sim, non opto ut sciatur qualis sim.*—
Card. in *vitâ propria.*

durations; and *Thersites* is like to live as long as *Agamemnon*, Who knows whether the best of men be known? or whether there be not more remarkable persons forgot, than any that stand remembred in the known account of time? Without the favour of the everlasting register, the first man had been as unknown as the last, and *Methuselahs* long life had been his only Chronicle.

Oblivion is not to be hired: The greater part must be content to be as though they had not been, to be found in the Register of God, not in the record of man. Twenty-seven Names make up the first story before the flood, and the recorded names ever since contain not one living Century. The number of the dead long exceedeth all that shall live. The night of time far surpasseth the day, and who knows when was the Æquinox? Every hour adds unto that current Arithmetique which scarce stands one moment. And since death must be the *Lucina* of life, and even Pagans[1] could doubt, whether thus to live, were to dye. Since our longest sunne sets at right descensions, and makes but winter arches, and therefore it cannot be long before we lie down in darknesse, and have our light in ashes.[2] Since the brother of death daily haunts us with dying *memento's,* and time that grows old in it self, bids us hope no long duration: Diuturnity is a dream and folly of expectation.

Darknesse and light divide the course of time, and oblivion shares with memory, a great part even of our living beings; we slightly remember our felicities, and the smartest stroaks of affliction leave but short smart upon us. Sense endureth no extremities, and sorrows destroy us or themselves. To weep into stones are fables. Afflictions induce callosities, miseries are slippery, or fall like snow upon us, which notwithstanding is no

---

[1] Euripides.
[2] According to the custom of the Jews, who place a lighted wax candle in a pot of ashes by the corpse.—Leo.

unhappy stupidity. To be ignorant of evils to come, and forgetfull of evils past, is a mercifull provision in nature, whereby we digest the mixture of our few and evil dayes, and our delivered senses not relapsing into cutting remembrances, our sorrows are not kept raw by the edge of repetitions. A great part of Antiquity contented their hopes of subsistency with a transmigration of their souls. A good way to continue their memories, while having the advantage of plurall successions, they could not but act something remarkable in such variety of beings, and enjoying the fame of their passed selves, make accumulation of glory unto their last durations. Others, rather then be lost in the uncomfortable night of nothing, were content to recede into the common being, and make one particle of the public soul of all things, which was no more then to return into their unknown and divine Originall again. Ægyptian ingenuity was more unsatisfied, contriving their bodies in sweet consistencies, to attend the return of their souls. But all was vanity,[1] feeding the winde, and folly. The Ægyptian Mummies, which *Cambyses* or time hath spared, avarice now consumeth. Mummie is become Merchandise, *Mizraim* cures wounds, and *Pharaoh* is sold for balsoms.

In vain do individuals hope for Immortality, or any patent from oblivion, in preservations below the Moon: Men have been deceived even in their flatteries above the Sun, and studied conceits to perpetuate their names in heaven. The various Cosmography of that part hath already varied the names of contrived constellations; *Nimrod* is lost in *Orion,* and *Osyris* in the Doggestarre. While we look for incorruption in the heavens, we finde they are but like the Earth; Durable in their main bodies, alterable in their parts: whereof beside Comets and new Stars, perspectives begin to tell tales. And the spots

---

[1] *Omnia vanitas et pastio venti, νομὴ ἀνέμου καὶ βόσκησις, ut olim Aquila et Symmachus.* v. Drus. *Eccles.*

that wander about the Sun, with *Phaetons* favour, would make clear conviction.

There is nothing strictly immortall, but immortality; whatever hath no beginning, may be confident of no end —which is the peculiar of that necessary essence that cannot destroy itself; And the highest strain of omnipotency, to be so powerfully constituted as not to suffer even from the power of itself: All others have a dependent being, and within the reach of destruction, But the sufficiency of Christian Immortality frustrates all earthly glory, and the quality of either state after death, makes a folly of posthumous memory. God who can only destroy our souls, and hath assured our resurrection, either of our bodies or names hath directly promised no duration. Wherein there is so much of chance, that the boldest Expectants have found unhappy frustration; and to hold long subsistence, seems but a scape in oblivion. But man is a Noble Animal, splendid in ashes, and pompous in the grave, solemnizing Nativities and Deaths with equal lustre, nor omitting Ceremonies of bravery in the infamy of his nature.

Life is a pure flame, and we live by an invisible Sun within us. A small fire sufficeth for life, great flames seemed too little after death, while men vainly affected precious pyres, and to burn like *Sardanapalus,* but the wisedom of funerall Laws found the folly of prodigall blazes, and reduced undoing fires unto the rule of sober obsequies, wherein few could be so mean as not to provide wood, pitch, a mourner, and an Urne.[1]

Five Languages secured not the Epitaph of *Gordi-*

---

[1] According to the epitaph of Rufus and Beronica, in Gruterus.

nec ex
Eorum bonis plus inventum est, quam
Quod sufficeret ad emendam pyram
Et picem quibus corpora cremarentur,
Et præfica conducta, et olla empta.

anus.[1] The man of God lives longer without a Tomb
then any by one, invisibly interred by Angels, and ad-
judged to obscurity, though not without some marks
directing humane discovery. *Enoch* and *Elias,* without
either tomb or buriall, in an anomalous state of being,
are the great Examples of perpetuity, in their long and
living memory, in strict account being still on this side
death, and having a late part yet to act upon this stage of
earth. If in the decretory term of the world we shall not
all dye but be changed, according to received translation;
the last day will make but few graves; at least quick
Resurrections will anticipate lasting Sepultures; Some
Graves will be opened before they be quite closed, and
Lazarus be no wonder. When many that feared to dye,
shall groane that they can dye but once, the dismall state
is the second and living death, when life puts despair
on the damned; when men shall wish the coverings of
Mountaines, not of Monuments, and annihilations shall
be courted.

While some have studied Monuments, others have
studiously declined them: and some have been so vainly
boisterous, that they durst not acknowledge their Graves;
wherein *Alaricus*[2] seems most subtle, who had a River
turned to hide his bones at the bottome. Even *Sylla,* that
thought himself safe in his Urne, could not prevent re-
venging tongues, and stones thrown at his Monument.
Happy are they whom privacy makes innocent, who deal
so with men in this world, that they are not afraid to meet
them in the next, who when they dye, make no com-
motion among the dead, and are not touched with that
poetical taunt of *Isaiah.*[3]

Pyramids, Arches, Obelisks, were but the irregularities
of vain-glory, and wilde enormities of ancient magnanim-

[1] In Greek, Latin, Hebrew, Egyptian, Arabic; defaced by Licinius
the emperor.
[2] Jornandes *de rebus Geticis.*
[3] Isa. xiv.

ity. But the most magnanimous resolution rests in the Christian Religion, which trampleth upon pride, and sits on the neck of ambition, humbly pursuing that infallible, perpetuity, unto which all others must diminish their diameters, and be poorly seen in Angles of contingency.[1]

Pious spirits who passed their dayes in raptures of futurity, made little more of this world, then the world that was before it, while they lay obscure in the Chaos of pre-ordination, and night of their fore-beings. And if any have been so happy as truly to understand Christian annihilation, extasis, exolution, liquefaction, transformation, the kisse of the Spouse, gustation of God, and ingression into the divine shadow, they have already had an handsome anticipation of heaven; the glory of the world is surely over, and the earth in ashes unto them.

To subsist in lasting Monuments, to live in their productions, to exist in their names and prædicament of *chymera's,* was large satisfaction unto old expectations, and made one part of their *Elyziums.* But all this is nothing in the Metaphysicks of true belief. To live indeed is to be again ourselves, which being not only an hope but an evidence in noble beleevers; 'Tis all one to lye in St. *Innocents*[2] churchyard, as in the Sands of *Ægypt:* Ready to be anything, in the ecstasie of being ever, and as content with six foot as the Mole of *Adrianus.*[3]

> ——*Tabesne cadavera solvat*
> *An rogus haud refert.*—LUCAN.

[1] *Angulus contingentiæ,* the least of Angles.
[2] In Paris, where bodies soon consume.
[3] A stately Mausoleum or sepulchral pyle, built by Adrianus in Rome, where now standeth the Castle of St. Angelo.

THE GARDEN OF CYRUS,

or,

the Quincunciall, Lozenge,
or Net-work Plantations of the Ancients,
Artificially, Naturally,
Mystically Considered.
With Sundry Observations.
1658

NICHOLAS BACON, OF GILLINGHAM, ESQUIRE.[1]

HAD I not observed that Purblind [2] men had discoursed well of Sight, and some without Issue,[3] excellently of Generation; I that was never Master of any considerable Garden, had not attempted this Subject. But the Earth is the Garden of Nature, and each fruitful Country a Paradise. Dioscorides made most of his Observations in His march about with Antonius; and Theophrastus raised his Generalities chiefly from the Field.

Besides, we write no Herbal, nor can this Volume deceive you, who have handled the Massiest[4] thereof; who know that three[5] Folios are yet too little, and how New Herbals fly from America upon us, from persevering Enquirers, and old [6] in those singularities, we expect such Descriptions. Wherein England [7] is now so exact, that it yields not to other Countries.

We pretend not to multiply Vegetable Divisions by Quincuncial and Reticulate Plants; or erect a New Phy-

---

[1] *Nicholas Bacon, of Gillingham, Esq.*] Created a baronet, Feb. 7, 1661, by Charles II. His father was the sixth son of Sir Nicholas Bacon, who was created premier baronet of England, May 22, 1611, by James I., and was the eldest son of the lord keeper of Queen Elizabeth, and half-brother of Francis, Lord Bacon, the lord keeper's youngest son by a second marriage.

[2] Plempius, Cabeus, &c.

[3] Dr. Harvey.

[4] Besleri *Hortus Eystetensis.*

[5] Bauhini *Theatrum Botanicum,* &c.

[6] My worthy friend M. Goodier, an ancient and learned Botanist.

[7] As in London and divers parts, whereof we mention none, lest we seem to omit any.

tology. The Field of Knowledge hath been so traced, it
is hard to spring any Thing new. Of old Things we
write something new, if Truth may receive addition, or
Envy will allow any Thing new; since the Ancients knew
the late Anatomical Discoveries, and Hippocrates the
Circulation.

You have been so long out of trite Learning, that it is
hard to find a Subject proper for you; and if you have met
with a Sheet upon this, we have missed our Intention. In
this Multiplicity of Writing, bye and barren Themes are
best fitted for Invention; Subjects so often discoursed
confine the Imagination, and fix our Conceptions unto
the Notions of Forewriters. Beside, such Discourses allow
Excursions, and venially admit of collateral Truths,
though at some distance from their Principals. Wherein
if we sometimes take wide liberty, we are not single, but
err by great Example.[1]

He that will illustrate the Excellency of this Order,
may easily fail upon so spruce a Subject, wherein we have
not affrighted the common reader with any other Dia-
grams, than of itself; and have industriously declined
Illustrations from rare and unknown Plants.

Your discerning Judgment, so well acquainted with
that Study, will expect herein no Mathematical Truths,
as well understanding how few Generalities and *U Finitas*
there are in Nature. How Scaliger hath found Exceptions
in most Universals of Aristotle and Theophrastus. How
botanical Maxims must have fair Allowance, and are tollerably Current, if not overballanced by Exceptions.

You have wisely ordered your Vegetable Delights, beyond the Reach of Exception. The Turks who passed
their Days in Gardens here, will have Gardens also hereafter; and delighting in Flowers on Earth, must have
Lillies and Roses in Heaven. In Garden Delights it is not
easy to hold a Mediocrity; that insinuating Pleasure is

[1] Hippocrates *de Superfœtatione, de Dentitione.*

seldom without some Extremity. The Ancients venially delighted in flourishing Gardens: Many were Florists that knew not the true Use of a Flower: And in Plinys Days none had directly treated of that Subject. Some commendably affected Plantations of venomous Vegetables; some confined their Delights unto single Plants; and Cato seemed to doat upon Cabbage; While the ingenious Delight of Tulipists, stands saluted with hard Language, even by their own Professors.[1]

That in this Garden Discourse, we range into extraneous Things, and many Parts of Art and Nature, we follow herein the Example of old and new Plantations, wherein noble Spirits contented not themselves with Trees; but by the Attendance of Aviaries, Fishponds, and all Variety of Animals, they made their Gardens the Epitome of the Earth, and some resemblance of the secular Shows of old.

That we conjoin these Parts of different Subjects[2] your Judgment will admit without impute of Incongruity; since the delightful World comes after Death, and Paradise succeeds the Grave. Since the verdant State of Things is the Symbol of the Resurrection, and to flourish in the State of Glory, we must first be sown in Corruption. Beside, the ancient Practice of Noble Persons, to conclude in Garden-Graves, and Urn themselves of old, to be wrapt up in Flowers and Garlands.

Nullum sine venia placuisse eloquium, is more sensibly understood by Writers, than by Readers; nor well apprehended by either, till Works have hanged out like Apelles his Pictures; wherein even common Eyes will find something for Emendation.

To wish all Readers of your Abilities, were unreason-

---

[1] Tulipo-mania, *Narrencruiid,* Laurenberg, Pet. Hondius *in lib. Belg.*
[2] Alluding to his joining this Tract to his Hydriotaphia, with which it was originally published.

ably to multiply the Number of Scholars beyond the Temper of these Times. But unto this ill-judging Age, we charitably desire a Portion of your Equity, Judgment, Candour, and Ingenuity; wherein you are so rich, as not to lose by diffusion. And being a flourishing branch of that noble family,[1] unto which we owe so much Observance, you are not new set, but long rooted in such Perfection; whereof having had so lasting confirmation in your worthy Conversation, constant Amity and Expression; and knowing you a serious Student in the highest *arcanas* of Nature, with much excuse we bring these low Delights, and poor Maniples to your Treasure.

Your affectionate Friend and Servant,

THOMAS BROWNE.

Norwich, May 1, 1658.

[1] Of the most worthy Sir Edmund Bacon, prime Baronet, my true and noble friend.

THE GARDEN OF CYRUS

CHAPTER I

THAT *Vulcan* gave arrows unto *Apollo* and *Diana* the fourth day after their Nativities, according to Gentile Theology, may passe for no blinde apprehension of the Creation of the Sunne and Moon, in the work of the fourth day; when the diffused light contracted into Orbes, and shooting rayes, of those Luminaries. Plainer Descriptions there are from Pagan pens, of the creatures of the fourth day; while the divine Philosopher[1] unhappily omitteth the noblest part of the third; and *Ovid* (whom many conceive to have borrowed his description from *Moses*) coldly deserting the remarkable account of the text, in three words[2] describeth this work of the third day; the vegetable creation, and first ornamentall scene of nature; the primitive food of animals, and first story of Physick, in Dietetical conservation.

For though Physick may pleade high, from that medicall act of God, in casting so deep a sleep upon our first Parent; and chirurgery[3] finde its whole art, in that one passage concerning the Rib of *Adam*, yet is there no rivality with Garden contrivance and Herbery. For if Paradise were planted the third day of the Creation, as wiser Divinity concludeth, the Nativity thereof was too early

[1] Plato in *Timæo*.
[2] *Fronde tegi silvas.*
[3] διαίρεσις, in opening the flesh; ἐξαίρεσις, in taking out the rib; σύνθεσις, in closing up the part again.

191

for Horoscopy; Gardens were before Gardiners, and but some hours after the earth.

Of deeper doubt is its Topography, and local designation, yet being the primitive garden, and without much controversie[1] seated in the East; it is more than proba-ble the first curiosity, and cultivation of plants, most flourished in those quarters. And since the Ark of *Noah* first toucht upon some mountains of *Armenia,* the plant-ing art arose again in the East, and found its revolution not far from the place of its Nativity, about the Plains of those Regions. And if *Zoroaster* were either *Cham, Chus,* or *Mizraim,* they were early proficients therein, who left (as *Pliny* delivereth,) a work of Agriculture.

However the account of the Pensill or hanging gardens of *Babylon,* if made by *Semiramis,* the third or fourth from *Nimrod,* is of no slender antiquity; which being not framed upon ordinary levell of ground, but raised upon pillars, admitting under-passages, we cannot accept as the first *Babylonian* Gardens; but a more eminent progress and advancement in that art, than any that went before it: Somewhat answering or hinting the old Opinion con-cerning Paradise itself, with many conceptions elevated, above the plane of the Earth.[2]

---

[1] For some there is from the ambiguity of the word *Mikedem,* whether *ab Oriente,* or *a principio.*

[2] In MS. SLOAN. 1847, occurs the following passage, evidently in-tended for this work:—"We are unwilling to diminish or loose the credit of Paradise, or only pass it over with [the Hebrew word for] *Eden,* though the Greek be of a later name. In this excepted, we know not whether the ancient gardens do equal those of late times, or those at present in Europe. Of the gardens of Hesperides, we know nothing singular, but some golden apples. Of Alcinous his garden, we read nothing beyond figgs, apples, and olives; if we allow it to be any more than a fiction of Homer, unhappily placed in Corfu, where the sterility of the soil makes men believe there was no such thing at all. The gardens of Adonis were so empty that they afforded proverbial expression, and the principal part thereof was empty spaces, with herbs and flowers in pots. I think we little under-stand the pensile gardens of Semiramis, which made one of the wonders of it [Babylon], wherein probably the structure exceeded

Nebuchodonosor whom some will have to be the famous *Syrian* King of *Diodorus,* beautifully repaired that City; and so magnificently built his hanging gardens,[1] that from succeeding Writers he had the honour of the first. From whence overlooking *Babylon,* and all the Region about it, he found no circumscription to the eye of his ambition, till overdelighted with the bravery of this Paradise; in his melancholy metamorphoris, he found the folly of that delight, and a proper punishment, in the contrary habitation, in wild plantations and wanderings of the fields.

The *Persian* Gallants who destroyed this Monarchy, maintained their Botanicall bravery. Unto whom we owe the very name of Paradise: wherewith we meet not in Scripture before the time of *Solomon,* and conceived originally *Persian.* The word for that disputed Garden, expressing in the Hebrew no more than a Field enclosed, which from the same Root is content to derive a garden and a Buckler.

Cyrus the elder brought up in Woods and Mountains, when time and power enabled, pursued the dictate of his education, and brought the treasures of the field into rule and circumscription. So nobly beautifying the hanging Gardens of *Babylon,* that he was also thought to be the authour thereof.

Ahasuerus (whom many conceive to have been *Artaxerxes Longi-manus*) in the Countrey and City of Flowers,[2] and in an open Garden, entertained his Princes and people, while *Vashti* more modestly treated the Ladies within the Palace thereof.

----

the plants contained in them. The excellency thereof was probably in the trees, and if the descension of the roots be equal to the height of trees, it was not [absurd] of Strebæus to think the pillars were hollow that the roots might shoot into them."

[1] Josephus.
[2] Sushan in Susiana.

But if (as some opinion) [1] King *Ahasuerus* were *Arta-xerxes Mnemon*, that found a life and reign answerable unto his great memory, our magnified *Cyrus* was his second Brother: who gave the occasion of that memorable work, and almost miraculous retreat of *Xenophon*. A person of high spirit and honour, naturally a King, though fatally prevented by the harmlesse chance of *post*-geniture: Not only a Lord of Gardens, but a man-uall planter thereof: disposing his trees, like his armies in regular ordination. So that while old *Laertes* hath found a name in Homer for pruning hedges, and clear-ing away thorns and bryars; while King *Attalus* lives for his poysonous plantations of *Aconites*, Henbane, Helle-bore, and plants hardly admitted within the walls of Paradise; While many of the ancients do poorly live in the single names of Vegetables; All stories do look upon *Cyrus* as the splendid and regular planter.

According whereto *Xenophon*[2] describeth his gallant plantation at *Sardis*, thus rendered by *Strebæus. Arbores pari intervallo sitas, rectos ordines, et omnia perpulchrè in Quincuncem directa.* Which we shall take for granted as being accordingly rendred by the most elegant of the *Latines*,[3] and by no made term, but in use before by *Varro.* That is the rows and orders so handsomely dis-posed; or five trees so set together, that a regular angu-larity, and through prospect, was left on every side. Owing this name not only unto the Quintuple number of Trees, but the figure declaring that number, which being doubled at the angle, makes up the letter X, that is the Emphatical decussation, or fundamentall figure.

Now though in some ancient and modern practice the *area* or decussated plot, might be a perfect square, an-

[1] Plutarch, in the *Life of Artaxerxes*.
[2] In *Œconomico*.
[3] *Cicero* in *Cat. Major*.

swerable to a *Tuscan* Pedestall, and the *Quinquernio* or Cinque point of a dye; wherein by diagonall lines the intersection was regular; accommodable unto Plantations of large growing Trees; and we must not deny ourselves the advantage of this order; yet shall we chiefly insist upon that of *Curtius* and *Porta*,[1] in their brief description hereof. Wherein the *decussis* is made within a longi-laterall square, with opposite angles, acute and obtuse at the intersection; and so upon progression making a *Rhombus* or Lozenge figuration, which seemeth very agreeable unto the Originall figure; Answerable where-unto we observe the decussated characters in many con-sulary Coynes, and even in those of *Constantine* and his Sons, which pretend their pattern in the Sky; the crucig-erous Ensigne carried this figure, not transversely or rec-tangularly intersected, but in a decussation, after the form of an *Andrean* or *Burgundian* cross, which answer-eth this description.

Where by the way we shall decline the old Theme, so traced by antiquity, of crosses and crucifixion: Whereof some being right, and of one single peece without trans-version or transome, do little advantage our subject. Nor shall we take in the mysticall *Tau*, or the Crosse of our blessed Saviour, which having in some descriptions an *Empedon* or crossing footstay, made not one single trans-version. And since the Learned *Lipsius* hath made some doubt even of the Crosse of *St. Andrew*, since some Martyrologicall Histories deliver his death by the general Name of a crosse, and *Hippolytus* will have him suffer by the sword; we should have enough to make out the received Crosse of that Martyr. Nor shall we urge the *labarum*, and famous Standard of *Constantine*, or make further use thereof, then as the first Letters in the Name of our Saviour Christ, in use among Christians, before

[1] Benedict. *Curtius de Hortis*. Bapt. Porta in *Villa*.

the dayes of *Constantine,* to be observed in Sepulchral
Monuments[1] of Martyrs, in the reign of *Adrian* and *Antoninus;* and to be found in the Antiquities of the Gentiles,
before the advent of Christ, as in the Medall of King
Ptolemy, signed with the same characters, and might be
the beginning of some word or name, which Antiquaries
have not hit on.

We will not revive the mysterious crosses of *Ægypt,*
with circles on their heads, in the breast of *Serapis,* and
the hands of their Geniall spirits, not unlike the character
of *Venus,* and looked on by ancient Christians, with relation unto Christ. Since however they first began, the
Ægyptians thereby expressed the processe and motion
of the spirit of the world, and the diffusion thereof upon
the Celestiall and Elementall nature; implyed by a circle
and right-lined intersection. A secret in their Telesmes
and magicall Characters among them. Though he that
considereth the plain cross[2] upon the head of the owl in
the Lateran obelisk, or the cross[3] erected upon a pitcher
diffusing streams of water into two basins, with sprinkling
branches in them, and all described upon a two-footed
Altar, as in the Hieroglyphicks of the brasen Table of
Bembus; will hardly decline all thought of Christian
signality in them.

We shall not call in the Hebrew *Tenupha,* or ceremony of their Oblations, waved by the Priest unto the
four quarters of the world, after the form of a cross; as in
the peace-offerings. And if it were clearly made out what
is remarkably delivered from the Traditions of the Rabbins, that as the Oyle was powred coronally or circularlly
upon the head of Kings, so the High-Priest was anointed
decussatively or in the form of an X; though it could not

[1] Of Marius, Alexander. *Roma Sotterranea.*

[2] Wherein the lower part is somewhat longer, as defined by Upton
de studio militari, and *Johannes de Bado Aureo, cum comment.
clariss. et doctiss. Bissæi.*

[3] Casal. *de Ritibus.* Bosio *nella Trionfante croce.*

escape a typicall thought of Christ, from mysticall considerators; yet being the conceit is Hebrew, we should rather
expect its verification from Analogy in that language,
than to confine the same unto the unconcerned Letters
of *Greece,* or make it out by the characters of *Cadmus*
or *Palamedes.*

Of this Quincuncial Ordination the Ancients practised
much, discoursed little; and the Moderns have nothing
enlarged; which he that more nearly considereth, in the
form of its square *Rhombus,* and decussation, with the
several commodities, mysteries, parallelismes, and resemblances, both in Art and Nature, shall easily discern the
elegancy of this order.

That this was in some wayes of practice in diverse and
distant Nations, hints or deliveries there are from no
slender Antiquity. In the hanging Gardens of *Babylon,*
from *Abydenus, Eusebius,* and others,[1] *Curtius* describeth
this Rule of decussation. In the memorable Garden of
Alcinous anciently conceived an orginall phancy, from
Paradise, mention there is of well-contrived order; For so
hath *Didymus* and *Eustachius* expounded the emphatical
word. *Diomedes* describing the Rural possessions of his
father, gives account in the same Language of Trees orderly planted. And *Ulysses* being a boy was promised
by his Father fourty figge-trees, and fifty[2] rows of Vines
producing all kinde of grapes.

That the Eastern Inhabitants of India, made use of
such order, even in open Plantations, is deducible from
Theophrastus; who describing the trees whereof they
made their garments, plainly delivereth that they were
planted κατ' ὄρχους, and in such order that at a distance
men would mistake them for Vineyards. The same seems
confirmed in *Greece* from a singular expression in *Aris-*

---

[1] *Decussatio ipsa jucundum ac peramœnum conspectum præbuit.*
Curt. Hortor. 1. 6.

[2] ὄρχοι, στίχοι ἀμπέλων, φυτῶν στίχος, ἡ κατὰ τάξιν φυτεία.
Phavorinus, Philoxenus.

totle[1] concerning the order of Vines, delivered by a military term representing the orders of Souldiers, which also confirmeth the antiquity of this form yet used in vineall plantations.

That the same was used in Latine plantations is plainly confirmed from the commending penne of *Varro Quintilian,* and handsome Description of *Virgil.*[2]

That the first Plantations not long after the Floud were disposed after this manner, the generality and antiquity of this order observed in Vineyards, and Wine plantations, affordeth some conjecture. And since from judicious enquiry, *Saturn,* who divided the world between his three sonnes, who beareth a Sickle in his hand, who taught the plantations of Vines, the setting, grafting of trees, and the best part of Agriculture, is discovered to be Noah, whether this early dispersed Husbandry in Vineyards had not its Originall in that Patriarch, is no such Paralogicall doubt.

And if it were clear that this was used by *Noah* after the Floud, I could easily beleeve it was in use before it; Not willing to fix to such ancient inventions no higher originall than *Noah;* nor readily conceiving those aged Heroes, whose diet was vegetable, and only, or chiefly consisted in the fruits of the earth, were much deficient in their splendid cultivations; or after the experience of fifteen hundred years, left much for future discovery in Botanicall Agriculture. Nor fully perswaded that Wine was the invention of *Noah,* that fermented Liquors, which often make themselves, so long escaped their Luxury or experience; that the first sinne of the new world was no sin of the old. That *Cain* and *Abel* were the first that offered Sacrifice; or because the Scripture is silent that *Adam* or *Isaac* offered none at all.

---

[1] συστάδας ἀμπέλων. Polit. vii.
[2] *Indulge ordinibus, nec secius omnis in unguem*
    Arboribus positis, secto via limite quadret. Georg. ii.

Whether *Abraham,* brought up in the first planting Countrey, observed not some rule hereof, when he planted a grove at *Beer-sheba;* or whether at least a like ordination were not in the Garden of *Solomon,* probability may contest. Answerably unto the wisedom of that eminent Botanologer, and orderly disposer of all his other works. Especially since this was one piece of Gallantry, wherein he pursued the specious part of felicity, according to his own description. "I made me Gardens and Orchards, and planted Trees in them of all kindes of fruits. I made me Pools of water, to water therewith the wood that bringeth forth Trees," [1] which was no ordinary plantation, if according to the Targum, or *Chaldee paraphrase,* it contained all kinds of Plants, and some fetched as far as *India;* and the extent thereof were from the wall of *Jerusalem* unto the water of *Siloah.*

And if *Jordan* were but *Jaar Eden,* that is, the River of *Eden, Genesar* but *Gansar* or the Prince of Gardens; and it could be made out, that the Plain of Jordan were watered not comparatively, but causally, and because it was the Paradise of God, as the Learned *Abramas*[2] hinteth, he was not far from the Prototype and originall of Plantations. And since even in Paradise itself, the tree of knowledge was placed in the middle of the Garden, whatever was the ambient figure, there wanted not a centre and rule of decussation. Whether the groves and sacred Plantations of Antiquity, were not thus orderly placed, either by *quaternios,* or quintuple ordinations, may favourably be doubted. For since they were so methodicall in the constitutions of their temples, as to observe the due scituation, aspect, manner, form, and order in Architectonicall relations, whether they were not as distinct in their groves and Plantations about them, in form and *species* respectively unto their Deities, is not with-

[1] Eccles. ii.
[2] *Vet. Testamenti Pharus.*

out probability of conjecture. And in their groves of the
Sunne this was a fit number, by multiplication to denote
the dayes of the year; and might Hieroglyphically speak
as much, as the mysticall *statua* of *Janus*[1] in the Language
of his fingers. And since they were so criticall in the number of his horses, the strings of his Harp, and rayes about
his head, denoting the orbes of heaven, the Seasons and
Moneths of the Yeare; witty Idolatry would hardly be flat
in other appropriations.

CHAPTER II

NOR was this only a form of practise in Plantations, but
found imitation from high Antiquity, in sundry artificiall
contrivances and manuall operations. For to omit the
position of squared stones, *cuneatim* or *wedgwise,* in the
Walls of *Roman* and *Gothick* buildings; and the *litho-
strata* or figured pavements of the ancients, which consisted not all of square stones, but were divided into
triquetrous segments, honeycombs, and sexangular figures, according to *Vitruvius;* The squared stones and
bricks, in ancient fabricks, were placed after this order.
And two above or below, conjoyned by a middle stone
or *Plinthus,* observable in the ruines of *Forum Nervæ,*
the *Mausoleum* of *Augustus,* the Pyramid of *Cestius,* and
the sculpture draughts of the larger Pyramids of Ægypt.
And therefore in the draughts of eminent fabricks, Paint-
ers do commonly imitate this order in the lines of their
description.

In the Laureat draughts of sculpture and picture, the
leaves and foliate works are commonly thus contrived,
which is but in imitation of the *Pulvinaria,* and ancient
pillow-work, observable in *Ionick* peeces, about columns,
temples and altars. To omit many other analogies, in

---

[1] Which King Numa set up, with his fingers so disposed that they
numerically denoted 365.—Pliny.

Architectonicall draughts, which art itself is founded upon[1] fives, as having its subject and most gracefull peeces divided by this number.

The Triumphal Oval, and Civicall Crowns of Laurel, Oake, and Myrtle, when fully made, were pleated after this order. And to omit the crossed Crowns of Christian Princes; what figure that was which *Anastatius* described upon the head of Leo the third; or who first brought in the Arched Crown; That of Charles the great (which seems the first remarkably closed Crown,) was framed after this[2] manner; with an intersection in the middle from the main crossing barres, and the interspaces, unto the frontal circle, continued by handsome net-work plates, much after this order. Whereon we shall not insist, because from greater Antiquity, and practice of consecration, we meet with the radiated, and starry Crown, upon the head of *Augustus,* and many succeeding Emperors. Since the Armenians and Parthians had a peculiar royall Capp; and the Grecians from *Alexander* another kinde of diadem. And even Diadems themselves were but fasciations, and handsome ligatures, about the heads of Princes; nor wholly omitted in the mitrall Crown, which common picture seems to set too upright and forward upon the head of *Aaron:* Worne[3] sometimes singly, or doubly by Princes, according to their Kingdomes; and no more to be expected from two Crowns at once upon the head of *Ptlomy.* And so easily made out when historians tell us, some bound up wounds, some hanged themselves with diadems.

The beds of the antients were corded somewhat after

---

[1] Of a structure five parts, *Fundamentum, parietes, aperturæ, Compartitio, tectum.* Leo Alberti. Five Columes, Tuscan, Dorick, Ionick, Corinthian, Compound. Five different inter-columniations, *Pycnostylos, dystylos, Systylos, Areostylos, Eustylos.* Vitruv.

[2] *Uti constat ex pergamena apud Chifflet.* in B. R. Bruxelli, & *Icon.* F. Stradae.

[3] Macc. i. xi.

this fashion: That is not directly, as ours at present, but obliquely, from side to side, and after the manner of network; whereby they strengthened the spondæ or bedsides, and spent less cord in the work: as is demonstrated by *Blancanus.*[1]

And as they lay in crossed beds, so they sat upon seeming crosselegg'd seats: in which form the noblest thereof were framed: Observable in the triumphall seats, the *sella curulis,* or *Ædyle Chayres;* in the coyns of *Cestius, Sylla,* and *Julius.* That they sat also crosselegg'd, many nobler draughts declare; and in this figure the sitting gods and goddesses are drawn in medalls and medallions. And, beside this kinde of work in Retiarie and hanging textures, in embroideries, and eminent needle-works; the like is obvious unto every eye in glass-windows. Nor only in Glassie contrivances, but also in Lattice and Stone work, conceived in the Temple of *Solomon;* wherein the windows are termed *fenestræ reticulatæ,* or lights framed like nets. And agreeable unto the Greek expression[2] concerning Christ in the Canticles,[3] looking through the nets, which ours hath rendered, "he looketh forth at the windows, shewing himself through the lattesse;" that is, partly seen and unseen, according to the visible and invisible sides of his nature. To omit the noble reticulate work, in the chapters of the pillars of *Solomon,* with Lillies, and Pomegranats upon a net-work ground; and the *Graticula* or grate through which the ashes fell in the altar of burnt offerings.

That the networks and nets of antiquity were little different in the form from ours at present, is confirmable from the nets in the hands of the Retiarie gladiators, the proper combatants with the *secutores.* To omit the ancient *Conopeion* or gnat-net, of the Ægyptians, the

[1] Aristot. *Mechan. Quæst.*
[2] δικτυωτά.
[3] Cant. ii.

inventors of that Artifice: the rushey labyrinths of *Theoc-ritus;* the nosegay nets, which hung from the head under the nostrils of Princes; and that uneasie metaphor of *Reticulum Jecoris,* which some expound the lobe, we the caule above the liver. As for that famous net-work of *Vulcan,* which inclosed *Mars* and *Venus,* and caused that[1] unextinguishable laugh in heaven; since the gods themselves could not discern it, we shall not prie into it; Although why *Vulcan* bound them, *Neptune* loosed them, and *Apollo* should first discover them, might afford no vulgar mythologie. Heralds have not omitted this order or imitation thereof, while they Symbollically adorn their Scuchions with Mascles, Fusils, and Saltyrs, and while they dispose the figures of Ermins, and vaired coats in this Quincuncial method.[2]

The same is not forgot by Lapidaries, while they cut their gemms pyramidally, or by æquicrural triangles. Perspective pictures, in their Base, Horison, and lines of distances, cannot escape these Rhomboidall decus-sations. Sculptors in their strongest shadows, after this order do draw their double Haches. And the very *Ameri-cans* do naturally fall upon it, in their neat and curious textures, which is also observed in the elegant artifices of *Europe.* But this is no law unto the woof of the neat *Retiarie* Spider, which seems to weave without trans-version, and by the union of right lines to make out a continued surface, which is beyond the common art of Textury, and may still nettle *Minerva,*[3] the goddesse of that mystery. And he that shall hatch the little seeds, either found in small webs, or white round Egges, carried under the bellies of some Spiders, and behold how at their first production in boxes, they will presently fill the

---

[1] Ἀσβεστος δ' ἀρ' ἐνῶρτο γέλως. Hom.
[2] *De armis Scaccatis, masculatis, invectis, fuselatis, vide* Spelm., *Aspilog.; et* Upton *cum erudit.* Byssaeo.
[3] As in the contention between Minerva and Arachne.

same with their webbs, may observe the early, and un-taught finger of nature, and how they are natively pro-vided with a stock, sufficient for such Texture.

The Rurall charm against *Dodder, Tetter,* and stran-gling weeds, was contrived after this order, while they placed a chalked Tile at the four corners, and one in the middle of their fields, which though ridiculous in the intention, was rational in the contrivance, and a good way to diffuse the magick through all parts of the *Area.*

Somewhat after this manner they ordered the little stones in the old game of *Pentalithismus,* or casting up five stones to catch them on the back of their hand. And with some resemblance hereof, the *Proci* or Prodi-gall Paramours disposed their men, when they played at *Penelope.*[1] For being themselves an hundred and eight, they set fifty-four stones on either sides, and one in the middle, which they called Penelope, which he that hit was master of the game.

In Chesse-boards and Tables we yet find Pyramids and Squares. I wish we had their true and ancient descrip-tion, farre different from ours, or the *Chet mat* of the *Persians,* which might continue some elegant remark-ables, as being an invention as High as *Hermes* the Secretary of *Osyris,* figuring the whole world, the motion of the Planets, with Eclipses of sunne and Moon.

Physicians are not without the use of this decussation in severall operations, in ligatures and union of dissolved continuities. Mechanicks make use hereof in forcipall Or-gans, and Instruments of Incision; wherein who can but magnifie the power of decussation, inservient to contrary ends, solution and consolidation, union, and division, illustrable from *Aristotle* in the old *Nucifragium* or nut-cracker, and the Instruments of Evulsion, compression or Incision; which consisting of two *Vectes* or armes, con-

---

[1] In Eustathius, his Comment upon Homer.

verted towards each other, the Innitency[1] and stresse being made upon the *hypomochlion,* or fulciment[2] in the decussation, the greater compression is made by the union of two impulsors.

The Romane *Battalia*[3] was ordered after this manner, whereof as sufficiently known *Virgil* hath left but an hint, and obscure intimation. For thus were the maniples and cohorts of the *Hastati, principes,* and *Triarii* placed in their bodies, wherein consisted the strength of the Roman battle. By this Ordination they readily fell into each other; the *Hastati* being pressed, handsomely retired into the intervalls of the *Principes,* these into that of the *Triarii,* which making as it were a new body, might joyntly renew the battle, wherein consisted the secret of their successes. And therefore it was remarkably[4] singular in the battle of *Africa,* that *Scipio,* fearing a rout from the Elephants of the Enemy, left not the *Principes* in their alternate distances, whereby the Elephants, passing the vacuities of the *Hastati,* might have run upon them, but drew his battle into right order, and leaving the passages bare, defeated the mischief intended by the Elephants. Out of this figure were made two remarkable forms of Battle, the *Cuneus* and *Forceps,* or the sheare and wedge battles, each made of half a *Rhombus,* and but differenced by position. The wedge invented to break or work into a body, the *forceps* to environ and defeat the power thereof, composed out of the selectest Souldiery, and disposed into the form of an V, wherein receiving the wedge, it inclosed it on both sides. After this form the famous Nasses[5] ordered his battle against the Franks,

[1] His own synonym for "stress."
[2] *Fulcrum.*
[3] In the disposure of the Legions in the Wars of the Republike, before the division of the Legion into ten Cohorts by the Emperours. Salmas. in his epistle *à Mounsieur de Peyresc. et de Re Militari Romanorum.*
[4] Polybius; Appianus.
[5] Agathius; Ammianus.

and by this figure the Almans were enclosed, and cut in peeces.

The *Rhombus* or Lozenge-figure so visible in this order, was also a remarkable form of battle in the *Grecian* Cavalry,[1] observed by the *Thessalians,* and *Philip* king of *Macedon,* and frequently by the *Parthians,* As being most ready to turn every way, and best to be commanded, as having its ductors, or Commanders at each Angle.

The *Macedonian Phalanx* (a long time thought invincible), consisted of a long square. For though they might be sixteen in Rank and file, yet when they shut close, so that the sixt pike advanced before the first, though the number might be square, the figure was oblong, answerable unto the Quincuncial quadrate of *Curtius.* According to this square, *Thucydides* delivers, the *Athenians* disposed their battle against the *Lacedemonians,* brickwise,[2] and by the same word the Learned *Guellius* expoundeth the quadrate of *Virgil,*[3] after the form of a brick or tile.

And as the first station and position of trees, so was the first habitation of men, not in round Cities, as of later foundation; For the form of *Babylon* the first City was square, and so shall also be the last, according to the description of the holy City in the Apocalyps. The famous pillars of *Seth,* before the floud, had also the like foundation, if they were but *antediluvian* Obelisks, and such as *Cham* and his *Ægyptian* race imitated after the Floud.

But *Nineveh* which Authours acknowledge to have exceeded *Babylon,* was of a longilaterall figure,[4] ninety-five Furlongs broad, and an hundred and fifty long, and so making about sixty miles in circuit, which is the measure of three dayes journey, according unto military marches, or castrensial mansions. So that if *Jonas* entred

[1] Ælian. *Tact.*
[2] ἐν πλαισίω.
[3] *Secto via limite quadret. Comment.* in Virgil.
[4] *Diod. Sic.*

at the narrower side, he found enough for one dayes
walk to attain the heart of the City, to make his Procla-
mation. And if we imagine a City extending from *Ware*
to *London,* the expression will be moderate of six score
thousand Infants, although we allow vacuities, fields, and
intervals of habitation, as there needs must be when the
monument of *Ninus* took up no lesse then ten furlongs.

And, though none of the seven wonders, yet a noble
peece of Antiquity, and made by a Copy exceeding all
the rest, had its principall parts disposed after this manner, that is, the Labyrinth of *Crete,* built upon a long
quadrate, containing five large squares communicating
by right inflexions, terminating in the centre of the middle square, and lodging of the *Minotaur,* if we conform
unto the description of the elegant medall thereof in
Agostino.[1] And though in many accounts we reckon grosly
by the square, yet is that very often to be accepted as
a long-sided quadrate, which was the figure of the Ark
of the Covenant, the table of the Shew-bread, and the
stone wherein the names of the twelve Tribes were en-
graved, that is, three in a row, naturally making a longi-
laterall Figure, the perfect quadrate being made by nine.

What figure the stones themselves maintained, tradition and Scripture are silent, yet Lapidaries in precious
stones affect a Table or long square, and in such proportion, that the two laterall and also the three inferiour
Tables are equall unto the superiour; and the angles
of the laterall Tables contain and constitute the *hypo-
thenusæ,* or broader sides subtending.

That the Tables of the Law were of this figure, general
imitation and tradition hath confirmed; yet are we unwilling to load the shoulders of *Moses* with such massie
stones, as some pictures lay upon them, since 'tis plainly
delivered that he came down with them in his hand;
since the word strictly taken implies no such massie hew-

[1] Antonio Agostino *delle Medaglie.*

ing, but cutting, and fashioning of them into shape and surface; since some will have them Emeralds, and if they were made of the materials of Mount *Sina,* not improbable that they were marble: Since the words were not many, the letters short of seven hundred, and the Tables, written on both sides, required no such capacity.

The beds of the Ancients were different from ours at present, which are almost square, being framed oblong, and about a double unto their breadth; not much unlike the *area,* or bed of this Quincuncial quadrate. The single beds of *Greece* were six foot[1] and a little more in length, three in breadth; the Giant-like bed of *Og,* which had four cubits of bredth, nine and a half in length, varied not much from this proportion. The Funeral bed of King *Cheops,* in the greater Pyramid, which holds seven in length, and four feet in bredth, had no great difformity from this measure; And whatsoever were the bredth, the length could hardly be lesse, of the tyrannical bed of *Procrustes,* since in a shorter measure he had not been fitted with persons for his cruelty of extension. But the old sepulchral bed, or *Amazonian* Tomb,[2] in the market place of *Megara,* was in the form of a Lozenge; readily made out by the composure of the body. For the arms not lying fasciated or wrapt up after the *Grecian* manner, but in a middle distention, the including lines will strictly make out that figure.

CHAPTER III

Now although this elegant ordination of vegetables, hath found coincidence or imitation in sundry works of Art, yet is it not also destitute of naturall examples, and, though overlooked by all, was elegantly observable, in severall works of nature.

[1] Aristot. *Mechan.*
[2] Plut. *in vit. Thes.*

Could we satisfie ourselves in the position of the lights above, or discover the wisedom of that order so invariably maintained in the fixed Stars of heaven; Could we have any light, why the stellary part of the first masse, separated into this order, that the Girdle of Orion should ever maintain its line, and the two Starres in *Charles's* Wain never leave pointing at the Pole-starre, we might abate the *Pythagoricall* Musick of the Spheres, the seven-fold Pipe of *Pan;* and the strange Cryptography of *Gaffarel* in his starrie Booke of Heaven.

But not to look so high as Heaven or the single Quin-cunx of the *Hyades* upon the neck of *Taurus,* the Tri-angle, and remarkable *Crusero* about the foot of the *Centaur;* observable rudiments there are hereof in sub-terraneous concretions, and bodies in the Earth; in the *Gypsum* or *Taleum Rhomboides,* in the Favaginites or honey-comb-stone, in the *Asteria* and *Astroites,* and in the crucigerous stone of *S. Iago* of *Gallicia.*

The same is observably effected in the *Julus, catkins,* or pendulous excrescencies of severall Trees, of Wallnuts, Alders, and Hazels, which hanging all the Winter, and maintaining their Net-worke close, by the expansion thereof are the early foretellers of the Spring discover-able also in long Pepper, and elegantly in the *Julus* of *Calamus Aromaticus,* so plentifully growing with us, in the first Palmes of Willowes, and in the Flowers of Sycamore, *Petasites, Asphodelus,* and *Blattaria,* before explication. After such order stand the flowery Branches in our best spread *Verbascum,* and the seeds about the spicous head or torch of *Tapsas Barbatus,* in as fair a regularity as the circular and wreathed order will admit, which advanceth one side of the square, and makes the same Rhomboidall.

In the squamous heads of *Scabious, Knapweed,* and the elegant *Jacea Pinea,* and in the Scaly composure of the *Oak-Rose,*[1] which some years most aboundeth. After this order hath Nature planted the Leaves in the Head of the common and prickled Artichoak; wherein the black and shining Flies do shelter themselves, when they retire from the purple Flower about it; The same is also found in the pricks, sockets, and impressions of the seeds, in the pulp or bottome thereof; wherein do elegantly stick the Fathers of their Mother.[2] To omit the Quincunciall Specks on the top of the Miscle-berry, especially that which grows upon the *Tilia,* or Lime-Tree. And the remarkable disposure of those yellow fringes about the purple Pestill of *Aaron,* and elegant clusters of Dragons, so peculiarly secured by nature, with an *umbrella* or skreening Leaf about them.

The Spongy leaves of some Sea-wracks, Fucus, Oaks, in their several kindes, found about the Shoar,[3] with ejectments of the Sea, are over-wrought with Network elegantly containing this order, which plainly declareth the naturality of this texture; And how the needle of nature delighteth to work, even in low and doubtful vegetations.

The *Arbustetum* or Thicket on the head of the Teazell, may be observed in this order: And he that considereth that fabrick so regularly palisadoed, and stemm'd with flowers of the royall colour; in the house of the solitary maggot, may finde the Seraglio of *Solomon.* And contemplating the calicular shafts, and uncous disposure of their extremities, so accommodable unto the office of abstersion, not condemne as wholly improbable the conceit of those who accept it, for the herbe *Borith.*[4] Where

---

[1] *Capitula squammata Quercum,* Bauhini, whereof though he saith *perraro reperiuntur bis tantum invenimus,* yet we finde them commonly with us and in great numbers.

[2] Anthol. *Græc. Inter Epigrammata.* γριφώδη ἐνδὸν ἐμῶν, λαγόνων μητρὸς ἔχω πατέρα.

[3] Especially the *porus cervinus, Imperati, Sporosa,* or Alga πλατύκερως. Bauhini.

[4] Jer. ii. 22.

by the way, we could with much inquiry never discover any transfiguration, in this abstemious insect, although we have kept them long in their proper houses, and boxes. Where some wrapt up in their webbs, have lived upon their own bowels, from September unto July.

In such a grove doe walke the little creepers about the head of the burre. And such an order is observed in the aculeous prickly plantation, upon the heads of several common thistles, remarkably in the notable palisados about the flower of the milk Thistle; and he that inquireth into the little bottome of the globe-thistle, may finde that gallant bush arise from a scalpe of like disposure.

The white umbrella or medicall bush of Elder, is an Epitome of this order: arising from five main stemms Quincuncially disposed, and tollerably maintained in their subdivisions. To omit the lower observations in the seminal spike of Mercurie wild, and plantane.

Thus hath nature ranged the flowers of Santfoyne, and French honeysuckle; and somewhat after this manner hath ordered the bush in *Jupiters* beard, or houseleek; which old superstition set on the tops of houses, as a defensative against lightning, and thunder. The like in Fenny Seagreen, or the water Souldier,[1] which, though a military name from Greece, makes out the Roman order.

A like ordination there is in the favaginous Sockets, and Lozenge seeds of the noble flower of the Sunne. Wherein in Lozenge figured boxes nature shuts up the seeds, and balsame which is about them.

But the firre and Pine tree from their fruits doe naturally dictate this position. The Rhomboidall protuberances in Pine apples maintaining this Quincuncial order unto each other, and each Rhombus in it selfe. Thus are also disposed the triangular foliations, in the conical fruit

[1] *Stratiotes.*

of the firre tree orderly shadowing and protecting the winged seeds below them.

The like so often occurreth to the curiosity of observers, especially in spicated seeds and flowers, that we shall not need to take in the single Quincunx of *Fuchsius* in the growth of the male[1] fearn, the seedy disposure of *Gramen Ischemon,* and the trunk or neat Reticulate work in the codde of the Sachell palme.

For even in very many round stalk plants, the leaves are set after a Quintuple ordination, the first leaf answering the fifth, in lateral disposition. Wherein the leaves successively rounding the stalke, in foure at the furthest the compass is absolved, and the fifth leafe or sprout, returns to the position of the other fifth before it; as in accounting upward is often observable in furze, pellitorye, Ragweed, the sproutes of Oaks, and thorns, upon pollards, and very remarkably in the regular disposure of the rugged excrescencies in the yearly shoots of the Pine.

But in square stalked plants, the leaves stand respectively unto each other, either in crosse or decussation to those above or below them, arising at crosse positions; whereby they shadow not each other, and better resist the force of winds, which in a parallel situation, and upon square stalkes would more forcibly bear upon them.

And to omit, how leaves and sprouts which compasse not the stalk, are often set in a Rhomboides, and making long and short Diagonals, doe stand like the leggs of Quadrupeds when they goe: Nor to urge the thwart enclosure and furdling of flowers, and blossomes, before explications, as in the multiplyed leaves of pionie; and the *Chiasmus* in five-leaved flowers, while one lies wrapt about the staminous beards, the other foure obliquely shutting and closing upon each other; and how even

[1] Orig. Masle.

flowers which consist of foure leaves, stand not ordinarily in three and one, but two, and two crossewise, unto the Stylus; even the Autumnal budds, which awaite the re-turne of the sun, doe after the winter solstice multiply their calicular leaves, making little Rhombuses, and net-work figures, as in the Sycamore and lilac.

The like is discoverable in the original production of plants, which first putting forth two leaves, those which succeed, bear not over each other, but shoot obliquely or crossewise, untill the stalke appeareth; which sendeth not forth its first leaves without all order unto them; and he that from hence can discover in what position the two first leaves did arise, is no ordinary observator.

Where by the way, he that observeth the rudimental spring of seeds, shall finde strict rule, although not after this order. How little is required unto effectual genera-tion, and in what diminutives the plastick principle lodg-eth, is exemplified in seeds, wherein the greater mass affords so little comproduction. In Beanes the leaf and root sprout from the Germen, the main sides split, and lye by, and in some pull'd up near the time of blooming, we have found the pulpous sides intire or little wasted. In Acorns the nebb dilating splitteth the two sides, which sometimes lye whole, when the Oak is sprouted two hand-fuls. In Lupins these pulpy sides do sometimes arise with the stalk in the resemblance of two fat leaves. Wheat and Rye will grow up, if after they have shot some tender Roots, the adhering pulp be taken from them. Beanes will prosper though a part be cut away, and so much set as sufficeth to contain and keep the Germen close. From this superfluous pulp in unkindely, and wet years, may arise that multiplicity of little insects, which infest the Roots and Sprouts of tender Graines and pulses.

In the little nebbe or fructifying principle, the motion is regular, and not transvertible, as to make that ever the leaf, which nature intended the root; observable from their conversion, until they attain their right position, if seeds be set inversedly.

In vain we expect the production of plants from different parts of the seed, from the same *corculum* or little original proceed both germinations; and in the power of this slender particle lye many Roots, that though the same be pull'd away, the generative particle will renew them again, and proceed to a perfect plant; And malt may be observed to grow, though the Cummes be fallen from it.

The seminall nebbe hath a defined and single place, and not extended unto both extremes. And therefore many too vulgarly conceive that Barley and Oats grow at both ends; For they arise from one *punctilio* or generative nebbe, and the speare sliding under the husk, first appeareth nigh the toppe. But in Wheat and Rye being bare the sprouts are seen together. If Barley unhulled would grow, both would appear at once. But in this and Oat-meal the nebbe is broken away, which makes them the milder food, and less apt to raise fermentation in Decoctions.

Men taking notice of what is outwardly visible, conceive a sensible priority in the Root. But as they begin from one part, so they seem to start and set out upon one signall of nature. In Beanes yet soft, in Pease while they adhere unto the Cod, the rudimentall Leafe and Root are discoverable. In the seeds of Rocket and Mustard, sprouting in Glasses of water, when the one is manifest the other is also perceptible. In muddy waters apt to breed Duckweed, and Periwinkles, if the first and rudimentall stroaks of Duckweed be observed, the Leaves and Root anticipate not each other. But in the Date-stone the first sprout is neither root nor leaf distinctly, but both together; For the Germination being to passe through the

narrow Navell and hole about the midst of the stone,
the generative germ is faine to enlengthen itself, and
shooting out about an inch, at that distance divideth
into the ascending and descending portion.

And though it be generally thought that Seeds will
root at the end, where they adhere to their Originals,
and observable it is that the nebbe sets most often next
the stalk, as in Grains, Pulses, and most small Seeds, yet
is it hardly made out in many greater plants. For in
Acornes, Almonds, Pistachios, Wallnuts, and accuminated
shells, the germ puts forth at the remotest part of the
pulp. And therefore to set Seeds in that posture, wherein
the Leaf and Roots may shoot right without contortion,
or forced circumvolution, which might render them
strongly rooted, and straighter, were a Criticisme in Agriculture. And nature seems to have made some provision
hereof in many from their figure, that as they fall from
the tree they may lye in Positions agreeable to such
advantages.

Besides the open and visible Testicles of plants, the
seminall powers lie in great part invisible, while the Sun
findes polypody in stone-wals, the little stinging Nettle,
and night-shade in barren sandy High-wayes, *Scurvy-
grasse* in *Greeneland,* and unknown plants in earth
brought from remote Countries. Beside the known longevity of some Trees, what is the most lasting herb, or
seed, seems not easily determinable. Mandrakes upon
known account have lived near an hundred yeares. Seeds
found in Wilde-Fowls Gizards have sprouted in the earth.
The Seeds of Marjorane and *stramonium* carelessly kept,
have grown after seven years. Even in Garden-plots long
fallow, and digged up, the seeds of *Blattaria* and yellow
henbane, after twelve years burial have produced themselves again.

That bodies are first spirits *Paracelsus* could affirm,

which in the maturation of Seeds and fruits, seem obscurely implied by *Aristotle,*[1] when he delivereth, that the spirituous parts are converted into water, and the water into earth, and attested by observation in the maturative progresse of Seeds, wherein at first may be discerned a flatuous distension of the husk, afterwards a thin liquor, which longer time digesteth into a pulp or kernell observable in Almonds and large Nuts. And some way answered in the progressionall perfection of animal semination, in its spermaticall maturation, from crude pubescency unto perfection. And even that seeds themselves in their rudimentall discoveries, appear in foliaceous surcles, or sprouts within their coverings, in a diaphanous gellie, before deeper incrassation, is also visibly verified in Cherries, Acorns, Plums.

From seminall considerations, either in reference unto one mother, or distinction from animall production, the holy Scripture describeth the vegetable creation; and while it divideth plants but into Herb and Tree, though it seemeth to make but an accidental division, from magnitude, it tacitely containeth the naturall distinction of vegetables, observed by Herbalists, and comprehending the four kinds. For since the most naturall distinction is made from the production of leaf or stalk, and plants after the two first seminall leaves, do either proceed to send forth more leaves, or a stalk, and the folious and stalky emission distinguisheth herbs and trees; in a large acception it compriseth all vegetables: for the *frutex* and *suffrute* are under the progression of tress, and stand Authentically differenced, but from the accidents of the stalk.

The Æquivocall production of things under undiscerned principles, makes a large part of generation, though they seem to hold a wide univocacy in their set and certain Originals, while almost every plant breeds its

[1] *In Met. cum* Cabeo.

peculiar insect, most a Butterfly, moth or fly, wherein the Oak seems to contain the largest seminality, while Julus, Oak, Apple, dill, woolly tuft, foraminous roundles upon the leaf, and grapes underground make a Fly with some difference. The great variety of Flyes lyes in the variety of their originals, in the seeds of Caterpillars or Cankers their lyeth not only a Butterfly or Moth, but if they be sterill or untimely cast, their production is often a Fly, which we have also observed from corrupted and mouldred Egges both of Hens and Fishes; to omit the generation of Bees out of the bodies of dead Heifers, or what is strange yet well attested, the production of Eeles in the backs of living Cods and Perches.[1]

The exiguity and smallnesse of some seed extending to large productions is one of the magnalities of nature, somewhat illustrating the work of the Creation, and vast production from nothing. The true[2] seeds of Cypresse and Rampions are indistinguishable by old eyes. Of the seeds of Tobacco a thousand make not one grain. The disputed seeds of Hartstongue and Maidenhair, require a great number. From such undiscernable seminalities arise spontaneous productions. He that would discern the rudimentall stroak of a plant, may behold it in the originall of Duckweed, at the bignesse of a pins point, from convenient water in glasses, wherein a watchfull eye may also discover the puncticular Originals of Periwincles and Gnats.

That seeds of some Plants are lesse than any animals, seems of no clear decision; That the biggest of Vegetables exceedeth the biggest of Animals, in full bulk, and all dimensions, admits exception in the Whale, which in length and above ground measure, will also contend with tall Oakes. That the richest odour of plants, surpasseth that of Animals, may seem of some doubt, since animall-

---

[1] Schoneveldus *de Pisc.*
[2] *Doctissim.* Laurenburg. *Hort.*

musk, seems to excell the vegetable, and we finde so noble a scent in the Tulip-fly, and Goat-Beetle.[1]

Now whether seminall nebbes hold any sure proportion unto seminall enclosures, why the form of the germe doth not answer the figure of the enclosing pulp, why the nebbe is seated upon the solid, and not the channeld side of the seed as in grains, why since we often meet with two yolks in one shell, and sometimes one egge within another, we do not oftener meet with two nebbes in one distinct seed: why since the Egges of a Hen laid at one course, do commonly out-weigh the bird, and some moths, coming out of their cases, without assistance of food, will lay so many egges as to out-weigh their bodies, trees rarely bear their fruit, in that gravity or proportion: Whether in the germination of seeds according to the *Hippocrates,* the lighter part ascendeth, and maketh the sprout, the heaviest tending downward frameth the root; Since we observe that the first shoot of seeds in water, will sink or bow down at the upper and leafing end: Whether it be not more rational Epicurisme to contrive whole dishes out of the nebbes and spirited particles of plants, then from the Gallatures and treddles of Egges; since that part is found to hold no seminal share Oval Generation, are quæries which might enlarge but must conclude this digression.

And though not in this order, yet now nature delighteth in this number, and what consent and coordination there is in the leaves and parts of flowers, it cannot escape our observation in no small number of plants. For the calicular or supporting and closing leaves, do answer the number of the flowers, especially in such as exceed not the number of Swallows Egges; as in Violets, Stichwort, Blossomes, and flowers of one leaf have often five divisions, answered by a like number of calicular leaves;

[1] The long and tender green *Capricornus,* rarely found, we could never meet with but two.

as *Gentianella, Convolvulus,* Bell-flowers. In many the flowers, blades, or staminous shootes and leaves are all equally five, as in cockle, mullein and *Blattaria;* wherein the flowers before explication are pentagonally wrapped up, with some resemblance of the *blatta* or moth from whence it hath its name: But the contrivance of nature is singular in the opening and shutting of Bindeweeds, performed by five inflexures, distinguishable by pyramidall figures, and also different colours.

The rose at first is thought to have been of five leaves, as it yet groweth wilde among us; but in the most luxuriant, the calicular leaves do still maintain that number. But nothing is more admired than the five Brethren of the Rose,[1] and the strange disposure of the Appendices or Beards, in the calicular leaves thereof, which in despair of resolution is tolerably salved from this contrivance, best ordered and suited for the free closure of them before explication. For those two which are smooth, and of no beard are contrived to lye undermost, as without prominent parts, and fit to be smoothly covered; the other two which are beset with Beards on either side, stand outward and uncovered, but the fifth or half-bearded leaf is covered on the bare side but on the open side stands free, and bearded like the other.

Besides a large number of leaves have five divisions, and may be circumscribed by a *pentagon* or figure of five Angles, made by right lines from the extremity of their leaves, as in Maple, Vine, Figge-tree: But five-leaved flowers are commonly disposed circularly about the *Stylus;* according to the higher Geometry of nature dividing a circle by five *radii, wh*ich concurre not to make Diameters, as in Quadrilaterall and sexangular Intersections.

---

[1] Alluding to a rustic rhyme:—

> On a summer's day, in sultry weather,
> Five brethren were born together,
> Two had beards, and two had none,
> And the other had but half a one.—*Jeff.*

Now the number of five is remarkable in every circle, not only as the first sphærical number, but the measure of sphærical motion. For sphærical bodies move by fives, and every globular figure placed upon a plane, in direct volutation, returns to the first point of contaction in the fifth touch, accounting by the Axes of the Diameters or Cardinall points of the four quarters thereof. And before it arriveth unto the same point again, it maketh five circles equall unto itself, in each progresse from those quarters absolving an equall circle.

By the same number doth nature divide the circle of the Sea-Starre, and in that order and number disposeth these elegant Semi-Circles, or dentall sockets and egges in the Sea Hedgehogge. And no mean Observations hereof there is in the Mathematicks of the neatest Retiary Spider, which concluding in fourty-four Circles, from five Semidiameters beginneth that elegant texture.

And after this manner both lay the foundation of the circular branches of the Oak, which being five-cornered, in the tender annual sprouts, and manifesting upon incision the signature of a Starre, is after made circular, and swel'd into a round body: Which practice of nature is become a point of art, and makes two Problemes in Euclide.[1] But the Bryar which sends forth shoots and prickles from its angles, maintain its pentagonall figure, and the unobserved signature of a handsome porch within it. To omit the five small buttons dividing the Circle of the Ivy-berry, and the five characters in the Winter stalk of the Walnut, with many other Observables, which cannot escape the eyes of signal discerners; Such as know where to find, *Ajax* his name in *Gallitricum*, or *Aarons* Mitre in Henbane.

Quincuncial forms and ordinations are also observable in animal figurations. For to omit the *hioides* or throatbone of animals, the *furcula* or *merry-thought* in birds,

[1] *Elem.* lib. 4.

which supporteth the *scapulæ,* affording a passage for the
winde-pipe and the gullet, the wings of Flyes, and disposure of their legges in their first formation from mag-
gots, and the position of their horns, wings and legges,
in their *Aurelian* cases and swadling clouts: The back
of the *Cimex Arboreus,* found often upon Trees and
lesser plants, doth elegantly discover the *Burgundian*
decussation; And the like is observable in the belly of
the *Notonecton,* or water-Beetle, which swimmeth on its
back, and the handsome *Rhombusses* of the Sea-poult
or weazel on either side the Spine.

The sexangular Cels in the Honeycombs of Bees, are
disposed after this order, much there is not of wonder
in the confused Houses of Pismires, though much in
their busie life and actions, more in the edificial Pal-
aces of Bees and Monarchical spirits; who make their
combs six-corner'd, declining a circle, whereof many
stand not close together, and compleatly fill the *area* of
the place; But rather affecting a six-sided figure, whereby
every cell affords a common side unto six more, and also
a fit receptacle for the Bee itself, which gathering into
a Cylindrical Figure, aptly enters its sexangular house,
more nearly approaching a circular Figure, then either
doth the Square or Triangle. And the Combes themselves so regularly contrived, that their mutual intersections make three Lozenges at the bottome of every Cell;
which severally regarded make three Rows of neat Rhomboidall Figures, connected at the angles, and so continue
three several chains throughout the whole comb.

As for the *Favago,* found commonly on the Sea shoar,
though named from an honey comb, it but rudely makes
out the resemblance, and better agrees with the round
Cels of humble Bees. He that would exactly discern the
shape of a Bees mouth, needs observing eyes, and good
augmenting glasses; wherein is discoverable one of the
neatest peeces in nature, and he must have a more pierc-

ing eye than mine, who finds out the shape of Buls heads, in the guts of Drones pressed out behinde, according to the experiment of *Gomesius;*[1] wherein notwithstanding there seemeth somewhat which might a pliant fancy to credulity of similitude.

A resemblance hereof there is in the orderly and rarely disposed Cels made by Flyes and Insects, which we have often found fastened about small sprigs, and in those cottonary and woolly pillows, which sometimes we meet with fastened unto Leaves, there is included an elegant Net-work Texture, out of which come many small Flies. And some resemblance there is of this order in the Egges of some Butterflies and moths, as they stick upon leaves, and other substances; which being dropped from be-hinde, nor directed by the eye, doth neatly declare how nature Geometrizeth and observeth order in all things.

A like correspondency in figure is found in the skins and outward teguments of animals, whereof a regardable part are beautiful by this texture. As the backs of several Snakes and Serpents, elegantly remarkable in the *Aspis,* and the Dart-snake, in the *Chiasmus an*d larger decussations upon the back of the Rattle-snake, and in the close and finer texture of the *mater formicarum,* or snake that delights in Ant-hils; whereby upon approach of outward injuries, they can raise a thicker Phalanx on their backs, and handsomely contrive themselves into all kindes of flexures; Whereas their bellies are commonly covered with smooth semicircular divisions, as best accommodable unto their quick and gliding motion.

This way is followed by nature in the peculiar and re-markable tayl of the Bever, wherein the scaly particles are disposed, somewhat after this order, which is the plainest resolution of the wonder of *Bellonius,* while he saith, with incredible Artifice hath Nature framed the tayl or *Oar* of the Bever: where by the way we can-

[1] Gom. *de Sale.*

not but wish a model of their houses, so much extolled by some Describers: wherein since they are so bold as to venture upon three stages, we might examine their Artifice in the contignations, the rule and order in the compartitions; or whether that magnified structure be any more than a rude rectangular pyle or meer hovell-building.

Thus works the hand of nature in the feathery planta-tion about birds. Observable in the skins of the breast,[1] legs, and Pinions of Turkies, Geese, and Ducks, and the Oars or finny feet of Water-Fowl: and such a naturall Net is the scaly covering of Fishes, of Mullets, Carps, Tenches, &c., even in such as are excoriable and consist of smaller scales, as Bretts, soals, and Flounders. The like Reticulate grain is observable in some *Russia* leather. To omit the ruder Figures of the ostracion, the triangular or cunny-fish, or the pricks of the Sea-Porcupine.

The same is also observable in some part of the skin of man, in habits of neat texture, and therefore not un-aptly compared unto a Net: We shall not affirm that from such grounds, the Ægyptian Embalmers imitated this texture, yet in their linnen folds the same is still observ-able among their neatest Mummies, in the figures of *Isis* and *Osyris,* and the Tutelary spirits in the Bembine Table. Nor is it to be overlooked how Orus, the Hiero-glyphick of the world, is described in a Net-work cover-ing, from the shoulder to the foot. And (not to enlarge upon the cruciated character of *Trismegistus,* or handed crosses, so often occurring in the Needles of Pharoah, and Obelisks of Antiquity) the *Statuæ Isiacæ,* Teraphims, and little Idols, found about the Mummies, do make a decus-sation of *Jacob's* Crosse, with their armes, like that on the head of *Ephraim* and *Manasses,* and this *decussis* is also graphically described between them.

[1] Elegantly conspicuous on the inside of the stripped skins of the Dive-Fowl, of Cormorant, Goshonder, Weasell, Loon, &c.

This Reticulate or Net-work was also considerable in the inward parts of man, not only from the first *subtegmen* or warp of his formation, but in the netty *fibres* of the veins and vessels of life; wherein according to common Anatomy the right and transverse *fibres* are decussated, by the oblique *fibres;* and so must frame a Reticulate and Quincuncial Figure by their Obliquations, Emphatically extending that Elegant expression of Scripture "Thou hast curiously embroydered me," thou hast wrought me up after the finest way of Texture, and as it were with a Needle.

Nor is the same observable only in some parts, but in the whole body of man, which upon the extension of arms and legges, doth make out a square, whose intersection is at the genitals. To omit the fantastical Quincunx in *Plato* of the first hermaphrodite or double man, united at the Loynes, which *Jupiter* after divided.

A rudimental resemblance hereof there is in the cruciated and rugged folds of the *Reticulum,* or Net-like Ventricle of ruminating horned animals, which is the second in order, and culinarily called the Honey-comb. For many divisions there are in the stomack of severall animals: what number they maintain in the *Scarus* and ruminating Fish, common description, or our own experiment hath made no discovery. But in the Ventricle of *Porpuses* there are three divisions. In many Birds a crop, Gizzard, and little receptacle before it; but in Cornigerous animals, which chew the cudd, there are no less than four of distinct position and office.

The *Reticulum* by these crossed cels, makes a further digestion, in the dry and exuccous part of the Aliment received from the first Ventricle. For at the bottom of the gullet there is a double Orifice; What is first received at the mouth descendeth into the first and greater stomack, from whence it is returned into the mouth again, and after a fuller mastication, and salivous mixture, what part thereof descendeth again, in a moist and succulent body, it slides down the softer and more permeable Orifice, into the Omasus or third stomack; and from thence conveyed into the fourth, receives its last digestion. The other dry and exuccous part after ruminating by the larger and stronger orifice beareth into the first stomack, from thence into the *Reticulum,* and so progressively into the other divisions. And therefore in Calves newly calved, there is little or no use of the two first Ventricles, for the milk and liquid aliment slippeth down the softer Orifice, into the third stomack; where making little or no stay, it passeth into the fourth, the seat of the *Coagulum,* or Runnet, or that division of stomack which seems to bear the name of the whole, in the Greek translation of the Priests Fee, in the Sacrifice of Peace-offerings.

As for those Rhomboidal Figures made by the cartilagineous part of the Wezon, in the Lungs of great Fishes, and other animals, as *Rondeletius* discovered, we have not found them so to answer our figure as to be drawn into illustration; Something we expected in the more discernable texture of the lungs of frogs, which notwithstanding being but two curious bladders not weighing above a grain, we found interwoven with veins, not observing any just order. More orderly situated are those cretaceous and chalky concretions found sometimes in the bignesse of a small vetch[1] on either side their spine; which being not agreeable unto our order, nor yet observed by any, we shall not here discourse on.

But had we found a better account and tolerable Anatomy of that prominent jowle of the *Sperma Ceti* Whale then questuary operation,[2] or the stench of the last cast upon our shoar, permitted, we might have perhaps discovered some handsome order in those Net-like

---

[1] Orig. fech.
[2] 1652, described in our *Pseudo. Epidem,* Edit. 3.

seases and sockets, made like honey combs, containing that medicall matter.

Lastly, The Incession or locall motion of animals is made with analogy unto this figure, by decussative diametrals, Quincuncial Lines and angles. For to omit the enquiry how Butterflies and breezes move their four wings, how birds and fishes in ayre and water move by joynt stroaks of opposite wings and Finnes, and how salient animals in jumping forward seem to arise and fall upon a square base; As the station of most Quadrupeds is made upon a long square, so in their motion they make a rhomboides; their common progression being performed Diametrally, by decussation and crosse advancement of their legges, which not observed, begot that remarkable absurdity in the position of the legges of *Castors* horse in the Capitol. The Snake which moveth circularly makes his spires in like order, the convex and concave spirals answering each other at alternate distances; In the motion of man the armes and legges observe this thwarting position, but the legges alone do move Quincuncially by single angles with some resemblance of a V measured by successive advancement from each foot, and the angle of indenture greater or lesse, according to the extent or brevity of the stride.

Studious Observators may discover more analogies in the orderly book of nature, and cannot escape the Elegancy of her hand in other correspondencies.[1] The

[1] In *MSS. Sloan.* 1847, occurs the following passage:—"Considerations are drawne from the signatures in the rootes of plants resembling sometimes orderly shapes and figures; those are made according as the pores or ascending fibres are posited in the plants. Whereby alimental juce and stablishing fibre ascend. The brake makes an handsome figure of a tree; the osmund royall a semicircle or raynebowe; the sedge a neate print; the annual surcles of the oake a five poynted starre according to the figure of the twigge; the stalk of the figge a triangle; carrots and many other a flosculous figure; the first rudiments of the sprouts of pyonie give starres of an handsome posie; the budds of plants with large leaves and many flowers cutt, show the artificiall complications in a wonderfull manner."

Figures of nails and crucifying appurtenances, are but precariously made out in the *Granadilla* or flower of Christs passion: And we despair to behold in these parts that handsome draught of crucifixion in the fruit of the *Barbado* Pine. The seminal Spike of *Phalaris,* or great shaking grasse, more nearly answers the tayl of a Rattle-Snake, then many resemblances in *Porta:* And if the man *Orchis*[1] of *Columna be* well made out, it excelleth all analogies. In young Wallnuts cut athwart, it is not hard to apprehend strange characters; and in those of somewhat elder growth, handsome ornamental draughts about a plain crosse. In the root of *Osmond* or Water-fern, every eye may discern the form of a Half Moon, Rain-bow, or half the character of Pisces. Some find Hebrew, Arabick, Greek, and Latine Characters in Plants; In a common one among us we seem to read *Acaia, Viviu, Lilil.*

Right lines and circles make out the bulk of plants; In the parts thereof we finde heliacal or spiral roundles, volutas, conicall Sections, circular Pyramids, and frus-tums of *Archimedes;* And cannot overlook the orderly hand of nature, in the alternate succession of the flat and narrower sides in the tender shoots of the Ashe, or the regular inequality of bignesse in the five-leaved flowers of Henbane, and something like in the calicular leaves of *Tutson.* How the spots of *Persicaria* do manifest them-selves between the sixth and tenth ribbe. How the trian-gular capp in the stemme or *stylus o*f Tuleps doth con-stantly point at three outward leaves. That spicated flowers do open first at the stalk. That white flowers have yellow thrums or knops. That the nebbe of Beans and Pease do all look downward, and so presst not upon each other; And how the seeds of many pappous or downy flowers lock-up in sockets after a *gomphosis* or *mortis-*articulation, diffuse themselves circularly into branches

[1] *Orchis Anthropophora,* Fabii Columnae.

of rare order, observable in *Tragopogon* or Goats-beard, conformable to the Spider's web, and the *Radii* in like manner telarely inter-woven.

And how in animall natures, even colours hold correspondencies, and mutual correlations. That the colour of the Caterpillar will shew again in the Butterfly, with some latitude is allowable. Though the regular spots in their wings seem but a mealie adhesion, and such as may be wiped away, yet since they come in this variety, out of their cases, there must be regular pores in those parts and membrances, defining such Exudations.

That *Augustus*[1] had native notes on his body and belly, after the order and number in the Starres of Charles' wayne, will not seem strange unto astral Physiognomy, which accordingly considereth moles in the body of man, or Physicall Observators, who from the position of moles in the face, reduce them to rule and correspondency in other parts. Whether after the like method medicall conjecture may not be raised, upon parts inwardly affected; since parts about the lips are the critical seats of Pustules discharged in Agues; and scrofulous tumours about the neck do so often speak the like about the Mesentery, may also be considered.

The russet neck in young Lambs seems but adventitious, and may owe its tincture to some contraction in the womb; But that if sheep have any black or deep russet in their faces, they want not the same about their legges and feet; that black Hounds have mealy mouths and feet; that black Cows which have any white in their tayls, should not misse of some in their bellies; and if all white in their bodies, yet if black-mouth'd, their ears and feet maintain the same colour, are correspondent tinctures not ordinarily failing in nature, which easily unites the accidents of extremities, since in some generations she transmutes the parts themselves, while in the

[1] Suet. in *vit. Aug.*

Aurelian Metamorphosis the head of the canker becomes the Tayl of the Butterfly. Which is in some way not beyond the contrivance of Art, in submersions and Inlays, inverting the extremes of the plant, and fetching the root from the top, and also imitated in handsome columnary work, in the inversion of the extremes; wherein the Capitel, and the Base, hold such near correspondency.

In the motive parts of animals may be discovered mutual proportions; not only in those of Quadrupeds, but in the thigh-bone, legge, foot-bone, and claws of Birds. The legs of spiders are made after a sesquitertian proportion, and the long legs of some locusts, double unto some others. But the internodial parts of Vegetables, or spaces between the joints, are contrived with more uncertainty; though the joints themselves, in many plants, maintain a regular number.

In vegetable composure, the unition of prominent parts seems most to answer the *Apophyses* or processes of Animall bones, whereof they are the produced parts or prominent explanations. And though in the parts of plants which are not ordained for motion, we do not expect correspondent Articulation: yet in the setting on of some flowers and seeds in their sockets, and the lineal commissure of the pulpe of severall seeds, may be observed some shadow of the Harmony; some show of the *Gomphosis* or *mortis*-articulation.

As for the *Diarthrosis* or motive Articulation, there is expected little Analogy, though long-stalked leaves doe move by long lines, and have observable motions, yet are they made by outward impulsion, like the motion of pendulous bodies, while the parts themselves are united by some kinde of symphysis unto the stock.

But standing vegetables, void of motive-Articulations, are not without many motions. For beside the motion of vegetation upward, and of radiation unto all quarters, that of contraction, dilation, inclination, and contortion, is discoverable in many plants. To omit the rose of *Jericho,* the ear of Rye, which moves with change of weather, and the Magical spit, made of no rare plants, which windes before the fire, and rosts the bird without turning.

Even Animals near the Classis of plants, seem to have the most restless motions. The Summer-worm of Ponds and plashes, makes a long waving motion, the hair-worm seldome lies still. He that would behold a very anomalous motion, may observe it in the Tortile and tiring stroaks of Gnat-worms.[1]

CHAPTER IV

As FOR the delights, commodities, mysteries, with other concernments of this order, we are unwilling to fly them over, in the short deliveries of *Virgil, Varro,* or others, and shall therefore enlarge with additionall ampliations.

By this position they had a just proportion of Earth, to supply an equality of nourishment. The distance being ordered, thick or thin, according to the magnitude or vigorous attraction of the plant, the goodnesse, leannesse or propriety of the soyle, and therefore the rule of *Solon,* concerning the territory of *Athens,* not extendible unto all; allowing the distance of six foot unto common Trees, and nine for the Figge and Olive.

They had a due diffusion of their roots on all or both sides, whereby they maintained some proportion to their height, in Trees of large radication. For that they strictly make good their *profundeur* or depth unto their height, according to common conceit, and that expression of *Virgil,*[2] though confirmable from the plane Tree in

---

[1] Found often in some form of red maggot in the standing waters *of Cisterns in the Summer.*

[2] *Quantum vertice ad auras Æthereas, tantum radice ad Tartara tendit.*

Pliny, and some few examples, is not to be expected from the generation of Trees almost in any kinde, either of side-spreading, or tap roots: Except we measure them by lateral and opposite diffusions: nor commonly to be found in *minor* or hearby plants; If we except Sea-holly, Liquorice, Sea-rush, and some others.

They had a commodious radiation in their growth; and a due expansion of their branches, for shadow or delight. For trees thickly planted, do runne up in height and branch with no expansion, shooting unequally or short, and thinne upon the neighbouring side. And therefore Trees are inwardly bare, and spring, and leaf from the outward and Sunny side of their branches.

Whereby they also avoided the peril of συνολεθρισμὸς or one tree perishing with another, as it happeneth ofttimes from the sick *effluviums* or entanglements of the roots, falling foul with each other. Observable in elmes set in hedges, where if one dieth, the neighbouring Tree prospereth not long after.

In this situation divided into many intervals and open unto six passages, they had the advantage of a fair perflation from windes, brushing and cleansing their surfaces, relaxing and closing their pores unto due perspiration. For that they afford large *effluviums* perceptible from odours, diffused at great distances, is observable from Onyons out of the earth; which though dry, and kept until the spring, as they shoot forth large and many leaves, do notably abate of their weight. And mint growing in glasses of water, until it arriveth unto the weight of an ounce, in a shady place, will sometimes exhaust a pound of water.

And as they send much forth, so may they receive somewhat in: For beside the common way and road of reception by the root, there may be a refection and imbibition from without; For gentle showrs refresh plants, though they enter not their roots; And the good and bad *efflu-*

viums of Vegetables, promote or debilitate each other. So *Epithymum* and *Dodder,* rootlesse and out of the ground, maintain themselves, upon Thyme, *Savory,* and plants whereon they hang. And *Ivy* divided from the root, we have observed to live some years, by the cirrous parts commonly conceived but as tenacles and holdfasts unto it. The stalks of mint cropt from the root stripped from the leaves, and set in *glasses* with the root end upward, and out of the water, we have observed to send forth sprouts and leaves without the aid of roots, and *scordium* to grow in like manner, the leaves set down-ward in water. To omit severall Sea plants, which grow on single roots from stones, although in very many there are side shoots and *fibres,* beside the fastening root.

By this open position they were fairly exposed unto the rayes of Moon and Sunne, so considerable in the growth of Vegetables. For though Poplars, Willows, and severall Trees be made to grow about the brinks of *Acha-ron,* and dark habitations of the dead; Though some plants are content to grow in obscure Wells; wherein also old elme pumps afford sometimes long bushy sprouts, not observable in any above ground: And large fields of Vegetables are able to maintain their verdure at the bot-tome and shady part of the Sea; yet the greatest number are not content without the actual rayes of the Sunne, but bend, incline, and follow them; As large lists of solisequious or sun following plants. And some observe the method of its motion in their owne growth and con-version, twining towards the West by the South,[1] as Bry-ony, Hops, Woodbine, and several kindes of Bindeweed, which we shall more admire; when any can tell us, they observe another motion, and twist by the North at the *Antipodes.* The same plants rooted against an erect

---

[1] *Flectat ad Aquilonem, et declinit ad Austrum,* is Solon's descrip-tion of the motion of the sun.—*Author's note, from MS. Sloan.* 1847.

North-wall full of holes, will finde a way through them to look upon the Sunne. And in tender plants from mustard seed, sown in the winter, and in a pot of earth placed inwardly against a South-window, the tender stalks of two leaves arose not erect, but bending towards the window, nor looking much higher than the Meridian Sun. And if the pot were turned they would work themselves into their former declinations, making their conversion by the East. That the Leaves of the Olive and some other Trees solstitially turn, and precisely tell us, when the Sun is entred *Cancer,* is scarce expectable in any Climate; and *Theophrastus* warily observes it; Yet somewhat thereof is observable in our own, in the leaves of Willows and Sallows, some weeks after the Solstice. But the great *Convolvulus,* or white flower'd *Bindweed,* observes both motions of the sunne, while the flower twists Æquinoctionally from the left hand to the right, according to the daily revolution; The stalk twineth ecliptically from the right to the left, according to the annual conversion.

Some commend the exposure of these orders unto the Western gales, as the most generative and fructifying breath of heaven. But we applaud the Husbandry of *Solomon,* whereto agreeth the doctrine of *Theophrastus.* Arise O north winde, and blow thou South upon my garden, that the spices thereof may flow out; For the north-winde closing the pores, and shutting up the *effluviums,* when the South doth after open and relax them; the Aromaticall gummes do drop, and sweet odours fly actively from them. And if his garden had the same situation, which mapps, and charts afford it, on the East side of *Jerusalem,* and having the wall on the west; these were the windes unto which it was well exposed.

By this way of plantation they increased the number of their trees, which they lost in *Quaternio's,* and square orders, which is a commodity insisted on by *Varro,* and one great intent of nature, in this position of flowers and seeds in the elegant formation of plants, and the former Rules observed in naturall and artificial Figurations.

Whether in this order and one Tree in some measure breaking the cold, and pinching gusts of windes from the other, trees will not better maintain their inward circles, and either escape or moderate their eccentricities, may also be considered. For the circles in Trees are naturally concentricall parallell unto the bark, and unto each other, till frost and piercing windes contract and close them on the weather side, the opposite semicircle widely enlarging, and at a comely distance, which hindreth ofttimes the beauty and roundnesse of Trees, and makes the Timber lesse serviceable; whiles the ascending juyce, not readily passing, settles in knots and inequalities. And therefore it is no new course of Agriculture, to observe the native position of Trees according to North and South in their transplantations.[1]

The same is also observable under ground in the circinations and sphærical rounds of Onyons, wherein the circles of the orbes are oft times larger, and the meridionall lines stand wider upon one side than the other. And where the largenesse will make up the number of planetical Orbes, that of *Luna,* and the lower planets exceed the dimensions of *Saturne,* and the higher; Whether the like be not verified in the Circles of the

---

[1] In *MS. Sloan.* 1847, is the following passage:—"The sap in trees observes the circle and right line. Trees being to grow up tall, were made long and strong; of the strongest columnar figure, round. The lines are strongest for the most part, and in many equidistant, as in firs; the circles homocentrical, except perverted by situation; the circles on the northern, or side exposed to cold winds, being more contracted. In the knots of fir, the right lines broken from their course do run into homocentrical circles, whether in round or oval knots."

In *MS. Sloan.* 1847, occurs also the following passage:—"Trees set under a north wall will be larger circled than that side exposed unto the weather: trees set in open high places, near the sea, will close their circles on that side which respecteth it."

large roots of Briony and Mandrakes, or why in the knotts of Deale or Firre, the Circles are often eccentricall, although not in a plane, but vertical and right position, deserves a further enquiry.

Whether there be not some irregularity of roundnesse in most plants according to their position? Whether some small compression of pores be not perceptible in parts which stand against the current of waters, as in Reeds, Bullrushes, and other vegetables toward the streaming quarter, may also be observed, and therefore such as are long and weak, are commonly contrived into a roundnesse of figure, whereby the water presseth lesse, and slippeth more smoothly from them, and even in flags of flat-figured leaves, the greater part obvert their sharper sides unto the current in ditches.

But whether plants which float upon the surface of the water, be for the most part of cooling qualities, those which shoot above it of heating vertues, and why? whether *Sargasso* for many miles floating upon the Western Ocean, or Sea-Lettuce and *Phasganium* at the bottome of our Seas, make good the like qualities? Why Fenny waters afford the hottest and sweetest plants, as *Calamus, Cyperus,* and Crow-foot, and mudd cast out of ditches most naturally produceth Arsmart? Why plants so greedy of water so little regard oyl? Why since many seeds contain much oyle within them, they endure it not well without, either in their growth or production? Why since Seeds shoot commonly under ground, and out of the ayre, those which are let fall in shallow glasses, upon the surface of the water, will sooner sprout than those at the bottom? And if the water be covered with oyle, those at the bottome will hardly sprout at all, we have not room to conjecture.

Whether Ivy would not lesse offend the Trees in this clean ordination, and well-kept paths, might perhaps deserve the question. But this were a quæry only unto

some habitations, and little concerning *Cyrus* or the
Babylonian territory; wherein by no industry *Harpalus*
could make Ivy grow; And *Alexander* hardly found it
about those parts to imitate the pomp of *Bacchus*. And
though in these Northern Regions we are too much
acquainted with one Ivy, we know too little of another,
whereby we apprehend not the expressions of Antiquity,
the Splenetick medicine[1] of Galen, and the Emphasis of
the Poet, in the beauty of the white Ivy.[2]

The like concerning the growth of Misseltoe, which
dependeth not only of the *species*, or kinde of Tree, but
much also of the Soil. And therefore common in some
places, not readily found in others, frequent in *France*,
not so common in *Spain*, and scarce at all in the Territory of *Ferrara;* Nor easily to be found where it is most
required, upon Oaks, less on Trees continually verdant.
Although in some places the Olive escapeth it not, requiting its detriment, in the delightfull view of its red
Berries; as *Clusius* observed in *Spain*, and *Bellonius*
about *Hierusalem*. But this Parasiticall plant suffers
nothing to grow upon it, by any way of art; nor could we
ever make it grow where nature had not planted it; as
we have in vain attempted by inoculation and incision,
upon its native or forreign stock. And though there seems
nothing improbable in the seed, it hath not succeeded
by sation in any manner of ground, wherein we had no
reason to despair, since we reade of vegetable horns,
and how Rams horns will root about Goa.[3]

But besides these rurall commodities, it cannot be
meanly delectable in the variety of Figures, which these
orders, open and closed, do make. Whilest every inclosure
makes a *Rhombus*, the figures obliquely taken a Rhomboides, the intervals bounded with parallell lines, and

---

[1] Galen *de Med. secundum loc.*
[2] *Hederâ formosior albâ.*
[3] *Linschoten.*

each intersection built upon a square, affording two Triangles or Pyramids vertically conjoyned; which in the strict Quincunciall order doe oppositely make acute and blunt Angles.

And though therein we meet not with right angles, yet every Rhombus containing four Angles equall unto two right, it virtually contains two right in every one. Nor is this strange unto such as observe the naturall lines of Trees, and parts disposed in them. For neither in the root doth nature affect this angle, which shooting downward for the stability of the plant, doth best effect the same by Figures of Inclination; Nor in the Branches and stalky leaves, which grow most at acute angles; as declining from their head the root, and diminishing their Angles with their altitude: Verified also in lesser Plants, whereby they better support themselves, and bear not so heavily upon the stalk; So that while near the root they often make an Angle of seventy parts, the sprouts near the top will often come short of thirty. Even in the nerves and master veins of the leaves the acute angle ruleth; the obtuse but seldome found, and in the backward part of the leaf, reflecting and arching about the stalk. But why ofttimes one side of the leaf is unequall unto the other, as in Hazell and Oaks, why on either side the master vein the lesser and derivative channels stand not directly opposite, nor at equall angles, respectively unto the adverse side, but those of one part do often exceed the other, as the Wallnut and many more, deserves another enquiry.

Now if for this order we affect coniferous and tapering Trees, particularly the Cypresse, which grows in a conicall figure; we have found a Tree not only of great Ornament, but, in its Essentials, of affinity unto this order. A solid Rhombus being made by the conversion of two Equicrural Cones, as *Archimedes* hath defined. And these were the common Trees about *Babylon,* and the East, whereof the Ark was made; and *Alexander* found no Trees so accommodable to build his Navy; and this we rather think to be the Tree mentioned in the Canticles, which stricter Botanology will hardly allow to be Camphire.

And if delight or ornamentall view invite a comely disposure by circular amputations, as is elegantly performed in Hawthorns; then will they answer the figures made by the conversion of a Rhombus, which maketh two concentricall Circles; the greater Circumference being made by the lesser angles, the lesser by the greater.

The Cylindrical figure of Trees is virtually contained and latent is this order. A Cylinder or long round being made by the conversion or turning of a Parallelogram, and most handsomely by a long square, which makes an equall, strong, and lasting figure in Trees, agreeable unto the body and motive parts of animals, the greatest number of Plants, and almost all roots, though their stalks be angular, and of many corners, which seem not to follow the figure of their Seeds; Since many angular Seeds send forth round stalks, and sphæricall seeds arise from angular spindles, and many rather conform unto their Roots, as the round stalks of bulbous Roots; and in tuberous Roots stemmes of like figure. But why since the largest number of Plants maintain a circular Figure, there are so few with teretous or long round leaves; why coniferous Trees are tenuifolious or narrow-leaved; why Plants of few or no joynts have commonly round stalks, why the greatest number of hollow stalks are round stalks; or why in this variety of angular stalks the quadrangular most exceedeth, were too long a speculation; Meanwhile obvious experience may finde, that in Plants of divided leaves above, nature often beginneth circularly in the two first leaves below, while in the singular plant of Ivy she exerciseth a contrary Geometry, and beginning with angular leaves below, rounds them in the upper branches.

Nor can the rows in this order want delight, as carrying an aspect answerable unto the *dipteros hypæthros,* or double order of columns open above; the opposite ranks of Trees standing like pillars in the *Cavedia* of the Courts of famous buildings, and the *Portico's* of the *Templa subdialia* of old; Somewhat imitating the *Peristylia* or Cloyster buildings, and the *Exedræ* of the Ancients, wherein men discoursed, walked and exercised; For that they derived the rule of Columnes from Trees, especially in their proportionall diminutions, is illustrated by Vitruvius from the shafts of Firre and Pine. And though the interarboration do imitate the *Areostylos,* or thin order, not strictly answering the proportion of intercolumniations; yet in many Trees they will not exceed the intermission of the Columnes in the Court of the Tabernacle; which being an hundred cubits long, and made up by twenty pillars, will afford no lesse than intervals of five cubits.

Beside, in this kinde of aspect the sight being not diffused but circumscribed between long parallels and the ἐπισκιασμὸς and adumbration from the branches, it frameth a penthouse over the eye, and maketh a quiet vision: And therefore in diffused and open aspects, men hollow their hand above their eye, and make an artificiall brow, whereby they direct the dispersed rayes of sight, and by this shade preserve a moderate light in the chamber of the eye; keeping the *pupilla* plump and fair, and not contracted or shrunk as in light and vagrant vision.

And therefore providence hath arched and paved the great house of the world, with colours of mediocrity, that is, blew and green, above and below the sight, moderately terminating the *acies* of the eye. For most plants, though green above ground, maintain their Originall white below it, according to the candour of their seminall pulp, and the rudimental leaves do first appear in that colour; observable in Seeds sprouting in water upon their first foliation. Green seeming to be the first supervenient, or above-ground complexion of Vegetables, separable in many upon ligature or inhumation, as Succory, Endive, Artichoaks, and which is also lost upon fading in the Autumn.

And this is also agreeable unto water itself, the alimental vehicle of plants, which first altereth into this colour; And containing many vegetable seminalities, revealeth their Seeds by greennesse; and therefore soonest expected in rain or standing water, not easily found in distilled or water strongly boiled; wherein the Seeds are extinguished by fire and decoction, and therefore last long and pure without such alteration, affording neither uliginous coats, gnat-worms, *Acari*, hair-worms, like crude and common water; And therefore most fit for wholesome beverage, and with malt makes Ale and Beer without boyling. What large water-drinkers some Plants are, the Canary-Tree and Birches in some Northern Countries, drenching the Fields about them, do sufficiently demonstrate. How water itself is able to maintain the growth of Vegetables, and without extinction of their generative or medicall vertues; Beside the experiment of *Helmonts* tree, we have found in some which have lived six years in glasses. The seeds of Scurvy-grasse growing in water-pots, have been fruitful in the Land; and *Asarum* after a year space, and once casting its leaves in water, in the second leaves, hath handsomely performed its vomiting operation.

Nor are only dark and green colours, but shades and shadows contrived through the great Volume of nature, and trees ordained not only to protect and shadow others, but by their shades and shadowing parts, to preserve

and cherish themselves. The whole radiation or branch-
ings shadowing the stock and the root, the leaves, the
branches and fruit, too much exposed to the windes and
scorching Sunne. The calicular leaves inclose the tender
flowers, and the flowers themselves lye wrapt about the
seeds, in their rudiment and first formations, which being
advanced the flowers fall away; and are therefore contrived in variety of figures, best satisfying the intention;
Handsomely observable in hooded and gaping flowers,
and the Butterfly bloomes of leguminous plants, the
lower leaf closely involving the rudimental Cod, and the
alary or wingy divisions embracing or hanging over it.

But Seeds themselves do lie in perpetual shades, either
under the leaf, or shut up in coverings; and such as lye
barest, have their husks, skins, and pulps about them,
wherein the nebbe and generative particle lyeth moist
and secured from the injury of ayre and Sunne. Darknesse and light hold interchangeable dominions, and al-
ternately rule the seminal state of things. Light unto
Pluto[1] is darkness unto *Jupiter*. Legions of seminall *Ideas*
lye in their second Chaos and *Orcus* of *Hipocrates;* till
putting on the habits of their forms, they shew themselves upon the stage of the world, and open dominion of
Jove. They that held the Stars of heaven were but rayes
and flashing glimpses of the Empyreall light, through
holes and perforations of the upper heaven, took of the
natural shadows of stars, while according to better discovery the poor Inhabitants of the Moone have but a
polary life,[2] and must passe half their dayes in the
shadow of that Luminary.

Light that makes things seen, makes some things invisible, were it not for darknesse and the shadow of the
earth, the noblest part of the Creation had remained
unseen, and the Stars in heaven as invisible as on the

[1] *Lux Orco, tenebræ Jovi; tenebræ Orco, lux Jovi.* Hippoc. *de Dieta.*
[2] J. Hevelii *Selenographia.*

fourth day, when they were created above the Horizon,
with the Sun, or there was not an eye to behold them.
The greatest mystery of Religion is expressed by adumbration, and in the noblest part of Jewish Types, we find
the Cherubims shadowing the Mercy-seat: Life itself is
but the shadow of death, and souls departed but the
shadows of the living: All things fall under this name.
The Sunne itself is but the dark *simulachrum,* and light
but the shadow of God.

Lastly, it is no wonder that this Quincunciall order
was first and is still affected as gratefull unto the eye: For
all things are seen Quincuncially; for at the eye the
Pyramidal rayes, from the object, receive a decussation,
and so strike a second base upon the *Retina* or hinder
coat, the proper organ of Vision; wherein the pictures
from objects are represented, answerable to the paper,
or wall in the dark chamber; after the decussation of
the rayes at the hole of the horny-coat, and their refrac-
tion upon the Christalline humour, answering the *fora-
men* of the window, and the *convex* or burning-glasses,
which refract the rayes that enter it. And if ancient Anatomy would hold, a like disposure there was of the optick
or visual nerves in the brain, wherein Antiquity conceived a concurrence by decussation. And this not only
observable in the Laws of direct Vision, but in some
part also verified in the reflected rayes of sight. For
making the angle of incidence equal to that of reflection,
the visuall raye returneth Quincuncially, and after the
form of a V, and the line of reflection being continued
unto the place of vision, there ariseth a semi-decussation,
which makes the object seen in a perpendicular unto
itself, and as farre below the reflectent, as it is from it
above; observable in the Sun and Moon beheld in water.

And this is also the law of reflection in moved bodies
and sounds, which though not made by decussation, observe the rule of equality between incidence and reflec-

tion; whereby whispering places are framed by Ellipticall arches laid sidewise; where the voice being delivered at the *focus* of one extremity, observing an equality unto the angle of incidence, it will reflect unto the *focus* of the other end, and so escape the ears of the standers in the middle.

A like rule is observed in the reflection of the vocall and sonorous line in Ecchoes, which cannot therefore be heard in all stations. But happening in woody plantations, by waters, and able to return some words if reacht by a pleasant and well-dividing voice, there may be heard the softest notes in nature.

And this not only verified in the way of sence, but in animall and intellectuall receptions. Things entring upon the intellect by a Pyramid from without, and thence into the memory by another from within, the common decussation being in the understanding as is delivered by *Bovillus*.[1] Whether the intellectual and phantastical lines be not thus rightly disposed, but magnified, diminished, distorted, and ill placed in the Mathematicks of some brains, whereby they have irregular apprehensions of things, perverted notions, conceptions, and incurable hallucinations, were no unpleasant speculation.

And if Ægyptian Philosophy may obtain, the scale of influences was thus disposed, and the geniall spirits of both worlds do trace their way in ascending and descending Pyramids, mystically apprehended in the letter X, and the open Bill and stradling Legges of a Stork, which was imitated by that Character.

Of this Figure *Plato* made choice to illustrate the motion of the soul, both of the world and man; while he delivereth that God divided the whole conjunction length-wise, according to the figure of a Greek χ, and then turning it about reflected it into a circle; By the circle implying the uniform motion of the first Orb, and

[1] Car. Bovillus *de Intellectu*.

by the right lines, the planetical and various motions within it. And this also with application unto the soul of man, which hath a double aspect, one right, whereby it beholdeth the body, and objects without; another circular and reciprocal, whereby it beholdeth itself. The circle declaring the motion of the indivisible soul, simple, according to the divinity of its nature, and returning into itself; the right lines respecting the motion pertaining unto sense, and vegetation, and the central decussation, the wondrous connexion of the severall faculties conjointly in one substance. And so conjoyned the unity and duality of the soul, and made out the three substances so much considered by him; That is, the indivisible or divine, the divisible or corporeal, and that third, which was the *Systasis* or harmony of those two, in the mystical decussation.

And if that were clearly made out which *Justin Martyr* took for granted, this figure hath had the honour to characterize and notifie our blessed Saviour, as he delivereth in that borrowed expression from *Plato; Decussavit eum in universo,* the hint whereof he would have *Plato* derive from the figure of the brazen Serpent, and to have mistaken the Letter X for T, whereas it is not improbable, he learned these and other mystical expressions in his Learned Observations of Ægypt, where he might obviously behold the Mercurial characters, the handed crosses, and other mysteries not thoroughly understood in the sacred Letter X; which being derivative from the Stork, one of the ten sacred animals, might be originally Ægyptian, and brought into *Greece* by *Cadmus* of that Countrey.

CHAPTER V

To ENLARGE this contemplation unto all the mysteries and secrets, accommodable unto this number, were inexcusable Pythagorisme, yet cannot omit the ancient conceit of five surnamed the number of justice;[1] as justly dividing between the digits, and hanging in the centre of Nine, described by square numeration, which angularly divided will make the decussated number; and so agreeable unto the Quincunciall Ordination, and rowes divided by Equality, and just *decorum,* in the whole complantation; And might be the originall of that common game among us, wherein the fifth place is Soveraigne, and carrieth the chief intention. The Ancients wisely instructing youth, even in their recreations unto virtue, that is, early to drive at the middle point and Central Seat of justice.

Nor can we omit how agreeable unto this number an handsome division is made in Trees and Plants, since *Plutarch,* and the Ancients have named it the Divisive Number, justly dividing the Entities of the world, many remarkable things in it, and also comprehending the generall division of Vegetables.[2] And he that considers how most blossomes of Trees, and greatest number of Flowers, consist of five leaves; and therein doth rest the setled rule of nature; So that in those which exceed there is often found, or easily made a variety; may readily discover how nature rests in this number, which is indeed the first rest and pause of numeration in the fingers, the naturall Organs thereof. Nor in the division of the feet of perfect animals doth nature exceed this account. And even in the joints of feet, which in birds are most multiplied, surpasseth not this number; So progressionally making them out in many, that from five in the fore-claw she descendeth unto two in the hindemost; and

---

[1] δίκη.

[2] Δένδρον, Θάμνος Φρύγανον, Πόα, *Arbor, frutex, suffrutex, herba,* and that fifth which comprehendeth the *fungi* and *tubera,* whether to be named Ἄσχιον or γύμνον, comprehending also *conferva marina salsa,* and Sea-cords, of so many yards length.

so in fower feet makes up the number of joynts, in the five fingers or toes of man.

Not to omit the Quintuple section of a Cone[1] of handsome practise in Ornamentall Garden-plots, and in some way discoverable in so many works of Nature; In the leaves, fruits, and seeds of Vegetables, and scales of some Fishes, so much considerable in glasses, and the optick doctrine; wherein the learned may consider the Crystalline humour of the eye in the cuttle-fish and *Loligo*.

He that forgets not how Antiquity named this the Conjugall or wedding number, and made it the Embleme of the most remarkable conjunction, will conceive it duely appliable unto this handsome Economy, and vegetable combination; May hence apprehend the allegoricall sence of that obscure expression of *Hesiod*,[2] and afford no improbable reason why *Plato* admitted his Nuptiall guests by fives, in the kindred of the married couple.[3]

And though a sharper mystery might be implied in the Number of the five wise and foolish Virgins, which were to meet the Bridegroom, yet was the same agreeable unto the Conjugal Number, which ancient Numerists made out by two and three, the first parity and imparity, the active and passive digits, the materiall and formall principles in generative Societies. And not discordant even from the customs of the *Romans,* who admitted but five Torches in their Nuptiall solemnities.[4] Whether there were any mystery or not implied, the most generative animals were created on this day, and had accordingly the largest benediction: And under a Quintuple consideration, wanton Antiquity considered the Circum-

---

[1] *Elleipsis, parabola, Hyperbole, Circulus, Triangulum.*
[2] πέμπτας, *id est, nuptias, multas.* Rhodig.
[3] Plato *de Leg.* 6.
[4] Plutarch. *Problem. Rom.* i.

stances of generation, while by this number of five they naturally divided the Nectar of the fifth Planet.[1]

The same number in the Hebrew mysteries and Cabalistical accounts was the character of generation;[2] declared by the Letter *He,* the fifth in their Alphabet; According to that Cabalistical *Dogma:* If *Abram* had not had this Letter added unto his Name, he had remained fruitlesse, and without the power of generation: Not only because hereby the number of his Name attained two hundred fourty eight, the number of the affirmative precepts, but because as in created natures there is a male and female, so in divine and intelligent productions, the mother of Life and Fountain of souls in Cabalisticall Technology is called *Binah;* whose seal and character was *He.* So that being sterill before, he received the power of generation from that measure and mansion in the Archetype; and was made conformable unto *Binah.* And upon such involved considerations, the ten of *Sarai* was exchanged into five.[3] If any shall look upon this as a stable number, and fitly appropriable unto Trees, as Bodies of Rest and Station, he hath herein a great Foundation in nature, who observing much variety in legges and motive Organs of Animals, as two, four, six, eight, twelve, fourteen, and more, hath passed over five and ten, and assigned them unto none, or very few, as the *Phalangium montsrosum Brasilianum* (*Clusii et Jac. de Laet. Cur. Poster. Americæ Descript.*). If perfectly described. And for the stability of this Number, he shall not want the sphericity of its nature, which multiplied in itself, will return into its own denomination, and bring up the reare of the account. Which is also one of the Numbers that makes up the mysticall Name of God,

---

[1] . . . . . . *oscula quæ Venus*
   Quinta parte sui nectaris imbuit.—*Hor.* lib. i. od. 13.
[2] *Archang. Dog. Cabal.*
[3] *Jod* into *He.*

which consisting of Letters denoting all the sphæricall
Numbers, ten, five, and six; Emphatically sets forth the
Notion of *Trismegistus,* and that intelligible Sphere,
which is the Nature of God.

Many Expressions by this Number occurre in Holy
Scripture, perhaps unjustly laden with mysticall Exposi-
tions, and little concerning our order. That the Israelites
were forbidden to eat the fruit of their new planted
Trees, before the fifth yeare, was very agreeable unto the
naturall Rules of Husbandry: Fruits being unwholsome
and lash, before the fourth, or fifty Yeare. In the second
day or Feminine part of five, there was added no appro-
bation. For in the third or masculine day, the same is
twice repeated: and a double benediction inclosed both
Creations, whereof the one, in some part was but an
accomplishment of the other. That the Trespasser[1] was
to pay a fifth part above the head or principall, makes
no secret in this Number, and implied no more than one
part above the principall; which being considered in
four parts, the additional forfeit must bear the Name of
a fift. The five golden mice had plainly their determination from the number of the Princes; That five should
put to flight an hundred might have nothing mystically
implyed; considering a rank of Souldiers could scarce
consist of a lesser number. Saint *Paul* had rather speak
five words in a known than ten thousand in an un-
knowne tongue: That is as little as could well be spoken.
A simple proposition consisting of three words and a
complexed one not ordinarily short of five.

More considerable there are in this mysticall account,
which we must not insist on. And therefore why the radi-
call Letters in the Pentateuch, should equall the number
of the Souldiery of the Tribes; Why our Saviour in the
wilderness fed five thousand persons with five Barley
Loaves, and again, but four thousand with no lesse than

[1] Lev. vi.

seven of Wheat? Why *Joseph* designed five changes of
Rayment unto *Benjamin* and *David* took just five pib-
bles[1] out of the Brook against the Pagan Champion? We
leave it unto Arithmeticall Divinity, and Theologicall
explanation.

Yet if any delight in new Problemes, or think it
worth the enquiry, whether the Criticall Physician hath
rightly hit the nominall notation of *Quinque;* Why the
Ancients mixed five or three but not four parts of water
unto their Wine: And *Hippocrates* observed a fifth proportion in the mixture of water with milk, as in *Dysenteries* and bloudy fluxes? Under what abstruse foundation Astrologers do Figure the good or bad fate from our
Children, in good Fortune;[2] or the fifth house of their
Celestiall Schemes. Whether the Ægyptians described a
Starre by a Figure of five points, with reference unto the
five Capitall aspects,[3] whereby they transmit their Influences, or abstruser Considerations? Why the Cabalisticall Doctors, who conceive the whole *Sephiroth,* or divine emanations to have guided the ten-stringed Harp of
David, whereby he pacified the evil spirit of *Saul,* in
strict numeration doe begin with the *Perihypate Meson,*
or *si fa ut,* and so place the *Tiphereth* answering *C sol fa
ut,* upon the fifth string: Or whether this number he
oftner applied unto bad things and ends, then good in
holy Scripture, and why? He may meet with abstrusities
of no ready resolution.

If any shall question the rationality of that Magick, in
the cure of the blind man by *Serapis,* commanded to
place five fingers on his Altar, and then his hand on his
Eyes? Why since the whole Comœdy is primarily and
naturally comprised in four parts,[4] and Antiquity per-

---

[1] τέσσαρα ἔνκε four and one, or five.—Scalig.
[2] Ἀγαθὴ τυχὴ *bona fortuna,* the name of the fifth house.
[3] Conjunct, opposite, sextile, triagonal, tetragonal.
[4] Πρότασις, ἐπίτασις, κατάστασις, καταστροφή.

mitted not so many persons to speak in one Scene, yet
would not comprehend the same in more or lesse then
five acts? Why amongst Sea-starres nature chiefly delighteth in five points? And since there are found some of
no fewer than twelve, and some of seven, and nine, there
are few or none discovered of six or eight? If any shall
enquire why the Flowers of *Rue* properly consist of four
Leaves, The first and third Flower have five? Why since
many Flowers have one leaf or none,[1] as *Scaliger* will
have it, diverse three, and the greatest number consist of
five divided from their bottoms; there are yet so few of
two: or why nature generally beginning or setting out
with two opposite leaves at the Root, doth so seldome
conclude with that order and number at the Flower? he
shall not pass his hours in vulgar speculations.

If any shall further quæry why magneticall Philosophy
excludeth decussations, and needles transversely placed
do naturally distract their verticities? Why Geomancers
do imitate the Quintuple Figure, in their Mother Characters of Acquisition and Admission, &c., somewhat answering the Figures in the Lady or speckled Beetle?
With what Equity, Chiromantical conjecturers decry
these decussations in the Lines and Mounts of the hand?
What that decussated Figure intendeth in the medall
of *Alexander* the Great? Why the goddesses sit commonly crosse-legged in ancient draughts, Since *Juno* is
described in the same as a veneficial posture to hinder
the birth of *Hercules?* If any shall doubt why at the
Amphidromicall Feasts, on the fifth day after the Childe
was born, presents were sent from friends, of *Polipusses*
and Cuttle-fishes? Why five must be only left in that Symbolicall mutiny among the men of *Cadmus?* Why
Proteus in *Homer* the Symbole of the first matter, before
he setled himself in the midst of his Sea-monsters, doth
place them out by fives? Why the fifth years Oxe was

[1] *Unifolium, nullifolium.*

acceptable Sacrifice unto *Jupiter?* Or why the Noble *Antoninus* in some sence doth call the soul itself a Rhombus? He shall not fall on trite or triviall disquisitions. And these we invent and propose unto acuter enquirers, nauseating crambe verities and questions over-queried. Flat and flexible truths are beat out by every hammer; but *Vulcan* and his whole forge sweat to work out *Achilles* his armour. A large field is yet left unto sharper discerners to enlarge upon this order, to search out the *quaternios* and figured draughts of this nature, and moderating the study of names, and meer nomenclature of plants, to erect generalities, disclose unobserved proprieties, not only in the vegetable shop, but the whole volume of nature; affording delightful Truths, confirmable by sense and ocular Observation, which seems to me the surest path, to trace the Labyrinth of Truth. For though discursive enquiry and rationall conjecture, may leave handsome gashes and flesh-wounds; yet without conjunction of this expect no mortal or dispatching blows unto errour.

But the Quincunx[1] of Heaven runs low, and 'tis time to close the five ports of knowledge; We are unwilling to spin out our awaking thoughts into the phantasmes of sleep, which often continueth præcogitations; making Cables of Cobwebbes, and Wildernesses of handsome Groves. Beside *Hippocrates*[2] hath spoke so little, and the Oneirocriticall[3] Masters, have left such frigid Interpretations from plants, that there is little encouragement to dream of Paradise itself. Nor will the sweetest delight of Gardens afford much comfort in sleep; wherein the dulnesse of that sense shakes hands with delectable odours; and though in the Bed of *Cleopatra*,[4] can hardly with any delight raise up the ghost of a Rose.

[1] *Hyades,* near the Horizon about midnight, at that time.
[2] *De Insomniis.*
[3] Artemidorus, et Apomazar.
[4] Strewed with roses.

Night which Pagan Theology could make the daughter of Chaos, affords no advantage to the description of order: Although no lower then that Masse can we derive its Genealogy. All things began in order, so shall they end, and so shall they begin again; according to the ordainer of order and mystical Mathematicks of the City of Heaven.

Though *Somnus* in *Homer* be sent to rowse up *Agamemnon*, I finde no such effects in these drowsy approaches of sleep. To keep our eyes open longer were but to act our *Antipodes*. The Huntsmen are up in *America*, and they are already past their first sleep in *Persia*. But who can be drowsie at that howr which freed us from everlasting sleep? or have slumbering thoughts at that time, when sleep itself must end, and as some conjecture all shall awake again.

THE STATIONER TO THE READER

I CANNOT omit to advertise, that a Book was published not long since, Entituled, *Natures Cabinet Unlockt,* bearing the name of this Authour: If any man have been benefited thereby this Authour is not so ambitious as to challenge the honour thereof, as having no hand in that Work. To distinguish of true and spurious Peeces was the Originall Criticisme, and some were so handsomely counterfeited, that the Entitled Authours needed not to disclaime them. But since it is so, that either he must write himself, or Others will write for him, I know no better Prevention then to act his own part with lesse intermission of his Pen.

CHRISTIAN MORALS
1716

THE PREFACE

IF ANY One, after he has read Religio Medici and the ensuing Discourse, can make Doubt, whether the same Person was the Author of them both, he may be Assured by the Testimony of Mrs. Littleton, Sir Thomas Browne's Daughter, who Lived with her Father, when it was composed by Him; and who, at the time, read it written by his own hand; and also by the Testimony of Others, (of whom I am One) who read the MS. of the Author, immediately after his Death, and who have since Read the Same; from which it hath been faithfully and exactly Transcribed for the Press. The Reason why it was not Printed sooner is, because it was unhappily Lost, by being Mislay'd among Other MSS., for which Search was lately made in the Presence of the Lord Arch Bishop of Canterbury, of which his Grace, by Letter, informed Mrs. Littleton, when he sent the MS. to her. There is nothing printed in the Discourse, or in the short notes, but what is found in the Original MS. of the Author, except only where an Oversight had made the Addition or Transposition of some words necessary.

JOHN JEFFERY,
Archdeacon of Norwich.

CHRISTIAN MORALS

PART THE FIRST

TREAD SOFTLY and circumspectly in this funambulatory Track and narrow Path of Goodness: Pursue Virtue virtuously: Leven not good Actions nor render Virtues disputable. Stain not fair Acts with foul Intentions: Maim not Uprightness by halting Concomitances, nor circumstantially deprave substantial Goodness.

Consider whereabout thou art in *Cebes's* table, or that old Philosophical *Pinax*[1] of the Life of Man: whether thou art yet in the Road of uncertainties; whether thou hast yet entred the narrow Gate, got up the Hill and asperous way, which leadeth unto the House of Sanity, or taken that purifying Potion from the hand of sincere Erudition, which may send Thee clear and pure away unto a virtuous and happy Life.

In this virtuous Voyage of thy Life hull not about like the Ark, without the use of Rudder, Mast, or Sail, and bound for no Port. Let not Disappointment cause Despondency, nor difficulty despair. Think not that you are Sailing from *Lima* to *Manillia*, when you may fasten up the Rudder, and sleep before the Wind; but expect rough Seas, Flaws, and contrary Blasts: and 'tis well, if by many cross Tacks and Veerings, you arrive at the Port; for we sleep in lyons Skins in our Progress unto Virtue, and we slide not, but climb unto it.

Sit not down in the popular Forms and common Level of Virtues. Offer not only Peace-Offerings but Holocausts unto God: where all is due make no reserve,

[1] *Pinax*. Picture.—*Dr. J.*

and cut not a Cummin-seed with the Almighty: to serve
Him singly to serve ourselves were too partial a piece of
Piety, not like to place us in the illustrious Mansions
of Glory.

SECT. II.—Rest not in an Ovation[1] but a Triumph
over thy Passions. Let Anger walk hanging down the
head; Let Malice go Manicled, and Envy fetter'd after
thee. Behold within thee the long train of thy Trophies
not without thee. Make the quarrelling Lapithytes sleep,
and Centaurs within lye quiet. Chain up the unruly
Legion of thy breast. Lead thine own captivity captive,
and be *Cæsar* within thyself.

SECT. III.—He that is Chast and Continent not to impair his strength, or honest for fear of Contagion, will
hardly be Heroically virtuous. Adjourn not this virtue
untill that temper when Cato could lend out his Wife,
and impotent Satyrs write Satyrs upon Lust; but be
chast in thy flaming Days, when *Alexander* dar'd not trust
his eyes upon the fair Sisters of *Darius,* and when so
many think there is no other way but *Origen's.*[2]

SECT. IV.—Show thy Art in Honesty, and loose not
thy Virtue by the bad Managery of it. Be Temperate and
Sober, not to preserve your body in an ability for wanton
ends, not to avoid the infamy of common transgressors
that way, and thereby to hope to expiate or palliate obscure and closer vices, not to spare your purse, nor sim-
ply to enjoy health; but in one word that thereby you
may truly serve God, which every sickness will tell you
you cannot well do without health. The sick Man's Sacrifice is but a lame Oblation. Pious Treasures, lay'd up in
healthful days, plead for sick non-performances: without which we must needs look back with anxiety upon
the lost opportunities of health, and may have cause
rather to envy than pity the ends of penitent publick

[1] Ovation, a petty and minor Kind of Triumph.
[2] Who is said to have Castrated himself.

Sufferers, who go with healthfull prayers unto the last
Scene of their lives, and in the Integrity of their faculties
return their Spirit unto God that gave it.

SECT. V.—Be Charitable before wealth make thee covetous, and loose not the glory of the Mite. If Riches en-
crease, let thy mind hold pace with them, and think it
not enough to be Liberal, but Munificent. Though a
Cup of cold water from some hand may not be without
it's reward, yet stick not thou for Wine and Oyl for the
Wounds of the Distressed; and treat the poor, as our
Saviour did the Multitude, to the reliques of some bas-
kets. Diffuse thy beneficence early, and while thy Treasures call thee Master: there may be an Atropos of thy
Fortunes before that of thy Life, and thy wealth cut off
before that hour, when all Men shall be poor; for the
Justice of Death looks equally upon the dead, and *Charon*
expects no more from *Alexander* than from *Irus*.

SECT. VI.—Give not only unto seven, but also unto
eight, that is unto more than many.[1] Though to give
unto every one that asketh may seem severe advice,[2]
yet give thou also before asking, that is, where want
is silently clamorous, and men's Necessities not their
Tongues do loudly call for thy Mercies. For though sometimes necessitousness be dumb, or misery speak not out,
yet true Charity is sagacious, and will find out hints for
beneficence. Acquaint thyself with the Physiognomy of
Want, and let the Dead colours and first lines of necessity suffise to tell thee there is an object for thy bounty.
Spare not where thou canst not easily be prodigal, and
fear not to be undone by mercy. For since he who hath
pity on the poor lendeth unto the Almighty Rewarder,
who observes no Ides but every day for his payments;
Charity becomes pious Usury, Christian Liberality the
most thriving industry, and what we adventure in a

[1] Ecclesiasticus.
[2] Luke.

Cockboat may return in a Carrack unto us. He who thus casts his bread upon the Water shall surely find it again; for though it falleth to the bottom, it sinks but like the Ax of the Prophet, to arise again unto him.

SECT. VII.—If Avarice be thy Vice, yet make it not thy Punishment. Miserable men commiserate not themselves, bowelless unto others, and merciless unto their own bowels. Let the fruition of things bless the possession of them, and think it more satisfaction to live richly than dye rich. For since thy good works, not thy goods, will follow thee; since wealth is an appertinance of life, and no dead Man is Rich; to famish in Plenty, and live poorly to dye Rich, were a multiplying improvement in Madness, and use upon use in Folly.

SECT. VIII.—Trust not to the Omnipotency of Gold, and say not unto it Thou art my Confidence. Kiss not thy hand to that Terrestrial Sun, nor bore thy ear unto its servitude. A Slave unto Mammon makes no servant unto God. Covetousness cracks the sinews of Faith; nummes the apprehension of anything above sense, and only affected with the certainty of things present makes a peradventure of things to come; lives but unto one World, nor hopes but fears another; makes their own death sweet unto others, bitter unto themselves; brings formal sadness, scenical mourning, and no wet eyes at the grave.

SECT. IX.—Persons lightly dipt, not grain'd in generous Honesty, are but pale in Goodness, and faint hued in Integrity. But be thou what thou vertuously art, and let not the Ocean wash away thy Tincture. Stand magnetically upon that Axis, when prudent simplicity hath fixt there; and let no attraction invert the Poles of thy Honesty. That Vice may be uneasy and even monstrous unto thee, let iterated good Acts and long-confirmed habits make Virtue almost natural, or a second nature in thee. Since virtuous superstructions have commonly generous

foundations, dive into thy inclinations, and early discover what nature bids thee to be, or tells thee thou
may'st be. They who thus timely descend into themselves,
and cultivate the good seeds which nature hath set in
them, prove not shrubs but Cedars in their generation.
And to be in the form of the best of the Bad [1] or the
worst of the Good, will be no satisfaction unto them.

Sect. x.—Make not the consequence of Virtue the ends
thereof. Be not beneficent for a name or Cymbal of applause, nor exact and just in Commerce for the advantages of Trust and Credit, which attend the reputation
of true and punctual dealing. For these Rewards, though
unsought for, plain Virtue will bring with her. To have
other by-ends in good actions sowers Laudable performances, which must have deeper roots, motives, and insti-
gations, to give them the stamp of Virtues.

Sect. xi.—Let not the Law of thy Country be the non
ultra of thy Honesty; nor think that always good enough
which the Law will make good. Narrow not the Law of
Charity, Equity, Mercy. Joyn Gospel Righteousness with
Legal Right. Be not a mere *Gamaliel* in the Faith, but
let the Sermon in the Mount be thy *Targum* unto the
Law of *Sinah*.

Sect. xii.—Live by old Ethicks and the classical Rules
of Honesty. Put no new names or notions upon Authentic Virtues and Vices. Think not that Morality is Ambu-
latory; that Vices in one age are not Vices in another;
or that Virtues, which are under the everlasting Seal of
right Reason, may be Stamped by Opinion. And therefore, though vicious times invert the opinions of things,
and set up new Ethicks against Virtue, yet hold thou
unto old Morality; and rather than follow a multitude
to do evil, stand like *Pompey's* Pillar conspicuous by thyself, and single in Integrity. And since the worst of times
afford imitable Examples of Virtue; since no Deluge of

[1] *Optimi malorum pessimi bonorum.*

Vice is like to be so general, but more than eight will escape; Eye well those Heroes who have held their Heads above Water, who have touched Pitch, and not been defiled, and in the common Contagion have remained uncorrupted.

SECT. XIII.—Let Age not Envy draw wrinkles on thy cheeks, be content to be envy'd, but envy not. Embulation may be plausible and Indignation allowable, but admit no treaty with that passion which no circumstance can make good. A displacency at the good of others because they enjoy it, though not unworthy of it, is an absurd depravity, sticking fast unto corrupted nature, and often too hard for Humility and Charity, the great Suppressors of Envy. This surely is a lyon not to be strangled but by *Hercules* himself, or the highest stress of our minds, and an Atom of that power *which subdueth all things unto itself.*

SECT. XIV.—Owe not thy Humility unto humiliation from adversity, but look humbly down in that State when others look upwards upon thee. Think not thy own shadow longer than that of others, nor delight to take the Altitude of thyself. Be patient in the age of Pride, when Men live by short intervals of Reason under the dominion of Humour and Passion, when it's in the Power of every one to transform thee out of thyself, and run thee into the short madness. If you cannot imitate *Job,* yet come not short of *Socrates,* and those patient Pagans who tired the Tongues of their Enemies, while they perceived they spit their malice at brazen Walls and Statues.

SECT. XV.—Let *not the sun* in Capricorn[1] *go down upon thy wrath,* but write thy wrongs in Ashes. Draw the curtain of Night upon injuries, shut them up in the Tower

[1] Even when the Days are shortest.

of Oblivion,[1] and let them be as though they had not been. To forgive our Enemies, yet hope that God will punish them, is not to forgive enough. To forgive them ourselves, and not to pray God to forgive them, is a partial piece of Charity. Forgive thine enemies totally, and without any reserve, that however God will revenge thee.

SECT. XVI.—While thou so hotly disclaimest the Devil, be not guilty of Diabolism. Fall not into one name with that unclean Spirit, nor act his nature whom thou so much abhorrest; that is, to Accuse, Calumniate, Backbite, Whisper, Detract, or sinistrously interpret others. Degenerous depravities, and narrow-minded vices! not only below St. *Paul's* noble Christian but *Aristotle's* true Gentleman.[2] Trust not with some that the Epistle of St. *James* is Apocryphal, and so read with less fear than Stabbing Truth, that in company with this vice thy Religion is in vain. *Moses* broke the Tables without breaking of the Law; but where Charity is broke, the Law itself is shattered, which cannot be whole without Love, which is the fulfilling of it. Look humbly upon thy Virtues, and though thou art Rich in some, yet think thyself Poor and Naked without that Crowning Grace, which thinketh no evil, which envieth not, which beareth, hopeth, believeth, endureth all things. With these sure Graces, while busy Tongues are crying out for a drop of cold Water, mutes may be in happiness, and sing the *Trisagion*[3] in Heaven.

SECT. XVII.—However thy understanding may waver in the Theories of True and False, yet fasten the Rudder of thy Will, steer strait unto good and fall not foul on evil. Imagination is apt to rove, and conjecture to keep

[1] Alluding unto the Tower of Oblivion mentioned by Procopius, which was the name of a Tower of Imprisonment among the Persians; whoever was put therein was as it were buried alive, and it was death for any but to name him.

[2] See Aristotle's *Ethics,* chapter of Magnanimity.

[3] Holy, holy, holy.

no bounds. Some have run out so far, as to fancy the Stars might be but the light of the Crystalline Heaven shot through perforations on the bodies of the Orbs. Others more Ingeniously doubt whether there hath not been a vast tract of Land in the *Atlantick* Ocean, which Earthquakes and violent causes have long ago devoured. Speculative Misapprehensions may be innocuous, but immorality pernicious; Theoretical mistakes and Physical Deviations, may condemn our Judgments, not lead us into Judgment. But perversity of Will, immoral and sinfull enormities walk with *Adraste* and *Nemesis* at their Backs, pursue us into Judgment, and leave us viciously miserable.

Sect. xviii.—Bid early defiance unto those Vices which are of thine inward Family, and having a root in thy Temper plead a right and propriety in thee. Raise timely batteries against those strongholds built upon the Rock of Nature, and make this a great part of the Militia of thy life. Delude not thyself into iniquities from participation or community, which abate the sense but not the obliquity of them. To conceive sins less, or less of sins, because others also Transgress, were Morally to commit that natural fallacy of Man, to take comfort from Society, and think adversities less, because others also suffer them. The politick nature of Vice must be opposed by Policy. And therefore, wiser Honesties project and plot against it. Wherein, notwithstanding, we are not to rest in generals, or the trite Stratagems of Art. That may succeed with one which may prove successless with another: There is no community or commonweal of Virtue: Every man must study his own œconomy, and adapt such rules unto the figure of himself.

Sect. xix.—Be substantially great in thyself, and more than thou appearest unto others; and let the World be deceived in thee, as they are in the Lights of Heaven. Hang early plummets upon the heels of Pride, and let

Ambition have but an Epicycle and narrow circuit in thee. Measure not thyself by thy morning shadow, but by the extent of thy grave, and Reckon thyself above the Earth by the line thou must be contented with under it. Spread not into boundless Expansions either of designs or desires. Think not that mankind liveth but for a few, and that the rest are born but to serve those Ambitions, which make but flies of Men and wildernesses of whole Nations. Swell not into vehement actions which imbroil and confound the Earth; but be one of those violent ones which force the kingdom of heaven.[1] If thou must needs rule, be *Zeno's* king, and enjoy that Empire which every Man gives himself. He who is thus his own Monarch contentedly sways the Sceptre of himself, not envying the Glory of Crowned Heads and Elohims of the Earth. Could the World unite in the practice of that despised train of Virtues, which the Divine Ethicks of our Saviour hath so inculcated upon us, the furious face of things must disappear, Eden would be yet to be found, and the Angels might look down, not with pity, but Joy upon us.

SECT. xx.—Though the Quickness of thine Ear were able to reach the noise of the Moon, which some think it maketh in it's rapid revolution; though the number of thy ears should equal *Argus* his Eyes; yet stop them all with the wise man's wax, and be deaf unto the suggestions of Tale-bearers, Calumniators, Pickthank or Malevolent Delators, who while quiet Men sleep, sowing the Tares of discord and division, distract the tranquillity of Charity and all friendly Society. These are the Tongues that set the world on fire, cankers of reputation, and like that of *Jonas* his Gourd, wither a good name in a night. Evil Spirits may sit still, while these Spirits walk about and perform the business of Hell. To speak more strictly, our corrupted hearts are the Factories of the Devil, which may be at work without his presence. For when that cir-

[1] Matthew xi.

cumventing Spirit hath drawn Malice, Envy, and all un-
righteousness unto well rooted habits in his disciples,
iniquity then goes on upon its own legs, and if the gate
of Hell were shut up for a time, Vice would still be fertile
and produce the fruits of Hell. Thus when God forsakes
us, Satan also leaves us. For such offenders he looks upon
as sure and sealed up, and his temptations then needless
unto them.

SECT. XXI.—Annihilate not the Mercies of God by the
Oblivion of Ingratitude. For Oblivion is a kind of Annihilation, and for things to be as though they had not
been is like unto never being. Make not thy Head a
Grave, but a Repository of God's mercies. Though thou
hadst the Memory of *Seneca,* or *Simonides,* and Conscience, the punctual Memorist within us, yet trust not
to thy Remembrance in things which need Phylacteries.
Register not only strange but merciful occurrences: Let
Ephemerides not *Olympiads* give thee account of his mercies. Let thy Diaries stand thick with dutiful Mementos
and Asterisks of acknowledgment. And to be complete
and forget nothing, date not his mercy from thy nativity,
Look beyond the World, and before the Æra of Adam.

SECT. XXII.—Paint not the sepulcher of thyself, and
strive not to beautify thy corruption. Be not an Advocate
for thy Vices, nor call for many Hour-Glasses to justify
thy imperfections. Think not that always good which
thou thinkest thou canst always make good, nor that concealed which the Sun doth not behold. That which the
Sun doth not now see will be visible when the Sun is out,
and the Stars are fallen from Heaven. Meanwhile there
is no darkness unto Conscience, which can see without
Light, and in the deepest obscurity give a clear Draught
of things, which the Cloud of dissimulation hath conceal'd from all eyes. There is a natural standing Court
within us, examining, acquitting, and condemning at
the Tribunal of ourselves, wherein iniquities have their

natural Thetas[1] and no nocent[2] is absolved by the verdict of himself. And therefore although our transgressions shall be tryed at the last bar, the process need not be long: for the judge of all knoweth all, and every Man will nakedly know himself. And when so few are like to plead not Guilty, the Assize must soon have an end.

SECT. XXIII.—Comply with some humors, bear with others, but serve none. Civil complacency consists with decent honesty: Flattery is a Juggler, and no Kin unto Sincerity. But while thou maintainest the plain path, and scornest to flatter others, fall not into self Adulation, and become not thine own Parasite. Be deaf unto thy self, and be not betrayed at home. Self-credulity, pride, and levity lead unto self-Idolatry. There is no *Damocles* like unto self opinion, nor any *Siren* to our own fawning Conceptions. To magnify our minor things, or hug ourselves in our apparitions; to afford a credulous Ear unto the clawing suggestions of fancy; to pass our days in painted mistakes of ourselves; and though we behold our own blood, to think ourselves sons of *Jupiter;*[3] are blandishments of self-love, worse than outward delusion. By this Imposture Wise Men sometimes are Mistaken in their Elevation, and look above themselves. And Fools, which are Antipodes unto the Wise, conceive themselves to be but their *Periœci,* and in the same parallel with them.

SECT. XXIV.—Be not a *Hercules furens* abroad, and a Poltroon within thyself. To chase our Enemies out of the Field, and be led captive by our Vices; to beat down our Foes, and fall down to our Concupiscences; are Solecisms in Moral Schools, and no Laurel attends them. To well manage our Affections, and wild Horses of *Plato,*

---

[1] Θ a theta inscribed upon the judge's tessera or ballot was a mark for death or capital condemnation.—*Dr. J.*

[2] Se

Judice nemo nocens absolvitur.—JUV.—*Dr. J.*

[3] As Alexander the Great did.

are the highest Circenses: and the noblest Digladiation[1] is in the Theater of ourselves; for therein our inward Antagonists, not only like common Gladiators, with ordinary Weapons and down right Blows make at us, but also like Retiary and Laqueary[2] Combatants, with Nets, Frauds, and Entanglements fall upon us. Weapons for such combats are not to be forged at *Lipara: Vulcan's* Art doth nothing in this internal Militia; wherein not the armour of *Achilles,* but the Armature of St. *Paul,* gives the Glorious day, and Triumphs not Leading up into Capitols, but up into the highest Heavens. And therefore while so many think it the only valour to command and master others, study thou the Dominion of thyself, and quiet thine own Commotions. Let Right reason be thy *Lycurgus,* and lift up thy hand unto the Law of it: move by the Intelligences of the superior Faculties, not by the Rapt of Passion, nor merely by that of Temper and Constitution. They who are merely carried on by the Wheel of such inclinations, without the Hand and Guidance of Sovereign Reason, are but the Automatous part of mankind, rather lived than living, or at least underliving themselves.

SECT. XXV.—Let not Fortune, which hath no name in Scripture, have any in thy Divinity. Let Providence, not Chance have the honour of thy acknowledgments, and be thy *Œdipus* in Contingencies. Mark well the Paths and winding Ways thereof; but be not too wise in the Construction, or sudden in the Application. The Hand of Providence writes often by Abbreviatures, Hieroglyphics or short Characters, which, like the Laconism on the Wall, are not to be made out but by a Hint or Key from that Spirit which indicted them. Leave future occurrences to their uncertainties, think that which is present thy

[1] *Digladiation.* Fencing match.—*Dr. J.*

[2] *Retiary and laqueary.* The *retiarius* or *laquearius* was a prize-fighter, who entangled his opponent in a net, which by some dextrous management he threw upon him.—*Dr. J.*

own; and since 'tis easier to foretell an Eclipse, than a foul Day at some distance, Look for little Regular below. Attend with patience the uncertainty of Things, and what lieth yet unexerted in the Chaos of Futurity. The uncertainty and ignorance of Things to come makes the World new unto us by unexpected Emergences, whereby we pass not our days in the trite road of affairs affording no Novity; for the novellizing Spirit of Man lives by variety, and the new Faces of Things.

SECT. XXVI.—Though a contented Mind enlargeth the dimension of little things, and unto some 'tis Wealth enough not to be Poor, and others are well content, if they be but Rich enough to be Honest, and to give every Man his due: yet fall not into that obsolete Affectation of Bravery to throw away thy Money, and to reject all Honours or Honourable stations in this courtly and splendid World. Old Generosity is superannuated, and such contempt of the World out of date. No Man is now like to refuse the favour of great ones, or be content to say unto Princes, stand out of my sun. And if any there be of such antiquated Resolutions, they are not like to be tempted out of them by great ones; and 'tis fair if they escape the name of Hypochondriacks from the Genius of latter times, unto whom contempt of the World is the most contemptible opinion, and to be able, like *Bias,* to carry all they have about them were to be the eighth wise-man. However, the old tetrick Philosophers look'd always with Indignation upon such a Face of Things, and observing the unnatural current of Riches, Power, and Honour in the World, and withal the imperfection and demerit of persons often advanced unto them, were tempted into angry Opinions, that Affairs were ordered more by Stars than Reason, and that things went on rather by Lottery, than Election.

SECT. XXVII.—If thy Vessel be but small in the Ocean of this World, if Meanness of Possessions be thy allotment upon Earth, forget not those Virtues which the great disposer of all bids thee to entertain from thy Quality and Condition; that is, Submission, Humility, Content of mind, and Industry. Content may dwell in all Stations. To be low, but above contempt, may be high enough to be Happy. But many of low Degree may be higher than computed, and some Cubits above the common Commensuration; for in all States Virtue gives Qualifications, and Allowances, which make out defects. Rough Diamonds are sometimes mistaken for Pebbles, and Meanness may be Rich in Accomplishments, which Riches in vain desire. If our merits be above our Stations, if our intrinsical Value be greater than what we go for, or our Value than our Valuation, and if we stand higher in God's than in the Censor's book; it may make some equitable balance in the inequalities of this World, and there may be no such vast Chasm or Gulf between disparities as common Measures determine. The Divine Eye looks upon high and low differently from that of Man. They who seem to stand upon *Olympus,* and high mounted unto our eyes, may be but in the Valleys, and low Ground unto his; for he looks upon those as highest who nearest approach his Divinity, and upon those as lowest, who are farthest from it.

SECT. XXVIII.—When thou lookest upon the Imperfections of others, allow one Eye for what is Laudable in them, and the balance they have from some excellency, which may render them considerable. While we look with fear or hatred upon the Teeth of the Viper, we may behold his Eye with love. In venomous Natures something may be amiable: Poysons afford Antipoysons: nothing is totally, or altogether uselessly bad. Notable Virtues are sometimes dashed with notorious Vices, and in some vicious tempers have been found illustrious Acts of Virtue; which makes such observable worth in some actions of King *Demetrius, Antonius,* and *Ahab,* as are not to be found in the same kind in *Aristides, Numa,* or *David.* Constancy, Generosity, Clemency, and Liberality have been highly conspicuous in some Persons not marked out in other concerns for Example or Imitation. But since Goodness is exemplary in all, if others have not our Virtues, let us not be wanting in theirs, nor scorning them for their Vices whereof we are free, be condemned by their Virtues, wherein we are deficient. There is Dross, Alloy, and Embasement in all human Temper; and he flieth without Wings, who thinks to find Ophyr or pure Metal in any. For perfection is not like Light center'd in any one Body, but like the dispersed Seminalities of Vegetables at the Creation scattered through the whole Mass of the Earth, no place producing all and almost all some. So that 'tis well, if a perfect Man can be made out of many Men, and, to the perfect Eye of God, even out of Mankind. Time, which perfects some Things, imperfects also others. Could we intimately apprehend the Ideated Man, and as he stood in the intellect of God upon the first exertion by Creation, we might more narrowly comprehend our present Degeneration, and how widely we are fallen from the pure Exemplar and Idea of our nature: for after this the corruptive Elongation from a primitive and pure Creation, we are almost lost in Degeneration; and *Adam* hath not only fallen from his Creator, but we ourselves from *Adam,* our Tycho and primary Generator.

SECT. XXIX.—Quarrel not rashly with Adversities not yet understood; and overlook not the Mercies often bound up in them: for we consider not sufficiently the good of Evils, nor fairly compute the Mercies of Providence in things afflictive at first hand. The famous *Andreas Doria* being invited to a Feast by *Aloysio Fieschi,* with design to Kill him, just the night before, fell mercifully into a fit of the Gout and so escaped that mischief. When *Cato* intended to Kill himself, from a blow which he gave his servant, who would not reach his Sword unto him, his Hand so swell'd that he had much ado to Effect his design. Hereby any one but a resolved Stoick might have taken a fair hint of consideration, and that some mercifull Genius would have contrived his preservation. To be sagacious in such intercurrences is not Superstition, but wary and pious Discretion, and to contemn such hints were to be deaf unto the speaking hand of God, wherein *Socrates* and *Cardan* would hardly have been mistaken.

SECT. XXX.—Break not open the gate of Destruction, and make no haste or bustle unto Ruin. Post not heedlessly on unto the *non ultra* of Folly, or precipice of Perdition. Let vicious ways have their Tropicks and Deflections, and swim in the Waters of Sin but as in the *Asphaltick* Lake, though smeared and defiled, not to sink to the bottom. If thou hast dipt thy foot in the Brink, yet venture not over *Rubicon*. Run not into Extremities from whence there is no regression. In the vicious ways of the World it mercifully falleth out that we become not extempore wicked, but it taketh some time and pains to undo our selves. We fall not from Virtue, like *Vulcan* from Heaven, in a day. Bad Dispositions require some time to grow into bad Habits, bad Habits must undermine good, and often-repeated acts make us habitually evil: so that by gradual depravations, and while we are but staggeringly evil, we are not left without Parentheses of considerations, thoughtful rebukes, and merciful interventions, to recall us unto our selves. For the Wisdom of God hath methodiz'd the course of things unto the best advantage of goodness, and thinking Considerators overlook not the tract thereof.

SECT. XXXI.—Since Men and Women have their proper Virtues and Vices; and even Twins of different sexes have not only distinct coverings in the Womb, but differing qualities and Virtuous Habits after; transplace not their

Proprieties and confound not their Distinctions. Let Masculine and feminine accomplishments shine in their proper Orbs, and adorn their Respective subjects. However unite not the Vices of both Sexes in one; be not Monstrous in Iniquity, nor Hermaphroditically Vitious.

SECT. XXXII.—If generous Honesty, Valour, and plain Dealing be the Cognisance of thy Family or Characteristick of thy Country, hold fast such inclinations suckt in with thy first Breath, and which lay in the Cradle with thee. Fall not into transforming degenerations, which under the old name create a new Nation. Be not an Alien in thine own Nation; bring not Orontes into Tiber; learn the Virtues not the Vices of thy foreign Neighbours, and make thy imitation by discretion not contagion. Feel something of thyself in the noble Acts of thy Ancestors, and find in thine own Genius that of thy Predecessors. Rest not under the Expired merits of others, shine by those of thy own. Flame not like the central fire which enlightneth no Eyes, which no Man seeth, and most men think there's no such thing to be seen. Add one Ray unto the common Lustre; add not only to the Number, but the Note of thy Generation; and prove not a Cloud but an Asterisk in thy region.

SECT. XXXIII.—Since thou hast an Alarum in thy Breast, which tells thee thou hast a Living Spirit in thee above two thousand times in an hour; dull not away thy Days in sloathful supinity and the tediousness of doing nothing. To strenuous Minds there is an inquietude in over quietness, and no laboriousness in labour; and to tread a mile after the slow pace of a Snail, or the heavy measures of the Lazy of Brazilia, were a most tiring Pennance, and worse than a Race of some furlongs at the Olympicks. The rapid courses of the heavenly bodies are rather imitable by our Thoughts than our corporeal Motions; yet the solemn motions of our lives amount unto a greater measure than is commonly apprehended. Some few men have surrounded the Globe of the Earth; yet many in the set Locomotions and movements of their days have measured the circuit of it, and twenty thousand miles have been exceeded by them. Move circumspectly not meticulously, and rather carefully sollicitous than anxiously sollicitudinous. Think not there is a Lyon in the way, nor walk with Leaden Sandals in the paths of Goodness; but in all Virtuous motions let Prudence determine thy measures. Strive not to run like *Hercules* a furlong in a breath: Festination may prove Precipitation; Deliberating delay may be wise cunctation, and slowness no sloathfulness.

SECT. XXXIV.—Since Virtuous Actions have their own Trumpets, and without any noise from thy self will have their resound abroad; busy not thy best Member in the Encomium of thy self. Praise is a debt we owe unto the Virtues of others, and due unto our own from all, whom Malice hath not made Mutes, or Envy struck Dumb. Fall not however into the common prevaricating way of self-commendation and boasting, by denoting the imperfections of others. He who discommendeth others obliquely commendeth himself. He who whispers their infirmities proclaims his own Exemptions from them, and consequently says, I am not as this Publican, or *Hic Niger*,[1] whom I talk of. Open ostentation and loud vain-glory is more tolerable than this obliquity, as but containing some Froath, no Ink, as but consisting of a personal piece of folly, nor complicated with uncharitableness. Superfluously we seek a precarious applause abroad: every good Man hath his plaudite within himself; and though his Tongue be silent, is not without loud Cymbals in his Breast. Conscience will become his Panegyrist, and never forget to crown and extol him unto himself.

SECT. XXXV.—Bless not thyself only that thou wert born

[1] *Hic Niger est, hunc tu Romane caveto.*—Horace.

in *Athens;*[1] but, among thy multiplyed acknowledgments lift up one hand unto Heaven, that thou wert born of Honest Parents, that Modesty, Humility, Patience, and Veracity, lay in the same Egg, and came unto the World with thee. From such foundations thou may'st be Happy in a virtuous precocity, and make an early and long walk in Goodness; so may'st thou more naturally feel the contrariety of Vice unto Nature, and resist some by the Antidote of thy Temper. As charity covers, so Modesty preventeth a multitude of sins; withholding from noon day Vices and brazen-brow'd Iniquities, from sinning on the house-top, and painting our follies with the rays of the Sun. Where this Virtue reigneth, though Vice may show its Head, it cannot be in its Glory: where shame of sin sets, look not for Virtue to arise; for when Modesty taketh Wing, *Astrea*[2] goes soon after.

SECT. XXXVI.—The Heroical vein of Mankind runs much in the Souldiery, and courageous part of the World; and in that form we oftenest find Men above Men. History is full of the gallantry of that Tribe; and when we read their notable Acts, we easily find what a difference there is between a Life in *Plutarch* and in *Laertius.* Where true Fortitude dwells, Loyalty, Bounty, Friendship, and Fidelity may be found. A man may confide in persons constituted for noble ends, who dare do and suffer, and who have a Hand to burn for their Country and their Friend. Small and creeping things are the product of petty Souls. He is like to be mistaken, who makes choice of a covetous Man for a Friend, or relieth upon the Reed of narrow and poltron Friendship. Pityful things are only to be found in the cottages of such Breasts; but bright Thoughts, clear Deeds, Constancy, Fidelity, Bounty, and generous Honesty are the Gems

---

[1] As Socrates did. Athens a place of Learning and Civility.
[2] Astrea, Goddess of Justice and consequently of all Virtue.

of noble Minds; wherein, to derogate from none, the true Heroick English Gentleman hath no Peer.

PART THE SECOND

Sect. i.—Punish not thyself with Pleasure; Glut not thy sense with palative Delights; nor revenge the contempt of Temperance by the penalty of Satiety. Were there an Age of delight or any pleasure durable, who would not honour *Volupia?* but the Race of Delight is short, and Pleasures have mutable faces. The pleasures of one age are not pleasures in another, and their Lives fall short of our own. Even in our sensual days the strength of delight is in its seldomness or rarity, and sting in its satiety: Mediocrity is its Life, and immoderacy its Confusion. The Luxurious Emperors of old inconsiderately satiated themselves with the Dainties of Sea and Land, till, wearied through all varieties, their refections became a study unto them, and they were fain to feed by Invention. Novices in true Epicurism! which, by mediocrity, paucity, quick and healthful Appetite, makes delights smartly acceptable; whereby *Epicurus* himself found *Jupiter's* brain in a piece of Cytheridian Cheese,[1] and the Tongues of Nightingals in a dish of Onyons. Hereby healthful and temperate poverty hath the start of nauseating Luxury; unto whose clear and naked appetite every meal is a feast, and in one single dish the first course of Metellus;[2] who are cheaply hungry, and never loose their hunger, or advantage of a craving appetite, because obvious food contents it; while *Nero*,[3] half famish'd, could not feed upon a piece of Bread, and ling'ring after his snowed water, hardly got down an ordinary cup

---

[1] *Cerebrum Jovis,* for a Delicious bit.

[2] Metellus his riotous Pontifical Supper, the great variety whereat is to be seen in *Macrobius* (see note).

[3] Nero in his flight.—*Sueton.*

of Calda.[1] By such circumscriptions of pleasure the contemned Philosophers reserved unto themselves the secret
of Delight, which the *Helluos*[2] of those days lost in their
exorbitances. In vain we study Delight: It is at the command of every sober Mind, and in every sense born with
us: but Nature, who teacheth us the rule of pleasure,
instructeth also in the bounds thereof, and where its
line expireth. And therefore Temperate Minds, not
pressing their pleasures until the sting appeareth, enjoy
their contentations contentedly, and without regret,
and so escape the folly of excess, to be pleased unto displacency.

SECT. II.—Bring candid Eyes unto the perusal of men's
works, and let not *Zoilism* or Detraction blast well-intended labours. He that endureth no faults in men's
writings must only read his own, wherein for the most
part all appeareth White. Quotation mistakes, inadvertency, expedition, and human Lapses may make not only
Moles but Warts in Learned Authors, who notwithstanding being judged by the capital matter admit not
of disparagement. I should unwillingly afirm that *Cicero*
was but slightly versed in *Homer,* because in his work
De Gloria he ascribed those verses unto *Ajax,* which
were delivered by *Hector.* What if *Plautus,* in the account of *Hercules,* mistaketh nativity for conception?
Who would have mean thoughts of *Apollinaris Sido-
nius,* who seems to mistake the river *Tigris for Euphra-
tes;* and, though a good Historian and learned Bishop
of *Auvergne* had the misfortune to be out in the Story of
David, making mention of him when the Ark was sent
back by the *Philstins* upon a Cart; which was before his
time. Though I have no great opinion of *Machiavel's*
Learning, yet I shall not presently say, that he was but
a Novice in Roman History, because he was mistaken in

[1] *Caldæ gelidæque Minister.*
[2] *Helluos.* Gluttons.—*Dr. J.*

placing *Commodus* after the Emperor *Severus*. Capital Truths are to be narrowly eyed, collateral Lapses and circumstantial deliveries not to be too strictly sifted. And if the substantial subject be well forged out, we need not examine the sparks, which irregularly fly from it.

SECT. III.—Let well weighed Considerations, not stiff and peremptory Assumptions, guide thy discourses, Pen, and Actions. To begin or continue our works like *Trismegistus* of old, *verum certè verum atque verissimum est*,[1] would sound arrogantly unto present Ears in this strict enquiring Age, wherein, for the most part, Probably, and Perhaps, will hardly serve to mollify the Spirit of captious Contradictors. If *Cardan* saith that a Parrot is a beautiful Bird, *Scaliger* will set his Wits o' work to prove it a deformed Animal. The Compage of all Physical Truths is not so closely jointed, but opposition may find intrusion, nor always so closely maintained, as not to suffer attrition. Many Positions seem quodlibetically constituted, and like a *Delphian* Blade, will cut on both sides. Some Truths seem almost Falsehoods and some Falsehoods almost Truths; wherein Falsehood and Truth seem almost æquilibriously stated, and but a few grains of distinction to bear down the ballance. Some have digged deep, yet glanced by the Royal Vein, and a Man may come unto the *Pericardium*, but not the Heart of Truth. Besides, many things are known, as some are seen, that is by Parallaxis, or at some distance from their true and proper beings, the superficial regard of things having a different aspect from their true and central Natures. And this moves sober Pens unto suspensory and timorous assertions, nor presently to obtrude them as Sybils leaves, which after considerations may find to be but folious appearances, and not the central and vital interiours of Truth.

[1] *In Tabula Smaragdina.*

SECT. IV.—Value the Judicious, and let not mere acquests in minor parts of Learning gain thy pre-existimation. 'Tis an unjust way of compute to magnify a weak Head for some Latin abilities, and to undervalue a solid Judgment, because he knows not the genealogy of *Hector*. When that notable king of *France*[1] would have his Son to know but one sentence in Latin, had it been a good one, perhaps it had been enough. Natural parts and good Judgments rule the World. States are not governed by Ergotisms.[2] Many have Ruled well who could not perhaps define a Commonwealth, and they who understand not the Globe of the Earth, command a great part of it. Where natural logick prevails not, Artificial too often faileth. Where Nature fills the Sails, the Vessel goes smoothly on, and when Judgment is the Pilot, the Ensurance need not be high. When Industry builds upon Nature, we may expect Pyramids: where that foundation is wanting, the structure must be low. They do most by Books, who could do much without them, and he that chiefly owes himself unto himself, is the substantial Man.

SECT. V.—Let thy Studies be free as thy Thoughts and Contemplations: but fly not only upon the wings of Imagination; Joyn Sense unto Reason, and Experiment unto Speculation, and so give life unto Embryon Truths, and Verities yet in their Chaos. There is nothing more acceptable unto the Ingenious World, than this noble Eluctation[3] of Truth; wherein, against the tenacity of Prejudice and Prescription, this Century now prevaileth. What Libraries of new Volumes after times will behold, and in what a new World of Knowledge the eyes of our Posterity may be happy, a few Ages may joyfully declare; and is but a cold thought unto those, who cannot hope

[1] Lewis the Eleventh. *Qui nescit dissimulare nescit Regnare.*
[2] *Ergotisms.* Conclusions deduced according to the forms of logic.—Dr. J.
[3] *Eluctation.* Forcible eruption.—*Dr. J.*

to behold this Exantlation of Truth, or that obscured Virgin half out of the Pit. Which might make some content with a commutation of the time of their lives, and to commend the fancy of the *Pythagorean* metempsychosis; whereby they might hope to enjoy this happiness in their third or fourth selves, and behold that in *Pythagoras,* which they now but foresee in *Euphorbus.*[1] The World, which took but six days to make, is like to take six thousand to make out: meanwhile old Truths voted down begin to resume their places, and new ones arise upon us; wherein there is no comfort in the happiness of *Tully's* Elysium,[2] or any satisfaction from the Ghosts of the Ancients, who knew so little of what is now well known. Men disparage not antiquity, who prudently exalt new Enquiries, and make them the Judges of Truth, who were but fellow Enquirers of it. Who can but magnify the Endeavors of *Aristotle,* and the noble start which Learning had under him; or less than pity the slender progression made upon such advantages? while many Centuries were lost in repetitions and transcriptions sealing up the Book of Knowledge. And therefore rather than to swell the leaves of Learning by fruitless Repetitions, to sing the same Song in all Ages, nor adventure at Essays beyond the attempt of others, many would be content that some would write like *Helmont* or *Paracelsus;* and be willing to endure the monstrosity of some opinions, for diveres singular notions requiting such aberrations.

SECT. VI.—Despite not the obliquities of younger ways, nor despair of better things whereof there is yet no prospect. Who would imagine that *Diogenes,* who in his younger days was a falsifier of Money, should in the after

[1] Ipse ego, nam memini, Trojani tempore belli,
   Panthoides Euphorbus eram.—OVID.
[2] Who comforted himself that he should there converse with the old Philosophers.

course of his Life be so great a contemner of Metal? Some
Negros, who believe the Resurrection, think that they
shall rise white.[1] Even in this life Regeneration may imitate Resurrection, our black and vitious tinctures may
wear of, and goodness cloath us with candour. Good Admonitions Knock not always in vain. There will be signal
Examples of God's mercy, and the Angels must not want
their charitable Rejoyces for the conversion of lost Sinners. Figures of most Angles do nearest approach unto
Circles which have no Angles at all. Some may be near
unto goodness, who are conceived far from it, and many
things happen, not likely to ensue from any promises of Antecedencies. Culpable beginnings have found
commendable conclusions, and infamous courses pious
retractations. Detestable Sinners have proved exemplary Converts on Earth, and may be Glorious in the
Apartment of *Mary Magdalen* in Heaven. Men are not
the same through all divisions of their Ages. Time, experience, self Reflections, and God's mercies make in
some well-temper'd minds a kind of translation before
Death, and Men to differ from themselves as well as from
other Persons. Hereof the old World afforded many
Examples, to the infamy of latter Ages, wherein Men
too often live by the rule of their inclinations; so that,
without any Astral prediction, the first day gives the
last,[2] Men are commonly as they were, or rather, as bad
dispositions run into worser habits, the Evening doth not
crown, but sowerly conclude the Day.

SECT. VII.—If the Almighty will not spare us according to his merciful capitulation at *Sodom,* if his Goodness please not to pass over a great deal of Bad for a
small pittance of Good, or to look upon us in a Lump;
there is slender hope for Mercy, or sound presumption
of fulfilling half his Will, either in Persons or Nations:

[1] Mandelslo's travels.
[2] *Primusque dies dedit extremum.*

they who excel in some Virtues being so often defective
in others; few Men driving at the extent and amplitude
of Goodness, but computing themselves by their best
parts, and others by their worst, are content to rest in
those Virtues, which others commonly want. Which
makes this speckled Face of Honesty in the World; and
which was the imperfection of the old Philosophers and
great retenders unto Virtue, who well declining the
gaping Vices of Intemperance, Incontinency, Violence
and Oppression, were yet blindly peccant in iniquities of
closer faces, were envious, malicious, contemners, scoffers,
censurers, and stuffed with Wizard Vices, no less deprav-
ing the Ethereal particle and diviner portion of Man.
For Envy, Malice, Hatred, are the qualities of *Satan*,
close and dark like himself; and where such brands
smoak, the Soul cannot be White. Vice may be had at all
prices; expensive and costly iniquities, which make the
noise, cannot be every Man's sins: but the soul may be
foully inquinated [1] at a very low rate, and a Man may
be cheaply vitious, to the perdition of himself.

SECT. VIII.—Opinion rides upon the neck of Reason,
and Men are Happy, Wise, or Learned, according as that
Empress shall set them down in the Register of Reputation. However weigh not thyself in the scales of thy own
opinion, but let the Judgment of the Judicious be the
Standard of thy Merit. Self-estimation is a flatterer too
readily entitling us unto Knowledge and Abilities, which
others sollicitously labour after, and doubtfully think
they attain. Surely such confident tempers do pass their
days in best tranquillity, who, resting in the opinion of
their own abilities, who, resting in the opinion of their
own abilities, are happily gull'd by such contentation;
wherein Pride, Self-conceit, Confidence, and Opinia-
trity will hardly suffer any to complain of imperfection.
To think themselves in the right, or all that right, or only

[1] *Inquinated.* Defiled.—*Dr. J.*

that, which they do or think, is a fallacy of high content; though others laugh in their sleeves, and look upon them as in a deluded state of Judgment. Wherein, notwithstanding 'twere but a civil piece of complacency to suffer them to sleep who would not wake, to let them rest in their securities, nor by dissent or opposition to stagger their contentments.

SECT. IX.—Since the Brow speaks often true, since Eyes and Noses have Tongues, and the countenance proclaims the Heart and inclinations; let observation so far instruct thee in Physiognomical lines, as to be some Rule for thy distinction, and Guide for thy affection unto such as look most like Men. Mankind, methinks, is comprehended in a few Faces, if we exclude all Visages, which any way participate of Symmetries and Schemes of Look common unto other Animals. For as though Man were the extract of the World, in whom all were *in coagulato,* which in their forms were *in soluto* and at Extension; we often observe that Men do most act those Creatures, whose constitution, parts, and complexion do most predominate in their mixtures. This is a corner-stone in Physiognomy, and holds some Truth not only in particular Persons, but also in whole Nations. There are therefore Provincial Faces, National Lips and Noses, which testify not only the Natures of those Countries, but of those which have them elsewhere. Thus we may make *England* the whole Earth, dividing it not only into *Europe, Asia, Africa,* but the particular Regions thereof, and may in some latitude affirm, that there are *Ægyptians, Scythians, Indians* among us; who though born in *England,* yet carry the Faces and Air of those Countries, and are also agreeable and correspondent unto their Natures. Faces look uniformly unto our Eyes: how they appear unto some Animals of a more piercing or differing sight, who are able to discover the inequalities, rubbs, and hairiness of the Skin, is not without good doubt.

And, therefore in reference unto man *Cupid* is said to be blind. Affection should not be too sharp-Eyed, and Love is not to be made by magnifying Glasses. If things were seen as they truly are, the beauty of bodies would be much abridged. And therefore the wise Contriver hath drawn the pictures and outsides of things softly and amiably unto the natural Edge of our Eyes, not leaving them able to discover those uncomely asperities, which make Oyster-shells in good Faces, and Hedghoggs even in *Venus's* moles.

SECT. X.—Court not Felicity too far, and weary not the favourable hand of Fortune. Glorious actions have their times, extent, and *non ultras*. To put no end unto Attempts were to make prescription of Successes, and to bespeak unhappiness at the last. For the Line of our Lives is drawn with white and black vicissitudes, wherein the extremes hold seldom one complexion. That *Pompey* should obtain the sirname of Great at twenty five years, that Men in their young and active days should be fortunate and perform notable things, is no observation of deep wonder, they having the strength of their fates before them, nor yet acted their parts in the World, for which they were brought into it: whereas Men of years, matured for counsels and designs, seem to be beyond the vigour of their active fortunes, and high exploits of life, providentially ordained unto Ages best agreeable unto them. And therefore many brave men finding their fortune grow faint, and feeling its declination, have timely withdrawn themselves from great attempts, and so escaped the ends of mighty Men, disproportionable to their beginnings. But magnanimous Thoughts have so dimmed the eyes of many, that forgetting the very essence of Fortune, and the vicissitude of good and evil, they apprehend no bottom in felicity; and so have been still tempted on unto mighty Actions, reserved for their destructions. For Fortune lays the Plot of our Adversities in the foundation of our Felicities, blessing us in the first quadrate, to blast us more sharply in the last. And since in the highest felicities there lieth a capacity of the lowest miseries, she hath this advantage from our happiness to make us truly miserable. For to be become acutely miserable we are to be first happy. Affliction smarts most in the most happy state, as having somewhat in it of *Bellisarius* at Beggers bush, or *Bajazet* in the grate. And this the fallen Angels severely understand, who having acted their first part in Heaven, are made sharply miserable by transition, and more afflictively feel the contrary state of Hell.

SECT. XI.—Carry no careless Eye upon the unexpected scenes of things; but ponder the acts of Providence in the publick ends of great and notable Men, set out unto the view of all for no common *memorandums*. The Tragical Exits and unexpected periods of some eminent Persons cannot but amuse considerate Observators; wherein notwithstanding most Men seem to see by extramission, without reception or self-reflexion, and conceive themselves unconcerned by the fallacy of their Exemption: Whereas the Mercy of God hath singled out but few to be the signals of his Justice, leaving the generality of Mankind to the pedagogy of Example. But the inadvertency of our Natures not well apprehending this favourable method and merciful decimation, and that he sheweth in some what others also deserve; they entertain no sense of his hand beyond the stroak of themselves. Whereupon the whole becomes necessarily punished, and the contracted Hand of God extended unto universal Judgments: from whence nevertheless the stupidity of our tempers receives but faint impressions, and in the most Tragical state of times holds but starts of good motions. So that to continue us in goodness there must be iterated returns of misery, and a circulation in afflictions is necessary. And since we cannot be wise by warn-

ings, since plagues are insignificant, except we be per
sonally plagued, since also we cannot be punish'd unto
Amendment by proxy or commutation, nor by vicinity
but contraction; there is an unhappy necessity that we
must smart in our own Skins, and the provoked arm of
the Almighty must fall upon our selves. The capital suf
ferings of others are rather our monitions than acquit
ments. There is but one who dyed salvifically for us, and
able to say unto Death, hitherto shalt thou go and no
farther; only one enlivening Death, which makes Gar
dens of Graves, and that which was sowed in Corrup
tion to arise and flourish in Glory; when Death it self
shall dye, and living shall have no Period, when the
damned shall mourn at the funeral of Death, when Life
not Death shall be the wages of sin, when the second
Death shall prove a miserable Life, and destruction shall
be courted.

SECT. XII.—Although their Thoughts may seem too
severe, who think that few ill natur'd men go to Heaven
yet it may be acknowledged that good-natur'd Persons
are best founded for that place; who enter the World with
good Dispositions and natural Graces, more ready to be
advanced by impressions from above, and christianized
unto pieties; who carry about them plain and downright
dealing Minds, Humility, Mercy, Charity, and Virtues
acceptable unto God and Man. But whatever success
they may have as to Heaven, they are the acceptable Men
on Earth, and happy is he who hath his quiver full of
them for his Friends. These are not the Dens wherein
Falshood lurks, and Hypocrisy hides its Head, wherein
Frowardness makes its Nest, or where Malice, Hard
Heartedness, and Oppression love to dwell; nor those by
whom the Poor get little, and the Rich sometimes loose
all; Men not of retracted Looks, but who carry their
Hearts in their Faces, and need not to be look'd upon

with perspectives; not sordidly or mischievously ingrateful; who cannot learn to ride upon the neck of the afflicted, nor load the heavy laden, but who keep the Temple of *Janus* shut by peaceable and quiet tempers; who make not only the best Friends, but the best Enemies, as easier to forgive than offend, and ready to pass by the second offence, before they avenge the first; who make natural Royalists, obedient Subjects, kind and merciful Princes, verified in our own, one of the best natur'd kings of this Throne. Of the old Roman Emperours the best were the best-natur'd; though they made but a small number, and might be writ in a Ring. Many of the rest were as bad Men as Princes; Humorists rather than of good humors; and of good natural parts, rather than of good natures; which did but arm their bad inclinations, and make them wittily wicked.

SECT. XIII.—With what shift and pains we come into the World, we remember not; but 'tis commonly found no easy matter to get out of it. Many have studied to exasperate the ways of Death, but fewer hours have been spent to soften that necessity. That the smoothest way unto the grave is made by bleeding, as common opinion presumeth, beside the sick and fainting Languors, which accompany that effusion, the experiment in *Lucan* and *Seneca* will make us doubt; under which the noble Stoick so deeply laboured, that to conceal his affliction, he was fain to retire from the sight of his Wife, and not ashamed to implore the merciful hand of his Physician to shorten his misery therein. *Ovid*,[1] the old Heroes, and the Stoicks, who were so afraid of drowning, as dreading thereby the extinction of their Soul, which they conceived to be a Fire, stood probably in fear of an easier way of Death; wherein the Water, entring the possessions of Air, makes a temperate suffocation, and kills as it were

[1] *Demite naufragium, mors mihi munus erit.*

without a Fever. Surely many, who have had the Spirit
to destroy themselves, have not been ingenious in the
contrivance thereof. 'Twas a dull way practised by
Themistocles, to overwhelm himself with Bulls-blood,[1]
who, being an *Athenian,* might have held an easier
Theory of Death from the State potion of his Country;
from which *Socrates* in *Plato* seemed not to suffer much
more than from the fit of an Ague. *Cato* is much to be
pitied, who mangled himself with poyniards; and *Han-
nibal* seems more subtle, who carried his delivery, not in
the point, but the pummel of his sword.[2]

The *Egyptians* were merciful contrivers, who destroyed
their malefactors by Asps, charming their senses into an
invincible sleep, and killing as it were with *Hermes* his
rod. The Turkish Emperour,[3] odious for other Cruelty,
was herein a remarkable Master of Mercy, killing his
Favourite in his sleep, and sending him from the shade
into the house of darkness. He who had been thus
destroyed would hardly have bled at the presence of his
destroyer; when Men are already dead by metaphor, and
pass but from one sleep unto another, wanting herein
the eminent part of severity, to feel themselves to dye,
and escaping the sharpest attendant of Death, the lively
apprehension thereof. But to learn to dye is better than
to study the ways of dying. Death will find some ways to
unty or cut the most Gordian Knots of Life, and make
men's miseries as mortal as themselves: whereas evil
Spirits, as undying Substances, are unseparable from their
calamities; and therefore they everlastingly struggle under their *Angustias,* and bound up with immortality can
never get out of themselves.

---

[1] Plutarch.
[2] Pummel, wherein he is said to have carried something, whereby
upon a struggle or despair he might deliver himself from all misfortunes. Juvenal says, it was carried in a ring.
[3] Solyman.

PART THE THIRD

SECT. I.—'Tis hard to find a whole Age to imitate, or what Century to propose for Example. Some have been far more approveable than others; but Virtue and Vice, Panegyricks and Satyrs, scatteringly to be found in all. History sets down not only things laudable, but abominable; things which should never have been or never have been known: So that noble patterns must be fetched here and there from single Persons, rather than whole Nations, and from all Nations, rather than anyone. The World was early bad, and the first sin the most deplorable of any. The younger World afforded the oldest Men, and perhaps the Best and the Worst, when length of days made virtuous habits Heroical and immoveable, vitious, inveterate and irreclaimable. And since 'tis said that the imaginations of their hearts were evil, only evil, and continually evil; it may be feared that their sins held pace with their lives; and their Longevity swelling their Impieties, the Longanimity of God would no longer endure such vivacious abominations. Their Impieties were surely of a deep dye, which required the whole Element of Water to wash them away, and overwhelmed their memories with themselves; and so shut up the first Windows of Time, leaving no Histories of those longevous generations, when Men might have been properly Historians, when *Adam* might have read long Lectures unto *Methuselah,* and *Methuselah* unto *Noah.* For had we been happy in just Historical accounts of that unparallel'd World, we might have been acquainted with Wonders, and have understood not a little of the Acts and undertakings of *Moses* his mighty Men, and Men of renown of old; which might have enlarged our Thoughts, and made the World older unto us. For the unknown part of time shortens the estimation, if not the compute of it. What hath escaped our Knowledge, falls not under our Consideration, and what is and will be latent is little better than non-existent.

SECT. II.—Some things are dictated for our Instruction, some acted for our Imitation, wherein 'tis best to ascend unto the highest conformity, and to the honour of the Exemplar. He honours God who imitates him. For what we virtuously imitate we approve and Admire; and since we delight not to imitate Inferiors, we aggrandize and magnify those we imitate; since also we are most apt to imitate those we love, we testify our affection in our imitation of the Inimitable. To affect to be like may be no imitation. To act, and not to be what we pretend to imitate, is but a mimical conformation, and carrieth no Virtue in it. *Lucifer* imitated not God, when he said he would be like the Highest, and he imitated not *Jupiter,* who counterfeited thunder. Where Imitation can go no farther, let Admiration step on, whereof there is no end in the wisest form of Men. Even Angels and Spirits have enough to admire in their sublimer Natures, Admiration being the act of the Creature, and not of God, who doth not Admire himself. Created Natures allow of swelling Hyperboles; nothing can be said Hyperbolically of God, nor will his Attributes admit of expressions above their own Exuperances. *Trismegistus* his Circle, whose center is everywhere, and circumference nowhere, was no Hyperbole. Words cannot exceed, where they cannot express enough. Even the most winged Thoughts fall at the setting out, and reach not the portal of Divinity.

SECT. III.—In Bivious Theorems, and *Janus*-faced Doctrines, let Virtuous considerations state the determination. Look upon Opinions as thou dost upon the Moon, and chuse not the dark hemisphere for thy contemplation. Embrace not the opacous and blind side of Opinions, but that which looks most Luciferously or influ-

entially unto Goodness. 'Tis better to think that there
are Guardian Spirits, than that there are no Spirits to
Guard us; that vicious Persons are Slaves, than that there
is any servitude in Virtue; that times past have been better than times present, than that times were always bad,
and that to be Men it sufficeth to be no better than Men
in all Ages, and so promiscuously to swim down the tur-
bid stream, and make up the grand confusion. Sow not
thy understanding with Opinions, which make nothing
of Iniquities, and fallaciously extenuate Transgressions.
Look upon Vices and vicious Objects with Hyperbolical
Eyes, and rather enlarge their dimensions, that their unseen Deformities may not escape thy sense, and their
Poysonous parts and stings may appear massy and monstrous unto thee; for the undiscerned Particles and Atoms
of Evil deceive us, and we are undone by the Invisibles
of seeming Goodness. We are only deceived in what is
not discerned, and to Err is but to be Blind or Dim-
sighted as to some Perceptions.

SECT. IV.—To be Honest in a right Line,[1] and Virtuous by Epitome, be firm unto such Principles of Goodness, as carry in them Volumes of instruction and may
abridge thy Labour. And since instructions are many,
hold close unto those, whereon the rest depend. So may
we have all in a few, and the Law and the Prophets in
a Rule, the Sacred Writ in Stenography, and the Scripture
in a Nut-Shell. To pursue the osseous and solid part
of Goodness, which gives Stability and Rectitude to all
the rest; To settle on fundamental Virtues, and bid early
defiance unto Mother-Vices, which carry in their Bowels
the seminals of other Iniquities, makes a short cut in
Goodness, and strikes not off an Head but the whole Neck
of *Hydra*. For we are carried into the dark Lake, like the
Ægyptian River into the Sea, by seven principal Ostiaries.
The mother-sins of that number are the Deadly engins

---

[1] Linea Recta brevissima.

of Evil Spirits that undo us, and even evil Spirits themselves, and he who is under the Chains thereof is not
without a possession. *Mary Magdalen* had more than
seven Devils, if these with their Imps were in her, and
he who is thus possessed may literally be named *Legion*.
Where such Plants grow and prosper, look for no Cham-
pain or Region void of Thorns, but productions like the
tree of *Goa*,[1] and Forrests of abomination.

SECT. v.—Guide not the Hand of God, nor order the
Finger of the Almighty unto thy will and pleasure; but
sit quiet in the soft showers of Providence, and Favourable distributions in this World, either to thyself or others. And since not only Judgments have their Errands,
but Mercies their Commissions; snatch not at every Favour, nor think thyself passed by, if they fall upon thy
Neighbour. Rake not up envious displacences at things
successful unto others, which the wise Disposer of all
thinks not fit for thyself. Reconcile the events of things
unto both beings, that is, of this World and the next: so
will there not seem so many Riddles in Providence, nor
various inequalities in the dispensation of things below.
If thou doest not anoint thy Face, yet put not on sack-
cloth at the felicities of others. Repining at the Good
draws on rejoicing at the evils of others, and so falls into
that inhumane vice,[2] for which so few Languages have a
name. The blessed Spirits above rejoice at our happiness below; but to be glad at the evils of one another
is beyond the malignity of Hell, and falls not on evil
Spirits, who, though they rejoice at our unhappiness.
takes no pleasure at the afflictions of their own Society
or of their fellow Natures. Degenerous Heads! who

---

[1] *Arbor Goa de Ruyz*, or *Ficus Indica*, whose branches send down
shoots which root in the ground, from whence there successively
rise others, till one Tree becomes a wood.

[2] Ἐπικαιρεκακία.

must be fain to learn from such Examples, and to be Taught from the School of Hell.

SECT. VI.—Grain not thy vicious stains, nor deepen those swart Tinctures, which Temper, Infirmity, or ill habits have set upon thee; and fix not, by iterated depravations what time might Efface, or Virtuous washes expunge. He, who thus still advanceth in Iniquity, deepneth his deformed hue, turns a Shadow into Night, and makes himself a *Negro* in the black Jaundice; and so becomes one of those Lost ones, the disproportionate pores of whose Brains afford no entrance unto good Motions, but reflect and frustrate all Counsels, Deaf unto the Thunder of the Laws, and Rocks unto the Cries of charitable Commiserators. He who hath had the Patience of *Diogenes,* to make Orations unto Statues, may more sensibly apprehend how all Words fall to the Ground, spent upon such a surd and Earless Generation of Men, stupid unto all Instruction, and rather requiring an Exorcist, than an Orator for their Conversion.

SECT. VII.—Burden not the back of *Aries, Leo,* or *Taurus,* with thy faults, nor make *Saturn, Mars,* or *Venus,* guilty of thy Follies. Think not to fasten thy imperfections on the Stars, and so despairingly conceived thy self under a fatality of being evil. Calculate thyself within, seek not thyself in the Moon, but in thine own Orb or Microcosmical Circumference. Let celestial aspects admonish and advertise, not conclude and determine thy ways. For since good and bad Stars moralize not our Actions, and neither excuse or commend, acquit or condemn our Good or Bad Deeds at the present or last Bar, since some are Astrologically well disposed who are morally highly vicious; not Celestial Figures, but Virtuous Schemes, must denominate and state our Actions. If we rightly understood the Names whereby God calleth the Stars, if we knew his Name for the Dog-Star, or by what appellation *Jupiter, Mars,* and *Saturn* obey his Will, it might be a welcome accession unto Astrology, which speaks great things, and is fain to make use of appellations from Greek and Barbarick Systems. Whatever Influences, Impulsions, or Inclinations there be from the Lights above, it were a piece of wisdom to make one of those Wise men who overrule their Stars,[1] and with their own Militia contend with the Host of Heaven. Unto which attempt there want not Auxiliaries from the whole strength of Morality, supplies from Christian Ethicks, influences also and illuminations from above, more powerful than the Lights of Heaven.

SECT. VIII.—Confound not the distinctions of thy Life which Nature hath divided: that is, Youth, Adolescence, Manhood, and old Age, nor in these divided Periods, wherein thou art in a manner Four, conceive thyself but One. Let every division be happy in its proper Virtues, nor one Vice run through all. Let each distinction have its salutary transition, and critically deliver thee from the imperfections of the former, so ordering the whole, that Prudence and Virtue may have the largest Section. Do as a Child but when thou art a Child, and ride not on a Reed at twenty. He who hath not taken leave of the follies of his Youth, and in his maturer state scarce got out of that division, disproportionately divideth his Days, crowds up the latter part of his Life, and leaves too narrow a corner for the Age of Wisdom, and so hath room to be a Man scarce longer than he hath been a Youth. Rather than to make this confusion, anticipate the Virtues of Age, and live long without the infirmities of it. So mayst thou count up thy days as some do *Adams,*[2] that is, by anticipation; so mayst thou be

---

[1] *Sapiens dominabitur Astris.*
[2] Adam thought to be created in the State of Man about thirty years Old.

coetaneous unto thy Elders, and a Father unto thy contemporaries.

Sect. ix.—While others are curious in the choice of good Air, and chiefly sollicitous for healthful habitations, Study thou Conversation, and be critical in thy Consortion. The aspects, conjunctions, and configurations of the Stars, which mutually diversify, intend, or qualify their influences, are but the varieties of their nearer or farther conversation with one another, and like the Consortion of Men, whereby they become better or worse, and even Exchange their Natures. Since Men live by Examples, and will be imitating something; order thy imitation to thy Improvement, not thy Ruin. Look not for Roses in *Attalus* his garden,[1] or wholsome Flowers in a venomous Plantation. And since there is scarce any one bad, but some others are the worse for him; tempt not Contagion by proximity, and hazard not thy self in the shadow of Corruption. He who hath not early suffered this Shipwrack, and in his Younger Days escaped this *Charybdis,* may make a happy Voyage, and not come in with black Sails into the port. Self conversation, or to be alone, is better than such Consortion. Some School-men tell us, that he is properly alone, with whom in the same place there is no other of the same Species. *Nabuchodonozor* was alone, though among the Beasts of the Field; and a Wise Man may be tolerably said to be alone though with a Rabble of People, little better than Beasts about him. Unthinking Heads, who have not learn'd to be alone, are in a Prison to themselves, if they be not also with others: Whereas on the contrary, they whose thoughts are in a fair, and hurry within, are sometimes fain to retire into Company, to be out of the crowd of themselves. He who must needs have Company, must needs have sometimes bad company. Be able to

[1] Attalus made a Garden which contained only venomous Plants.

be alone. Loose not the advantage of Solitude, and the
Society of thy self, nor be only content, but delight to
be alone and single with Omnipresency. He who is
thus prepared, the Day is not uneasy nor the Night black
unto him. Darkness may bound his Eyes, not his Imagination. In his Bed he may ly, like *Pompey* and his Sons,[1]
in all quarters of the Earth, may speculate the Universe,
and enjoy the whole World in the Hermitage of himself.
Thus the old *Ascetick* Christians found a Paradise in a
Desert, and with little converse on Earth held a conversation in Heaven; thus they Astronomiz'd in Caves, and,
though they beheld not the Stars, had the Glory of
Heaven before them.

SECT. x.—Let the Characters of good things stand in-
delibly in Thy mind, and thy Thoughts be active on
them. Trust not too much unto suggestions from Reminiscential Amulets, or Artificial *Memorandums*. Let
the mortifying *Janus* of *Covarrubias*[2] be in thy daily
Thoughts, not only on thy Hand and Signets. Rely not
alone upon silent and dumb remembrances. Behold not
Death's Heads till thou doest not see them, nor look
upon mortifying Objects till thou overlook'st them.
Forget not how assuefaction unto anything minorates
the passion from it, how constant Objects lose their hints,
and steal an inadvertisement upon us. There is no
excuse to forget what everything prompts unto us. To
thoughtful Observators, the whole World is a Phylactery,
and everything we see an Item of the Wisdom, Power, or
Goodness of God. Happy are they who verify their Amu-

---

[1] *Pompeios Juvenes Asia atque Europa, sed ipsum Terra tegit
Libyes.*

[2] Don Sebastian de Covarrubias writ three Centuries of moral
Emblems in Spanish. In the 88th of the second Century he sets
down two Faces averse, and conjoined Janus-like; the one, a
Gallant Beautiful Face, the other, a Death's Head Face, with this
Motto out of *Ovid's Metamorphosis:*—

Quid fuerim quid simque vide.

lets, and make their Phylacteries speak in their Lives and Actions. To run on in despight of the Revulsions and Pul-backs of such Remoras aggravates our transgressions. When Death's Heads on our Hands have no influence upon our Heads, and fleshless Cadavers abate not the exorbitances of the Flesh; when Crucifixes upon Men's Hearts suppress not their bad Commotions, and his Image who was murdered for us withholds not from Blood and Murder; Phylacteries prove but formalities, and their despised hints sharpen our condemnation.

Sect. xi.—Look not for *Whales* in the *Euxine* Sea, or expect great matters where they are not to be found. Seek not for Profundity in Shallowness, or Fertility in a Wilderness. Place not the expectations of great Happiness here below, or think to find Heaven on Earth; wherein we must be content with Embryon-felicities, and fruitions of doubtful Faces. For the Circle of our felicities makes but short Arches. In every clime we are in a periscian state, and with our Light our Shadow and Darkness walk about us. Our Contentments stand upon the tops of Pyramids ready to fall off, and the insecurity of their enjoyments abrupteth our Tranquillities. What we magnify is Magnificent, but like to the *Colossus,* noble without, stuft with rubbidge and coarse Metal within. Even the Sun, whose Glorious outside we behold, may have dark and smoaky Entrails. In vain we admire the Lustre of anything seen: that which is truly glorious is invisible. *Paradise* was but a part of the Earth, lost not only to our Fruition but our Knowledge. And if, according to old Dictates, no Man can be said to be happy before Death, the happiness of this Life goes for nothing before it be over, and while we think ourselves happy we do but usurp that Name. Certainly true Beatitude groweth not on Earth, nor hath this World in it the Expectations we have of it. He Swims in Oil, and can hardly avoid sinking, who hath such light Foundations to support him. 'Tis therefore happy that we have two Worlds to hold on. To enjoy true happiness we must travel into a very far Countrey, and even out of ourselves; for the Pearl we seek for is not to be found in the *Indian* but in the *Empyrean* ocean.

SECT. XII.—Answer not the Spur of Fury, and be not prodigal or prodigious in Revenge. Make not one in the *Historia Horribilis;*[1] Flay not thy Servant for a broken Glass, nor pound him in a Mortar who offendeth thee; supererogate not in the worst sense, and overdo not the necessities of evil; humour not the injustice of Revenge. Be not Stoically mistaken in the equality of sins, nor commutatively iniquitous in the valuation of transgressions; but weigh them in the Scales of Heaven, and by the weights of righteous Reason. Think that Revenge too high, which is but level with the offence. Let thy Arrows of Revenge fly short, or be aimed like those of *Jonathan,* to fall beside the mark. Too many there be to whom a *dead enemy* smells well, and who find Musk and Amber in Revenge. The ferity of such minds holds no rule in Retaliations, requiring too often a Head for a Tooth, and the Supreme revenge for trespasses, which a night's rest should obliterate. But patient Meekness takes injuries like Pills, not chewing but swallowing them down, Laconically suffering, and silently passing them over, while angered Pride makes a noise, like *Homerican Mars,*[2] at every scratch of offences. Since Women do most delight in Revenge, it may seem but feminine manhood to be vindictive. If thou must needs have thy Revenge of thine enemy, with a soft Tongue break his Bones,[3] heap Coals of Fire on his Head, forgive him, and enjoy it. To forgive our Enemies is a charming way of Revenge, and

---

[1] A Book so entituled wherein are sundry horrid accounts.
[2] Tu tamen exclamas ut Stentora vincere possis
Vel saltem quantum Gradivus Homericus.—JUV.
[3] A soft Tongue breaketh the bones.—PROV. xxv. 15.

a short *Cæsarian* Conquest overcoming without a blow; laying our Enemies at our Feet, under sorrow, shame, and repentance; leaving our Foes our Friends, and solicitously inclined to grateful Retaliations. Thus to Return upon our Adversaries is a healing way of Revenge, and to do good for evil a soft and melting ultion, a method Taught from Heaven to keep all smooth on Earth. Common forceable ways make not an end of Evil, but leave Hatred and Malice behind them. An Enemy thus reconciled is little to be trusted, as wanting the foundation of Love and Charity, and but for a time restrained by disadvantage or inability. If thou hast not Mercy for others, yet be not Cruel unto thyself. To ruminate upon evils, to make critical notes upon injuries, and to be too acute in their apprehensions, is to add unto our own Tortures, to feather the Arrows of our Enemies, to lash our selves with the Scorpions of our Foes, and to resolve to sleep no more. For injuries long dreamt on take away at last all rest; and he sleeps but like *Regulus* who busieth his Head about them.

SECT. XIII.—Amuse not thyself about the Riddles of future things. Study Prophecies when they are become Histories, and past hovering in their causes. Eye well things past and present, and let conjectural sagacity suffise for things to come. There is a sober Latitude for prescience in contingences of discoverable Tempers, whereby discerning Heads see sometimes beyond their Eyes, and Wise Men become Prophetical. Leave Cloudy predictions to their Periods, and let appointed Seasons have the lot of their accomplishments. 'Tis too early to study such Prophecies before they have been long made, before some train of their causes have already taken Fire, laying open in part what lay obscure and before buryed unto us. For the voice of Prophecies is like that of Whispering-places: They who are near or at a little distance hear nothing, those at the farthest extremity will understand all. But a Retrograde cognition of times past, and things which have already been, is more satisfactory than a suspended Knowledge of what is yet unexistent. And the greatest part of Time being already wrapt up in things behind us; it's now somewhat late to bait after things before us; for futurity still shortens, and time present sucks in time to come. What is Prophetical in one Age proves Historical in another, and so must hold on unto the last of time; when there will be no room for Prediction, when *Janus* shall loose one Face, and the long beard of time shall look like those of *David's* Servants, shorn away upon one side, and when, if the expected *Elias* should appear, he might say much of what is past, not much of what's to come.

SECT. XIV.—Live unto the Dignity of thy Nature, and leave it not disputable at last, whether thou hast been a Man or since thou art a composition of Man and Beast, how thou hast predominantly passed thy days, to state the denomination. Un-man not therefore thy self by a Beastial transformation, nor realize old Fables. Expose not thyself by four-footed manners unto monstrous draughts, and *Caricatura* representations. Think not after the old *Pythagorean* conceit, what Beast thou may'st be after death. Be not under any Brutal *metempsychosis* while thou livest, and walkest about erectly under the scheme of Man. In thine own circumference, as in that of the Earth, let the Rational Horizon be larger than the sensible, and the Circle of Reason than of Sense. Let the Divine part be upward, and the Region of Beast below. Otherwise, 'tis but to live invertedly, and with thy Head unto the Heels of thy *Antipodes*. Desert not thy title to a Divine particle and union with invisibles. Let true Knowledge and Virtue tell the lower World thou art a part of the higher. Let thy Thoughts be of things which have not entred into the Hearts of Beasts: Think of things long past, and long to come: Acquaint thyself with the *choragium* of the Stars, and consider the vast expansion beyond them. Let Intellectual Tubes give thee a glance of things, which visive Organs reach not. Have a glimpse of incomprehensibles, and Thoughts of things, which Thoughts but tenderly touch. Lodge immaterials in thy Head: ascend unto invisibles: fill thy Spirit with Spirituals, with the mysteries of Faith, the magnalities of Religion, and thy Life with the Honour of God; without which, though Giants in Wealth and Dignity, we are but Dwarfs and Pygmies in Humanity, and may hold a pitiful rank in that triple division of mankind into Heroes, Men, and Beasts. For though human Souls are said to be equal, yet is there no small inequality in their operations; some maintain the allowable Station of Men; many are far below it; and some have been so divine, as to approach the *Apogeum* of their Natures, and to be in the *Confinium* of Spirits.

SECT. XV.—Behold thyself by inward Opticks and the Crystalline of thy Soul. Strange it is, that in the most perfect sense there should be so many fallacies, that we are fain to make a doctrine, and often to see by Art. But the greatest imperfection is in our inward sight, that is, to be Ghosts unto our own Eyes, and while we are so sharp-sighted as to look thorough others, to be invisible unto ourselves; for the inward Eyes are more fallacious than the outward. The Vices we scoff at in others laugh at us within ourselves. Avarice, Pride, Falsehood lye undiscerned and blindly in us, even to the Age of blindness: and, therefore, to see ourselves interiourly, we are fain to borrow other Men's Eyes; wherein true Friends are good Informers, and Censurers no bad Friends. Conscience only, that can see without Light, sits in the *Areopagy* and dark Tribunal of our Hearts, surveying our Thoughts and condemning their obliquities. Happy is that state of vision that can see without Light, though all should look as before the Creation, when there was not an Eye to see, or Light to actuate a Vision: wherein notwith-standing obscurity is only imaginable respectively unto Eyes; for unto God there was none, Eternal Light was ever, created Light was for the creation, not himself, and as he saw before the Sun may still also see without it. In the City of the new *Jerusalem* there is neither Sun nor Moon; where glorifyed Eyes must see by the *Archetypal* Sun, or the Light of God, able to illuminate intellectual Eyes, and make unknown Visions. Intuitive perceptions in Spiritual beings may perhaps hold some Analogy unto Vision: but yet how they see us, or one another, what Eye, what Light, or what perception is required unto their intuition, is yet dark unto our apprehension; and even how they see God, or how unto our glorified Eyes the Beatifical Vision will be celebrated, another World must tell us, when perceptions will be new, and we may hope to behold invisibles.

SECT. XVI.—When all looks fair about, and thou seest not a cloud so big as a Hand to threaten thee, forget not the Wheel of things: Think of sullen vicissitudes, but beat not thy brains to fore know them. Be armed against such obscurities rather by submission than fore-knowl-edge. The Knowledge of future evils mortifies present felicities, and there is more content in the uncertainty or ignorance of them. This favour our Saviour vouchsafed unto *Peter,* when he fore told not his Death in plain terms, and so by an ambiguous and cloudy delivery dampt not the Spirit of his Disciples. But in the assured fore-knowledge of the Deluge, *Noah* lived many Years under the affliction of a Flood, and *Jerusalem* was taken unto *Jeremy* before it was besieged. And therefore the Wis-dom of Astrologers, who speak of future things, hath wisely softned the severity of their Doctrines; and even in their sad predictions, while they tell us of inclination not coaction from the Stars, they Kill us not with *Stygian*

Oaths and merciless necessity, but leave us hopes of evasion.

SECT. XVII.—If thou hast the brow to endure the Name of Traytor, Perjur'd, or Oppressor, yet cover thy Face when Ingratitude is thrown at thee. If that degenerous Vice possess thee, hide thyself in the shadow of thy shame, and pollute not noble society. Grateful Ingenuities are content to be obliged within some compass of Retribution, and being depressed by the weight of iterated favours may so labour under their inabilities of Requital, as to abate the content from Kindnesses. But narrow self-ended Souls make prescription of good Offices, and obliged by often favours think others still due unto them: whereas, if they but once fail, they prove so perversely ungrateful, as to make nothing of former courtesies, and to bury all that's past. Such tempers pervert the generous course of things; for they discourage the inclinations of noble minds, and make Beneficence cool unto acts of obligation, whereby the grateful World should subsist, and have their consolation. Common gratitude must be kept alive by the additionary fewel of new courtesies: but generous Gratitudes, though but once well obliged, without quickening repetitions or expectation of new Favours, have thankful minds for ever; for they write not their obligations in sandy but marble memories, which wear not out but with themselves.

SECT. XVIII.—Think not Silence the wisdom of Fools, but, if rightly timed, the honour of Wise Men, who have not the Infirmity, but the Virtue of Taciturnity, and speak not out of the abundance, but the well-weighed thoughts of their Hearts. Such Silence may be Eloquence, and speak thy worth above the power of Words. Make such a one thy friend, in whom Princes may be happy, and great Counsels successful. Let him have the Key of thy Heart, who hath the Lock of his own, which no

Temptation can open; where thy Secrets may lastingly ly, like the Lamp in *Olybius* his Urn,[1] alive, and light, but close and invisible.

SECT. XIX.—Let thy Oaths be sacred and Promises be made upon the Altar of thy Heart. Call not Jove[2] to witness with a Stone in one Hand, and a Straw in another, and so make Chaff and Stubble of thy Vows. Worldly Spirits, whose interest is their belief, make Cobwebs of Obligations, and, if they can find ways to elude the Urn of the *Prætor,* will trust the Thunderbolt of *Jupiter:* and therefore if they should as deeply swear as *Osman* to *Bethlem Gabor;*[3] yet whether they would be bound by those chains, and not find ways to cut such *Gordian* Knots, we could have no just assurance. But Honest Men's words are *Stygian* Oaths, and Promises inviolable. These are not the Men for whom the fetters of Law were first forged: they needed not the solemness of Oaths; by keeping their Faith they swear, and evacuate such confirmations.[4]

SECT. XX.—Though the World be Histrionical, and most Men live Ironically, yet be thou what thou singly art, and personate only thy self. Swim smoothly in the stream of thy Nature, and live but one Man. To single Hearts doubling is discruciating: such tempers must sweat to dissemble, and prove but hypocritical Hypocrites. Simulation must be short: Men do not easily continue a counterfeiting Life, or dissemble unto Death. He who counterfeiteth, acts a part, and is as it were out of himself: which, if long, proves so irckesome, that Men are glad to pull off their Vizards, and resume themselves again; no practice being able to naturalize such unnat-

[1] Which after many hundred years was found burning under ground, and went out as soon as the air came to it.

[2] *Jovem lapidem jurare.*

[3] See the Oath of Sultan Osman in his life, in the addition to Knolls his *Turkish History.*

[4] *Colendo fidem jurant.*—CURTIUS.

urals, or make a Man rest content not to be himself.
And, therefore, since Sincerity is thy Temper, let veracity
be thy Virtue, in Words, Manners, and Actions. To offer
at iniquities, which have so little foundations in thee,
were to be vitious up hill, and strain for thy condemnation. Persons vitiously inclined want no Wheels to
make them actively vitious; as having the Elater and
Spring of their own Natures to facilitate their Iniquities.
And therefore so many, who are sinistrous unto Good
Actions, are Ambi-dexterous unto bad, and *Vulcans* in
virtuous Paths, *Achilleses* in vitious motions.

SECT. XXI.—Rest not in the high strain'd Paradoxes
of old Philosophy, supported by naked Reason, and the
reward of mortal Felicity, but labour in the ethicks of
Faith, built upon Heavenly assistance, and the happiness
of both beings. Understand the Rules, but swear not unto
the Doctrines of *Zeno* or *Epicurus*. Look beyond *Antoninus,* and terminate not thy Morals in *Seneca* or *Epictetus*.
Let not the twelve but the two Tables be thy Law: let
Pythagoras be thy Remembrancer, not thy textuary and
final Instructor; and learn the Vanity of the World, rather
from *Solomon* than *Phocylydes*. Sleep not in the Dogmas
of the *Peripatus,* Academy, or *Porticus*. Be a moralist
of the Mount, an *Epictetus* in the faith, and christianize
thy Notions.

SECT. XXII.—In seventy or eighty years a Man may
have a deep Gust of the World, Know what it is, what it
can afford, and what 'tis to have been a Man. Such a
latitude of years may hold a considerable corner in the
general Map of Time; and a Man may have a curt Epitome of the whole course thereof in the days of his own
Life, may clearly see he hath but acted over his Fore-
fathers, what it was to live in Ages past, and what living
will be in all ages to come.

He is like to be the best judge of Time who hath lived
to see about the sixtieth part thereof. Persons of short

times may Know what 'tis to live, but not the life of Man, who, having little behind them, are but *Januses* of one Face, and Know not singularities enough to raise Axioms of this World: but such a compass of Years will show new Examples of old Things, Parallelisms of occurrences through the whole course of Time, and nothing be monstrous unto him; who may in that time understand not only the varieties of men, but the variation of himself, and how many Men he hath been in that extent of time.

He may have a close apprehension what is to be forgotten, while he hath lived to find none who could remember his Father, or scarce the friends of his youth, and may sensibly see with what a face in no long time oblivion will look upon himself. His Progeny may never be his Posterity; he may go out of the World less related than he came into it, and considering the frequent mortality in Friends and Relations, in such a Term of Time, he may pass away divers years in sorrow and black habits, and leave none to mourn for himself; Orbity may be his inheritance, and Riches his Repentance.

In such a thred of Time, and long observation of Men, he may acquire a *Physiognomical* intuitive Knowledge, Judge the interiors by the outside, and raise conjectures at first sight; and knowing what Men have been, what they are, what Children probably will be, may in the present Age behold a good part, and the temper of the next; and since so many live by the Rules of Constitution, and so few overcome their temperamental Inclinations, make no improbable predictions.

Such a portion of Time will afford a large prospect backward, and Authentic Reflections how far he hath performed the great intention of his Being, in the Honour of his Maker; whether he hath made good the Principles of his Nature, and what he was made to be; what Characteristick and special Mark he hath left, to be observable in his Generation; whether he hath Lived to purpose or in vain, and what he hath added, acted, or performed, that might considerably speak him a Man.

In such an Age Delights will be undelightful and Pleasures grow stale unto him; antiquated Theorems will revive, and *Solomon's* Maxims be Demonstrations unto him; Hopes or presumptions be over, and despair grow up of any satisfaction below. And having been long tossed in the Ocean of this World, he will by that time feel the In-draught of another, unto which this seems but preparatory, and without it of no high value. He will experimentally find the Emptiness of all things, and the nothing of what is past; and wisely grounding upon true Christian Expectations, finding so much past, will wholly fix upon what is to come. He will long for Perpetuity, and live as though he made haste to be happy. The last may prove the prime part of his life, and those his best days which he lived nearest Heaven.

SECT. XXIII.—Live happy in the *Elizium* of a virtuously composed Mind, and let Intellectual Contents exceed the Delights wherein mere Pleasurists place their Paradise. Bear not too slack reins upon Pleasure, nor let complexion or contagion betray thee unto the exorbitancy of Delight. Make pleasure thy Recreation or intermissive Relaxation, not thy *Diana,* Life, and Profession. Voluptuousness is as insatiable as Covetousness. Tranquillity is better than jollity, and to appease pain than to invent pleasure. Our hard entrance into the World, our miserable going out of it, our sicknesses, disturbances, and sad Rencounters in it, do clamorously tell us we come not into the World to run a Race of Delight, but to perform the sober Acts and serious purposes of Man; which to omit were foully to miscarry in the advantage of humanity, to play away an uniterable Life, and to have lived in vain. Forget not the capital end, and frustrate not the opportunity of once Living. Dream not of any kind of *Metempsychosis* or transanimation, but into thine own

body, and that after a long time, and then also unto
wail or bliss, according to thy first and fundamental Life.
Upon a Curricle in this World depends a long course of
the next, and upon a narrow Scene here an endless expansion hereafter. In vain some think to have an end of
their Beings with their Lives. Things cannot get out of
their natures, or be or not be in despite of their constitutions. Rational existences in Heaven perish not at
all, and but partially on Earth: That which is thus once
will in some way be always: the first Living human Soul
is still alive, and all *Adam* hath found no Period.

SECT. XXIV.—Since the Stars of Heaven do differ in
glory; since it hath pleased the Almighty hand to honour
the North Pole with Lights above the South; since there
are some Stars so bright that they can hardly be looked
on, some so dim that they can scarce be seen, and vast
numbers not to be seen at all even by Artificial Eyes;
Read thou the Earth in Heaven, and things below from
above. Look contentedly upon the scattered difference of
things, and expect not equality in lustre, dignity, or perfection, in Regions or Persons below; where numerous
numbers must be content to stand like *Lacteous* or *Nebu-
lous* Stars, little taken notice of, or dim in their generations. All which may be contentedly allowable in the
affairs and ends of this World, and in suspension unto
what will be in the order of things hereafter, and the new
Systeme of Mankind which will be in the World to come;
when the last may be the first and the first the last; when
Lazarus may sit above *Cæsar,* and the just obscure on
Earth shall shine like the Sun in Heaven; when persona-
tions shall cease, and Histrionism of happiness be over;
when Reality shall rule, and all shall be as they shall be
for ever.

SECT. XXV.—When the *Stoick* said that life would not
be accepted, if it were offered unto such as knew it,[1] he

[1] *Vitam nemo acciperet si daretur scientibus.*—Seneca.

spoke too meanly of that state of being which placeth us in the form of Men. It more depreciates the value of this life, that Men would not live it over again; for although they would still live on, yet few or none can endure to think of being twice the same Men upon Earth, and some had rather never have lived than to tread over their days once more. *Cicero* in a prosperous state had not the patience to think of beginning in a cradle again. *Job* would not only curse the day of his Nativity, but also of his Renascency, if he were to act over his Disasters, and the miseries of the dung-hil. But the greatest underweening of this life is to undervalue that, unto which this is but Exordial or a Passage leading unto it. The great advantage of this mean life is thereby to stand in a capacity of a better; for the Colonies of Heaven must be drawn from Earth, and the Sons of the first *Adam* are only heirs unto the second. Thus *Adam* came into this World with the power also of another; not only to replenish the Earth, but the everlasting Mansions of Heaven. Where we were when the foundations of the Earth were layd, *when the morning Stars sang together, and all the Sons of God shouted for Joy,*[1] He must answer who asked it; who understands Entities of preordination, and beings yet unbeing; who hath in his Intellect the Ideal Existences of things, and Entities before their Extances. Though it looks but like an imaginary kind of existency to be before we are; yet since we are under the decree or prescience of a sure and Omnipotent Power, it may be somewhat more than a non-entity to be in that mind, unto which all things are present.

SECT. XXVI.—If the end of the World shall have the same foregoing Signs, as the period of Empires, States, and Dominions in it, that is, Corruption of Manners, inhuman degenerations, and deluge of iniquities; it may be doubted whether that final time be so far off, of whose

[1] Job xxxviii.

day and hour there can be no prescience. But while all men doubt and none can determine how long the World shall last, some may wonder that it hath spun out so long and unto our days. For if the Almighty had not determin'd a fixed duration unto it, according to his mighty and merciful designments in it, if he had not said unto it, as he did unto a part of it, hitherto shalt thou go and no farther; if we consider the incessant and cutting provocations from the Earth, it is not without amazement how his patience hath permitted so long a continuance unto it, how he, who cursed the Earth in the first days of the first Man, and drowned it in the tenth Generation after, should thus lastingly contend with Flesh and yet defer the last flames. For since he is sharply provoked every moment, yet punisheth to pardon, and forgives to forgive again; what patience could be content to act over such vicissitudes, or accept of repentances which must have after penitences, his goodness can only tell us. And surely if the Patience of Heaven were not proportionable unto the provocations from Earth; there needed an Intercessor not only for the sins, but the duration of this World, and to lead it up unto the present computation. Without such a merciful Longanimity, the Heavens would never be so aged as to grow old like a Garment; it were in vain to infer from the Doctrine of the Sphere, that the time might come, when *Capella,* a noble Northern Star, would have its motion in the *Æquator,* that the northern *Zodiacal* Signs would at length be the Southern, the Southern the Northern, and *Capricorn* become our *Cancer.* However therefore the Wisdom of the Creator hath ordered the duration of the World, yet since the end thereof brings the accomplishment of our happiness, since some would be content that it should have no end, since Evil Men and Spirits do fear it may be too short, since Good Men hope it may not be too long; the prayer of the Saints under the Altar will be the supplication of the Righteous World. That his mercy would abridge their languishing Expectation and hasten the accomplishment of their happy state to come.

SECT. XXVII.—Though Good Men are often taken away from the Evil to come, though some in evil days have been glad that they were old, nor long to behold the iniquities of a wicked World, or Judgments threatened by them; yet is it no small satisfaction unto honest minds to leave the World in virtuous well-temper'd times, under a prospect of good to come, and continuation of worthy ways acceptable unto God and Man. Men who dye in deplorable days, which they regretfully behold, have not their Eyes closed with the like content; while they cannot avoid the thoughts of proceeding or growing enormities, displeasing unto that Spirit unto whom they are then going, whose honour they desire in all times and throughout all generations. If *Lucifer* could be freed from his dismal place, he would little care though the rest were left behind. Too many there may be of *Nero's* mind, who, if their own turn were served, would not regard what became of others, and, when they dye themselves, care not if all perish. But good Men's wishes extend beyond their lives, for the happiness of times to come, and never to be known unto them. And therefore while so many question prayers for the .dead, they charitably pray for those who are not yet alive; they are not so enviously ambitious to go to heaven by themselves; they cannot but humbly wish, that the little Flock might be greater, the narrow Gate wider, and that, as many are called, so not a few might be chosen.

SECT. XXVIII.—That a greater number of Angels remained in Heaven, than fell from it, the School-men will tell us; that the number of blessed Souls will not come short of that vast number of fallen Spirits, we have the favourable calculation of others. What Age or Century hath sent most Souls unto Heaven, he can tell who vouchsafe that honour unto them. Though the Number of the blessed must be compleat before the World can pass away, yet since the World it self seems in the wane, and we have no such comfortable prognosticks of Latter times, since a greater part of time is spun than is to come, and the blessed Roll already much replenished; happy are those pieties, which solicitously look about, and hasten to make one of that already much filled and abbreviated List to come.

SECT. XXIX.—Think not thy time short in this World since the World itself is not long. The created World is but a small *parenthesis* in Eternity, and a short interposition for a time between such a state of duration as was before it and may be after it. And if we should allow of the old Tradition, that the World should last Six Thousand years, it could scarce have the name of old, since the first man lived near a sixth part thereof, and seven *Methuselas* would exceed its whole duration. However to palliate the shortness of our Lives, and somewhat to compensate our brief term in this World, it's good to know as much as we can of it, and also so far as possibly in us lieth to hold such a *Theory* of times past, as though we had seen the same. He who hath thus considered the World, as also how therein things long past have been answered by things present, how matters in one Age have been acted over in another, and how there is nothing new under the Sun may conceive himself in some manner to have lived from the beginning, and be as old as the world; and if he should still live on, 'twould be but the same thing.

SECT. XXX.—Lastly, if length of Days be thy Portion, make it not thy Expectation. Reckon not upon long Life: think every day the last, and live always beyond thy account. He that so often surviveth his Expectation lives many Lives, and will scarce complain of the shortness of his days. Time past is gone like a Shadow; make time to come present. Approximate thy latter times by present apprehensions of them: be like a neighbour unto the Grave, and think there is but little to come. And since there is something of us that will still live on, join both lives together, and live in one but for the other. He who thus ordereth the purposes of this Life will never be far from the next, and is in some manner already in it, by a happy conformity, and close apprehension of it. And if, as we have elsewhere declared, any have been so happy as personally to understand Christian Annihilation, Extasy, Exolution, Transformation, the Kiss of the Spouse, and Ingression into the Divine Shadow, according to Mystical Theology, they have already had an handsome Anticipation of Heaven; the World is in a manner over, and the Earth in Ashes unto them.

GLOSSARY

ABBREVIATIONS, ETC.

J.=Johnson.
H. E. D.=New "English Dictionary on Historical Principles" (Murray, Bradley).
Webster=International Dictionary.
Greenhill=Glossary to edition of "Hydriotaphia and Garden of Cyrus" (1896).

ABRUPT, to break off.
ABSTERSION, cleansing.
ABSUMPTION, consumption
ACCEPTIONS, acceptations.
ACCUMINATED, sharp-pointed.
ACTIVES, sub., active principles.
ACULEOUS, needle-like.
ADAM, QUID FECISTI? Adam, what hast thou done? 2 Esdras vii.
ADRASTE AND NEMESIS, the powers of vengeance (J.).
ADRIANUS ("the moles of"), "A stately mausoleum or sepulchral pile, built by Adrianus in Rome, where now standeth the castle of St. Angelo." [Note by Sir T. B.]
ADUMBRATION, faint resemblance, as of a shadow to the object it represents.
ADVISOES, admonitions.
ÆQUICRURAL, of equal length of leg.
ÆSON'S BATH, Son of Cretheus and Tyro, and father of Jason; according to Ovid, he survived the return of the Argonauts, and was made young again by Medea.
AFFECTION, influence.
AFFECTIONS, qualities, passions, feelings, men of affection.
ALCMENA'S nights, "one night as long as three." [Note by Sir T. B.]
AMAZED, confounded.
AMBIDEXTEROUS, able to use both hands alike.
AMBITIONS, ambitious men. This use of the abstract for the concrete in the plural occurs frequently in Sir Thomas Browne, as "desires," "affections," "devotions," "zeals," etc.
AMISSION, loss.
AMPHIBOLOGY, an ambiguous phrase.
AMPHIDROMICAL FEASTS, held at the naming of a child.

ANAXAGORAS. Several editors have wrongly printed "Anaxarchus," who actually held the opinions attributed by Browne to Anaxagoras.
ANGUSTIAS, agonies (J.).
ANIMA EST DEI, "the soul is the angel of man, the body of God."
ANIMOSITY, courage.
ANTICHRIST ("should be born of the tribe of Dan"). A belief held by the Ancient Church, based partly on the omission of the name of Dan from the list of tribes in the Apocalypse, and partly on the mention of him as "adder" and "serpent" in Jacob's last blessing of his sons. [Condensed from Greenhill.]
ANTICIPATIVELY, prematurely.
ANTICKS, clowns.
ANTINOMIES, contradictions to law.
ANTIPODES, opposites (J.).
APOGEUM, to the utmost point of distance from earth and earthly things (J.).
APPARITIONS, appearances without realities (J.).
APPREHEND, to dread, to conceive, comprehend.
APPREHENSION, reason, conception; PASSED APPREHENSION, former opinion; GROSSER APPREHENSIONS, men of grosser apprehension.
ARCANA, mysteries.
ARCHIDOXIS, a work of Paracelsus, translated into English in 1662.
ARCHIMIME, chief jester.
AREFACTION, drying.
AREOPAGY, the great court, like the Areopagus at Athens (J.).
ARUSPEX, soothsayer, diviner.
ASCENDENS ... NATURÆ (i.e., OPERA DEI). "A planet in the ascendant reveals to those who seek many of the great things of nature (i.e., the

works of God)." Paracelsus, "De Imaginibus." "Thereby is meant our good Angel appointed us from our nativity." [Note by Sir T. B.]

ASPEROUS, rough.

ASPHALTICK LAKE, Lake of Sodom, the waters of which, being very salt and therefore heavy, will scarcely suffer an animal to sink (J.).

ASPIRES, aspirations.

ASQUINT, askance.

ASSASSINE, vb., to assassinate.

ASSIZE ("to call to"), to summon to judgment.

ASSUCFACTION, habituation.

ASTERISK, small star.

ATTENDANCE, accompaniment.

ATTENUABLE, liable to diminution.

ATTRITION, friction.

AUDACITIES, bold persons.

AUDITORIES, lecture-rooms.

AURELIA, chrysalis, "aurelion."

AVE-MARY bell. "A church-bell, that tolls every day at six and twelve of the clock, at the hearing whereof, everyone, in what place soever, either of house or street, betakes himself to his prayer, which is commonly directed to the Virgin." [Note by Sir T. B.]

BASILISO, a piece of ordnance.

BELIEFS, believers.

BELISARIUS AND BAJAZET, the former, after many victories, said, owing to incurring the Emperor's displeasure, to have been reduced to beggary; the latter to have been made captive by Tamerlane and shut up in cage; "both stories are false" (J.).

BENEPLACIT, good pleasure.

BENEVOLOUS, favourable.

BEVIS, a famous giant-killer of Southampton, a hero of medieval English romances.

BEZO LES MANOS, a salute, a kiss of the hand.

BISHOP ("the miserable"). Virgilius, Bishop of Salzburg in the eighth century, said to have been burnt for asserting the existence of Antipodes.

BIVIOUS, which open different tracks to the mind; lead two ways (J.); "bivious theorems."

BLOOD, "though we behold our own blood," though we bleed when we are wounded (J.).

BOLARY, of the *nature of bole*, a clayey substance.

BOTTOM, a ship, a ball of yarn.

BOUFFAGE, "a satisfying meal" (H. E. D.).

BRAVACHE (French), boaster. The characteristic Scotchman.

BREEZE, gad-fly.

BUSHES, alluding to the bushes or wreaths of ivy formerly hung by vintners at their doors.

CACUS'S OXEN, stolen from Hercules, and drawn backwards by Cacus into his cave to avoid suspicion of theft.

CALDA, warm water (J.).

CALICULAR, in form of calix or cup.

CALLOSITIES, "calluses," or hard spots in the soul.

CANDLE, "by the candle," term borrowed from the auction-room where ceratin sales were held, at which the bidding went on as long as a small piece of candle continued to burn.

CANDOUR, whiteness.

CANTONS, corners of a shield in heraldry.

CARIOLA. "That part of the skeleton of a horse which is made by the haunch-bones." [Note by Sir T. B.]

CARNOUS, fleshy.

CARRACK, large merchantman.

CASTRENSIAL, belonging to a camp.

CATHOLICON, universal medicine.

CAUSALLY, for a special reason (Greenhill).

CAUSES ("four second"), of all things. That is, the "efficient," the "material," the "formal," and the "final."

CAUTELOUS, cautious.

CEBES' TABLE, an allegorical representation of the characters and conditions of mankind (J.).

CENTOES, patched garments, used metaphorically.

CERTUM EST QUIA IMPOSSIBLE, "it is certain, because it is impossible" (*i.e.*, to human reason). Tertullian, "De Carne Christi," c. 5.

CHIASMUS, decussation (Greenhill).

CHIONIA ("the King of"), Gumbrates, King of Chionia, a country near Persia.

CHIROMANCY, palmistry.

CHORAGIUM, dance (J.).

CHOROGRAPHY, description of places and countries.

CHYMICKS, chemists.

CIRCENSES, Roman horse-races (J.).

CIRCINNATIONS, spherical rounds (Greenhill).

CIRCUMSTANTIAL, accidental.

CIRROUS, bearing tendrils.

CIVILITY, state of civil society.

CLAMATION, shouting.

CLAWING, tickling, flattering.

CLIMACTER, the point in a man's life (supposed to be his sixty-third

year) when his powers begin to
fail.

CODRUS, the last King of Athens.

COMMISSURE, juncture, joining.

COMMODITIES, advantages.

COMPAGE, framework or system of
conjoined parts (H. E. D.).

COMPLEMENT, completeness.

COMPLEMENTAL, slight and subsid-
iary, merely making up weight.

COMPLEXIONALLY, by temperament.

COMPOSITION, compounding, but in
the next line (by a play of words)
composed=created.

COMPRODUCTION, joint production.

COMPROPORTIONS, proportions together.

COMPUTE, computation.

CONCEIT, conception, idea, jest.

CONCEIT, to imagine.

CONCLAMATION, noise made by several people shouting together.

CONCOMITANCIES, accompaniments.

CONCOURSE, help.

CONSIDERATION UNTO, value when
compared with.

CONSIDERATIONS, considerers.

CONSORTION, the consorting with
others.

CONSTELLATED UNTO, by the constel-
lation of my birth adaptive to.

CONTEMPERED, diluted.

CONTIGNATION, framing together of
beams.

CONTINGENCY (angles of), the small-
est angles.

CONTRACTION, "we cannot be punished . . . but contraction," by
having punishment brought to bear
upon ourselves.

CONVERSATION, behaviour.

CONVERSION, revolution, "annual conversion."

CONVINCIBLE, demonstrable.

CORNIGEROUS, horned.

CORPULENCY, solid character of
bodies.

CRAMBE, tiresome repetitions;
CRAMBE REPETITIA (Juvenal).

CRANY, cranium, skull.

CRASIS, lit. mixture; here, mixture of
bodily humours.

CRUCIATED, crossed.

CRUCIFEROUS, marked with a cross.

CRUSERO, Southern Cross (Greenhill).

CRYSTALLINE, alluding to the crystalline humour of the eye (J.).

CUNCTATION, delay.

CUPELS, refining glasses used in the
melting down of gold and silver
with lead.

DAMOCLES, a flatterer of Dionysius
(J.).

DASTARD, vb., to make craven.

DECIMATION, selection of every tenth
man for punishment (J.).

DECIPIENCY, state of being deceived,
hallucination (Webster).

DECUSSATION, crossing of lines in the
form of the figure X.

DELATOR, informer.

DEMONSTRATIONS, truths capable of
demonstration.

DEPRAVE, to malign, to spoil; DE-
PRAVEDLY, in a corrupt form.

DERIVED, secondary in source (i.e.,
from the sun?).

DESIRES, desirers.

DEVOTIONS, devout men.

DIAMETER WITH (to stand in), to be
diametrically opposed to.

DICHOTOMY, division into two.

DIFFERENCE, vb., to show the difference between, to define.

DIGLADIATION, fencing match (J.).

DIOGENES (testament of). "Who
willed his friend not to bury him,
but to hang him up, with a staffe in
his hand, to frighten away the
crowes." [Note by Sir T. B.]

DISCRUCIATING, excruciating.

DISSENTANEOUS UNTO, contrary to.

DITTY, speech.

DIUTURNITY, long duration.

DONATIVES, gifts.

DORADO, a fish, probably either the
gilt-head or dorade or the gold-
fish. IGNORANT DORADOES are rich
men of no education. [Condensed
from Greenhill.]

DORMATIVE, sleeping draught.

DRAUGHT, drawing.

ECLIPTICALLY, in the direction of the
sun's apparent motion.

EDIFIED, formed.

EFFRONT, to embolden.

ELATER, "spring," "elasticity"
(H. E. D.).

ELEEMOSYNARIES, beggars.

ELEMENTAL COMPOSITION, "composition of elements" (Greenhill).

ELIAS (prophecy of), "That the world
may last but six thousand years."
[Note by Sir T. B.]

EMPHATICAL, "designated emphatically, or par excellence" (H. E. D.).

EMPYREAL, in old astronomy, all
beyond the tenth heaven.

ENOCH'S PILLARS. "Josephus does not
mention Enoch, but says the de-
scendants of Seth erected two pillars, on which were engraven all
the discoveries then known to mankind. [Condensed from Greenhill.]

ENQUIRIES, enquirers.

ENTELECHIA, the realized, as distinct
from the merely possible being of
anything.

EPHEMERIDES, NOT OLYMPIADS, particular journals of every day, not abstracts comprehending several years under one notation (J.).

EPHEMERIDES, schedules showing the position of the heavenly bodies from day to day, used for purposes of divination.

EPICYCLE, a small revolution made by one planet in the wider orbit of another planet (J.).

EQUABLE, just.

EQUAL, impartial; equitable.

EQUIVOCAL, doubtful.

ERGOTISMS, conclusions deduced according to the forms of logic (J.).

ETHNICK, gentile.

EVULSION, extraction by force.

EXALTATION, refining.

EXCEPTING ONE (king). Christian IV., King of Denmark, who began to reign in 1588, and was still on the throne when the book was written.

EXCEPTION, objection or reservation.

EXENTERATION, disembowelling.

EXEQUIES, funeral rites.

EXILITY, smallness.

EXISTIMATION, estimation.

EXOLUTION, in medicine, great physical weakness; in mystical theology, dreamy exaltation of mind.

EXPANSED, expanded.

EXPATIATE, to roam about.

EXPILATORS, pillagers.

EXPLICATION, unfolding.

EXPRESSIONS, marks.

EXUCCOUS, dry.

EXTANCES, existences.

EXTEMPORARY, intuitive.

EXTENUATION, emaciation.

EXTRAMISSION, by the passage of sight from the eye to the object (J.).

EXUPERANCES, exaggerations.

FACES ("so many imperial"), an allusion, probably to his collection of coins.

FACULTY, authority, power.

FAITH, believer, abstract for concrete.

FAMILIST, a member of the "family of love," a religious sect which appeared about 1575.

FASCIATIONS, bandages.

FATHER ("that great"), probably St. Chrysostom.

FAVAGINOUS, cellular, like a honeycomb.

FERITY, ferocity, savageness.

FESTINATION, haste.

FIAT LUX, let there be light.

FICTILE, moulded.

FILED, placed in order.

FINGER ("one little"). "According to the ancient arithmetick of the hand, wherein the little finger of the right hand contracted, signified an hundred." [Note by Sir T. B.]

FLAW, sudden gust of wind.

FLUX, flow.

FOL, mad, of the characteristic Englishman.

FORAMINOUS, full of holes.

FORM, the essence of anything apart from the actual material of which it is composed.

FOUGADE, "a small mine for blowing up walls" (Greenhill).

FRUSTRUM, any part except the vertex cut off from a cone (Greenhill).

FULCIMENT, fulcrum.

FUNAMBULATORY, narrow, like the walk of a rope-dancer (J.).

FURDLING, furling.

FUSIL, heraldic term, elongated lozenge.

GALLATURE, germ in an egg.

GALLIARDISE, merriment.

GARAGANTUA, or Gargantua, Rabelais' giant.

GEOMANCER, one who divines by the earth.

GERMANY ("defection of the Maid of"). Nothing is known of this personage except that she is mentioned in one of the MSS. as having "lived without meat on the smell of a rose." In default of any evidence concerning the Maid, the precise meaning of the word "defection" is not clear; "detection" has been suggsted in place of it. [Condensed from Greenhill.]

GLOME, a clue of yarn.

GOMPHOSIS, immovable articulations like teeth in their sockets (Greenhill).

GORDIANUS ("the epitaph of"). "In Greek, Latin, Hebrew, Arabic, Egyptian, defaced by Licinius the Emperor." [Note by Sir T. B.]

GRAFFS, grafts.

GRAIN, dye in grain. "Not grain'd," not deeply tinged (J.).

GRAPHICAL, composed of letters.

GUSTATION, tasting.

HAGGARD, wild, untamed, a term in falconry.

HANGING PLAYED BEFORE THEM. "A barbarous pastime at feasts [among the Thracians], when men stood upon a rolling globe, with their necks in a rope, and a knife in their hands, ready to cut it when the stone was rolled away; wherein if they failed they lost their lives,

to the laughter of their spectators."
[Note by Sir T. B.]

HELIACAL, spiral.

HELIX, a screw or spiral line: to run
upon a helix, to be continually
moving spirally.

HELLUOS, gluttons (J.).

HELMONT OR PARCELSUS, enthusiastic
authors of romantic chemistry (J.).

HERMES' ROD, which procured sleep
by a touch (J.).

HERMETICAL PHILOSOPHERS, follow-
ers of Hermes Trismegistus, addicted to chemistry and alchemy.

HIPPOCRATES PATIENTS. In some of
the treatises of the Hippocratic
collection rough notes of cases are
found giving the names and ad-
dresses of the patients. The point
of the comparison lies in its showing how the dead live only in their
names; nothing more is known of
them.

HISTRIONISM (of happiness), theatrical representation, mere show.

HORÆ COMBUSTÆ, the time when the
moon is in conjunction and obscured by the sun.

HOUR-GLASSES, "call for many hour-
glasses." Ancient pleaders talked
by a clepsydra, or measurer of time.

HUMOUROUS, the result of some humour or individual trait.

HYDROPICAL, dropsical.

HYPOSTASIS, distinct substance.

IDEATED, pictured in idea, in fancy.

IDES, time when money laid out at
interest was commonly repaid. (J.).

IMMORTALITY, exemption from death.

IMPASSIBLE, impregnable to suffering
and decay.

IMPOSTERS (the three). The Emperor
Ferdinand II. was accused by Pope
Gregory I. of maintaining that the
world had been deceived by three
imposters—Jesus Christ, Moses, and
Mahomet. A book with this title
was said to have existed, but no
trace of it remains (Greenhill).

IMPROPERATIONS, insulting language.

INCESSION, progression.

INCINERABLE, reducible to ashes; IN-
CINERATED, reduced to ashes.

INCRASSATION, thickening.

INCREMABLE, incombustible.

INCURVATE, to make crooked.

INDIFFERENCY, impartiality; (pl.) insignificant matters; of arguments,
exact balance.

INDIFFERENT, impartial.

INFLEXURES, bends or folds (Greenhill).

INGENUITIES, people of ingenuous disposition.

INGRESSION, entrance.

INHUMATION, burying.

INNITENCY, leaning, pressing, or resting upon something (H. E. D.).

INORGANICAL, without organs.

INQUINATED, defiled (J.).

INSENSIBLE, too small to be felt.

INSERVIENT TO, conducive to.

INSTANCES, instants.

INTELLIGENCES, unbodied angelic
spirits.

INTENTIONS, persons who intend.

IRONICALLY ("live ironically"), with
dissimilation or personation (H.
E. D.).

ITEM, earnest, specimen.

ITERATELY, repeatedly.

JUDGMENTS, men of judgment.

KELL, caul.

KINGDOMS, "fatal periods of." According to Plato about 500 years.

LACONISM, short sentence written on
wall of Belschazzar (J.).

LACRYMATORIES, tear-bottles.

LARRON (French), thief. The characteristic Gascon.

LASH, soft and watery, but without
flavour (Forby's vocabulary of East
Anglia).

LAUREAT DRAUGHT, a picture with
laurel (Greenhill).

LAZY OF BRAZIL, sloth (J.).

LIGATION, binding.

LION ("we sleep in lions' skins"), in
armour, in a state of military vigi-
lance (J.).

LIPARA, the Liparæan Islands, near
Italy, being volcanoes, were fabled
to contain the forges of the Cyclops
(J.).

LIQUATION, melting.

LIVELY, vividly.

LIVERY ("without a"), without rec-
ompense or fee.

LIXIVIOUS, impregnated with alkaline
salts.

LURE, bait, a term used in falconry.

LUX EST UMBRA DEI, "light is the
shadow of God."

MAGNÆ . . . VITIA, "Great virtues, and
no smaller vices."

MAGNALITIES, great works from small
beginnings (Greenhill).

MAGNETICALLY ("stand magnetically
upon that axis"), with a position as
immutable as that of the magnetical
axis (J.).

MALIZSPINI, born about 1540, the
author of the "Ducento Novelle."

MANIPLE, handful.

MARASMUS, wasting disease.

MASCLE, heraldic term: a lozenge voided.

MATERIAL (vb.), to materialize.

MATILDA. "A piece of Maud, the Empress, said to be found in Buckenham Castle, with this inscription: 'Elle n'a d'elle.'" [Note by Sir T. B.]

MATURATION, maturing, ripening.

MEANNESS, low estate.

MEDIOCRITY, moderation.

MEMORY (whose), recollection of which.

MERCURIAL, relating to Mercury ("mercurial characters").

MERCURISMS, communications.

MERITS, deserts (in a bad sense).

METELLUS. The supper was not given by Metellus, but by Lentulus when he was made priest of Mars, and recorded by Metellus (J.).

METEMPSUCHOSIS, transmigration of souls.

METRICULOUSLY, timidly (J.).

MINORATE, diminish.

MORTAL, deadly, fatal.

MOTIVES, motive forces.

MUTILATE, p.p. mutilated.

MUTIN (French), stubborn. The characteristic Englishman.

MYSTERY, trade, craft.

NATURA . . . FRUSTRA, "nature does nothing in vain."

NATURALITY, naturalness.

NEBB, nib, "generative particle" (Greenhill).

NEBUCHODONOSOR, so spelt in the most trustworthy MSS.

NEQUE EMIN . . . MIHI. "For when the study or the couch calls me, I do not fail." Misquoted from Horace (Sat., i. 4, 133), who has *lectulus aut me porticus excepit.*

NERO, the Emperor Tiberius.

NOCENT, criminal (Webster).

NON ACCIDES, "thou shall not kill."

NUMERICAL, individual.

NUNQUAM . . . SOLUS, "never less alone than when alone."

OBSERVATOR, observer.

OÏLEUS, the line in the "Odyssey," iv. 511, referring to the death of Ajax Oïleus is possibly spurious.

OLYMPICS, Olympic games.

OMNEITY, the All.

ONEIRO CRITICISM, interpretation of dreams.

OPINION (vb.), to consider.

ORBITY, loss of parents or children, bereavement.

ORDINATION, arrangement.

ORONTES INTO TIBER, "In Tiberim defluxit Orontes," says Juvenal, speaking of the confluence of foreigners to Rome (J.).

OSSUARIES, places for bones.

OSTIARIES, estuaries.

PANTAGRUEL'S library. Rabelais, in his "Pantagruel" (liv. ii., ch. vii.), gives a list of sham titles of books for an imaginary library.

PAPPOUS, downy.

PARALLAXIS, the parallax of a star is the difference between its real and apparent place (J.).

PARALOGICAL, illogical.

PARAMOURS, lovers.

PARTICULARITIES, peculiarities.

PASSIVES, passive principles.

PATRON, vb., to patronize.

PENDULOUS, hanging.

PERFLATION, blowing through of the air.

PERIOD, term, end.

PERIŒCI ("to be but their periœci"), only placed at a distance in the same line (J.).

PERISCIAN, with shadows all round us. The Periscii, living within the Polar circle, see the sun move round them, and consequently project their shadows in all directions (J.).

PERISH upon, to die for the sake of.

PERSPECTIVE, telescope.

PHILOPŒMEN, chief of the Achæan League in Rome's second Macedonian War.

PHILOSOPHER. "Alluding either to Antisthenes or Aristippus, for the story is told of each of these philosophers" (Greenhill).

PHYLACTERY, a writing bound upon the forehead containing something to be kept constantly in mind. This was practised by the Jewish doctors with regard to the Mosaic Law (J.).

PHYTOGNOMY, "discerning the nature of plants from their outward forms" (Greenhill).

PHYTOLOGY, science of plants.

PIAE FRAUDES, pious frauds.

PICKTHANK, flatterer.

PINAX, tablet, register; hence list or scheme inscribed on a tablet (Webster).

PINEDA. "Pineda, in his 'Monarchia Ecclesiastia,' quotes one thousand and fortie authors." [Note by Sir T. B.]

PLATO's year. "A revolution of certain thousand years, when all things should return unto their former estate, and he be teaching again in his school, as when he delivered this opinion." [Note by Sir T. B.]

PLAUDIT, *plaudite* was the term by which the ancient theatrical performers solicited a clap (J.).

PLAUSIBLE, praiseworthy.

POLTRON (French), coward. The characteristic of the modern Roman.

PONDERATION, weighing.

POPES ("four"). Leo XI., Paul V., Gregory XV., and Urban VIII. But Leo XI. died nearly six months before Browne was born.

POPULOSITY, populousness.

PORT, portal.

POSIE, motto on a ring.

POTOSI, the rich mountain of Peru.

PRACTISED, practical.

PRECEDENTS, signs.

PREGNANT, instructive.

PREJUDICATE, formed without knowledge of the facts.

PRELATES, "Presbyters" in the pirated editions of 1642.

PRESCIOUS, foreknowing.

PRESCRIPT, direction.

PRESENTLY, immediately.

PROCESS OF THE TEXT, context.

PROFOUND, to fathom.

PROGENY, lineage.

PROGNOSTICKS, fore-tokens.

PROPENSE, inclined to; PROPENSION unto, inclination towards.

PROPHAN'D, probably in the sense of "common," which the first edition has.

PROPRIETARIES, proprietors.

PROPRIETIES, properties.

PTOLOMY, the King of Egypt who had the Hebrew scriptures translated and put in his library.

PUCELLAGE, virginity.

PUNCTUAL, exact; PUNCTUALLY, exactly.

PUNCTICULAR, contained in, size of, a point.

PUNCTILIO, point, hence a very small body (Greenhill).

PYRRHUS HIS TOE, "which could not be burnt." [Sir T. B.]

PYTHAGORAS ("escapes in the fabulous Hell of Dante"), escapes condemnation, or, perhaps, escapes notice altogether.

QUADRATE, square, vb. and sub.

QUANTAM . . . AB ILLO, "how greatly changed from him."

QUESTUARY, studious of profit (J.).

QUINCUNX, arrangement of things by fives, one at each corner, and one in the centre.

QUINQUERNIO, set of five (Greenhill).

QUINTAPLE, fivefold.

QUODLIBETICALLY, determinable on either side (J.).

RADICAL LETTERS, "according to old tradition, Moses, by command of God, took the first letters of the names of the tribes, and found them equal to the number of the Israelites, deducting those who were slain in the affair of Korah, etc." (extract from Greenhill's note).

RADICATION, process of taking root.

RAMPIERS, ramparts.

REACTION, retaliation.

REASONS, reasonable persons.

REFLEX, reflection.

REFLUX, ebb.

REGIO-MONTANUS. John Müller of Königsberg (1436-75), "who constructed an iron fly and a wooden eagle, both of which were able to fly." [Condensed from Greenhill.]

RELENTMENT, dissolution.

RELISH OF, to taste of.

REMINISCENTIAL, relating to reminiscence.

REMORAS, obstacles.

REMOVE, step.

REPROBATED, condemned to eternal punishment.

RESOLUTION, solution; RESOLUTIONS, men of resolution.

RESPECTIVE, partial.

RESTRAINT (upon) OF TIME, impeded by the restrictions of time.

RETIARIUS, a prize-fighter who entangled his opponent in a net, which by some dexterous management he threw upon him (J.).

RETIARY, RETICULATE, in form of network.

RETRIBUTE UNTO, to restore.

RETRIBUTION, repayment.

REVERBERATED BY FIRE, "fused as in a reverberatory furnace" (Greenhill).

REVIVIFICATION, recalling to life.

RHAPSODIES, "extravagant nonsensical books" (Greenhill).

RIVALITY, equality.

ROUNDLES, steps of a ladder.

RUAT . . . TUA, "The sky may fall, thy will be done."

RUBICON, the river by crossing which Cæsar declared war against the Senate (J.).

SALAMANDER'S WOOL, a kind of asbestos.

SALIENT, leaping "salient animals."

SALTYR, heraldic term for cross blazoning of shield.

SALVE, explained by Gardiner as "cure," "remedy," but it means rather to make a reservation which saves. To *Salve Priscian's Pate* means to *avoid breaking* Priscian's head. In Sir T. B. the word has the general sense of solve, explain.

SALVIFICALLY, "so as to procure salvation" (J.).

SANCTUARY ("St. Paul's"). Several passages in St. Paul's writings have been quoted by various editors to explain this passage, but Greenhill points out that the Dutch translator was probably right in quoting Rom. xi. 33: "O the depth of the riches," etc., as the passage referred to, especially as Sir T. B. himself alluded to it, and that the sanctuary is "the incomprehensibility of God."

SATION, sowing.

SATURN (revolution of). "The planet Saturn maketh his revolution once in thirty years." [Note in one of the MSS.]

SCALES, ladders.

SCANDAL, ill odour.

SCHOOLS, the medieval schools of disputation and theology.

SEASES, a word not to be found in any dictionary (Greenhill).

SECONDINE, after-birth.

SENSIBLE, perceptible by the senses.

SEVEN YEARS PAST. The Address to the Reader was first published in 1643; according to this the "Religio Medici" was written about 1636.

SHADOWED, shadowed forth.

SHARP, a pointed weapon. To PLAY AT SHARP, to fight in earnest.

SIC . . . VELIM. "Thus would I wish to be gathered together when turned into bones," Tibullus, iii, 2, 26.

SI FORET . . . DEMOCRITUS. "If Democritus were still on earth he would laugh" (Horace, Ep. ii. 1, 194).

SIGIL, seal.

SIMPLE, vb., to botanize.

SINISTROUS, left-handed.

SOCIETY, co-operation.

SOCRATES AND CARDAX, Socrates and Cardax talked of an attendant spirit that hinted from time to time how they should act (J.).

SOLSTICIALLY, at the solstices (Greenhill).

SORITES, a series of elliptic syllogisms.

SORTILEGIES, divination by drawing lots.

SPERMATICAL, pertaining to the seed.

SPICATED, spiked.

SPINDLES, slender stalks.

SPINTRIAN, obscene.

SPRUCE, "formerly used of things with a *serious* meaning" (J.).

SQUAMOUS, scaly.

STATION, fixity.

STATISTS, politicians.

ST. INNOCENT'S CHURCHYARD, PARIS, where bodies decay quickly.

STINT, limit.

STRABO'S CLOAK. Strabo compared the then known world to a cloak.

SUPEREROGATE, to do more than is absolutely necessary.

SUPINITY, sloth.

SUPPOSED, undeniable.

SUPPUTATION, reckoning.

SURCLE, small shoot, sucker.

SURD, deaf.

TABLES (a game at), backgammon.

TABID, wasted by disease.

TARGUM, a paraphrase or amplification (J.).

TARTARETUS, a real person, a doctor of the Sorbonne and a writer of some celebrity in the fifteenth and sixteenth centuries (Greenhill).

TEGUMENT, covering.

TELARELY, in a weblike manner.

TELESMES, talisman.

TEMERARIOUS, rash.

TESTACEOUS, made of earthenware.

TESTIFY THEIR POSSESSIONS, show the Romans once inhabited them.

TETRICK, sour, morose (J.).

TEXTUARY, text-learned.

THETAS θ, a theta inscribed upon the judges' tessera or ballot was a mark for death or capital condemnation (J.).

THIRTY YEARS (nor hath my pulse beat). As Browne was born in October, 1605, the "Religio Medici" would thus seem to have been written about 1635.

THWART, THWARTING, transverse.

TINCTURE, touch, colour.

TORTILE, twisted.

TRADUCTION, propagation.

TRAJECTION, emission.

TRANSPECIATE, to transform into another species.

TRANSVERTIBLE, invertible.

TREASURE, treasury.

TREDDLES, albuminous cords in an egg.

TRIGUETROUS, trigonal; having three salient angles or edges.

TROPIC, the tropic is the point where the sun turns back (J.).

TROPICAL, figurative.

TYCHO, he that makes, or he that possesses; as Adam might be said to contain within him the race of mankind (J.).

U FINITAS, rules without exceptions.
ULIGINOUS, slimy.
ULTION, revenge.
UNCOUS, hooked.
UNITERABLE, incapable of repetition.
UNITION, union.
UNIVOCACY, regularity, certain order
(Greenhill).
UNRECLAIMED, untamed, a term in
falconry.
URGING, burning fiercely.
URN OF THE PRÆTOR, into which the
ticket of condemnation or acquittal
was cast (J.).

VAGRANT, wandering.
VAINGLORIES, vain-glorious men.
VAIR, skin of squirrel ("vaired
coats").
VAS USTRINUM, a vessel for burning.
VENEFICIAL, injurious, bewitching
(Greenhill).
VENICE (the Duke of), an ancient
ceremony formerly performed by
the Doge yearly to symbolize the
sovereignty of the State over the
Adriatic.
VENICE (the State of). In 1606 there
was a quarrel between the State of
Venice and Pope Paul V., which
was settled in the following year by
the intervention of France.

VENNY (venew), the lunge in fenc-
ing.
VENTILATION, fanning, influence.
VERTICITIES, rotations.
VESPILLOES, corpse-bearers.
VINOSITY, vinous nature.
VITIOSITY, viciousness.
VITRIFICATION, reduction of a body
into glass.
VOLÉE (à la), at random.
VOLUTATION, a rolling, as of a sphere
on a plane surface (Greenhill).
VOTES, wishes.

WAX ("the wise man's wax"), alluding to the story of Ulysses, who
stopped his companions' ears with
wax as they passed by the Sirens
(J.).

YVROGNE, drunken. The characteristic
German.

ZEALS, zealous men.
ZENO'S KING, "the King of the
Stoics," whose founder was Zeno,
and who held that the wise man
alone had power and royalty (J.).
ZOILISM, criticism in the style of
Zoilus.

THE END